AM I NORMAL?

AM I NORMAL

?

Your Personal Guide to Understanding Yourself and Others

SID CORMIER, Ph.D.

Carroll & Graf Publishers, Inc.
New York

Copyright © 1993 by Sid Cormier

First Carroll & Graf edition 1993

Carroll & Graf Publishers, Inc.
260 Fifth Avenue
New York, NY 10001

Library of Congress Cataloging-in-Publication Data is available.

ISBN: 0-88184-873-5

Manufactured in the United States of America

To my dad,
Sidney R. Cormier, Sr.,
the closest person to normal I have ever known

CONTENTS

ACKNOWLEDGMENTS

I wish to express my appreciation to my agent, Bob Siverstein, whose patience and support during the formulation of this book kept the project alive. To Kent Carroll and Herman Graf, for their editorial and marketing efforts. To Laura Langlie, for her support and encouragement. To my secretary, Dawn Kofford, for her tireless typing efforts. And to Judith McQuown, for bringing this manuscript into its final form.

INTRODUCTION

HAVE YOU EVER ASKED YOURSELF, "AM I NORMAL?" THIS IS NOT THE KIND OF question most of us go around asking each other, but at some level we could all probably use a little reassurance about our psychological health. More importantly, we or our loved ones may be suffering from a psychiatric problem and not even know it.

Terry knows something is wrong but can't figure out what it is. The slender 32-year-old receptionist, wife, and mother of two wiped the tears from her hazel eyes and said, "These last few months I just feel like the life is being sucked right out of me. It's all I can do just to get out of bed and get to work. I love my husband and children, but I just can't take care of them the way I used to." After talking over her problems with her husband, Dean, they decide to take a vacation. But after a week at the little thatch-roofed cottage on the coast where they spent their honeymoon, Terry gives up and takes a bottle of Valium that her well-meaning family doctor prescribed for her down moods.

Terry is spared and responds favorably to treatment for her depression. But she and her husband want to know what they could have done to prevent the near-tragedy.

Shannon was stunned, shaken, and confused. The 41-year-old freckle-faced strawberry blonde real-estate agent cups her hands over her eyes and mumbles, "God, I just hope he lives."

11

In the emergency room, her husband, Ben, hangs on desperately to life while doctors try to replace the blood he's lost as the result of an alcohol-damaged esophagus which has just ruptured.

A week later, during a family-therapy group at an alcohol-rehabilitation unit, Ben admits that he felt his drinking pattern was normal until he almost died. Shannon wants to know what she could have done to help him sooner.

Tom, a 38-year-old systems analyst thinks he's developing heart problems. A major reorganization in the Silicon Valley software company he works for has left him feeling very insecure about his career with the company. Tom begins to experience shortness of breath, dizziness, tingling in his hands and feet, and a sense of impending doom several times a week.

After a thorough cardiac workup, Tom is told by his doctor that his heart is fine. He is referred to a psychologist, who diagnoses him as having panic attacks.

Ralph, a 55-year-old investment banker, has been a rock-solid pillar of the community for over thirty years. His wife, children, and friends can't ever recall seeing Ralph get very emotionally upset, no matter what the circumstances. Yet sometimes late at night, in the quiet solitude of his study, Ralph thinks that he might be losing his mind.

No, Ralph is not going crazy. He is just experiencing the emergence of some long-buried feelings of fear and simply needs a little reassurance.

Am I Normal? consists of a series of psychological questionnaires to help people like the ones just discussed and like you figure out who may or may not be suffering from a psychiatric disorder. It is based on the assumption that you are honest and intelligent enough to answer questions very similar to those used by psychologists and psychiatrists to diagnose their patients.

WHO NEEDS *AM I NORMAL?*

There are three major audiences for this book:

First, people who are suffering from a psychiatric disorder and need help.

Second, people who are concerned about the mental health of a loved one.

And, finally, those millions of people who simply need the reassurance that they or people they love are psychologically okay.

SOME INTERESTING STATISTICS

One out of every three people in the United States will suffer from an emotional, alcohol-, or drug-abuse problem at some point in their lives.

In 1989 the American Psychological Association presented highlights from a survey designed to determine the prevalence of alcohol-, drug-abuse, and other mental disorders in the United States. The information was based on thousands of interviews using the National Institute of Mental Health's diagnostic interview schedule. This interview schedule is patterned on the *Diagnostic and Statistical Manual of Mental and Emotional Disorders—Revised* (DSM III–R), which is the standard reference used by psychologists and psychiatrists to evaluate their patients for psychological disorders.

Results of this survey suggests that over 15 percent of the adults in our country experience some form of alcohol- or drug-abuse or mental disorder during a one-month period. That translates to 37 million people. During a six-month period, that number increases to one in every five adults. And, over the course of a lifetime, approximately 80 million people will have a diagnosable psychological disorder. Other statistics indicate that 12.8 million Americans will suffer from anxiety disorders, 10 million from depression, and over 20 million from alcoholism.

Yet, of these 80 million people with psychological problems, only 20 million will ever seek help. Some 60 million will suffer needlessly.

Are you or people you love among these psychologically walking wounded?

For some people, the problems will go away by themselves eventually. For others, the problems will escalate, leading into a downward spiral of disability and possibly even suicide. But most people will develop a grin-and-bear-it attitude, thinking that their suffering is a necessary part of the human condition.

But is it?

YOUR RIGHT TO KNOW

One of the biggest criticisms I received when I began to write this book was: "What right did I have to allow people to figure out for themselves whether or not they had a psychiatric disorder?" This evaluation could be performed only by a qualified professional during psychological or psychiatric interview.

Fortunately for most professionals, and unfortunately for consumers of mental-health services, the cost of an average evaluation ranges between $400 and $1,200. I know because I have been making these evaluations for the past twelve years and have helped more than 2,000 people figure out if they are—as they put it—"normal."

But, costs aside, most people with psychological problems will never seek help. Could this be because they don't know that they have a problem?

All experts in diagnosing human emotional and behavioral problems and any psychologist or psychiatrist of merit would have to admit honestly that the bulk of the information we use to formulate our diagnostic impressions is based on the patient's own reports to us.

And, if you can respond to questions posed to you by a professional, why can't you respond to similar questions posed to you in a book? In fact, wouldn't you be a lot more likely to answer the questions honestly when taking them for your own self-knowledge, as opposed to trying to look good to some evaluator who doesn't even know you?

Yes, I firmly believe that you have not only the *right* but the *need to know* whether you or someone you love is in need of help.

No, you are not a professional psychologist or psychiatrist, and no one is asking you to pretend to be one. But the questions I will be giving you a little later are based on the *actual questions* professionals use to make their diagnostic impressions.

Perhaps more important than helping *you* sort out whether you have a problem is the fact that this book can be an extremely valuable guide to helping you recognize problems in *people you love*.

For example, how do you know when it's time to take your husband into an alcohol-rehab center? Should you wait until he's thrown in jail for drunk driving?

How do you know if your daughter has an amphetamine problem? Is the excessive energy and activity she and her friends display typical of teen-agers, or is it a drug induced state that needs treatment?

What about your parents? Does the apparent gradual decline of their memory mean that they have Alzheimer's disease?

Remember, all of the disorders discussed in this book are treatable, and most are curable. But to know if something needs fixing, first you need to know whether or not it is broken.

WHAT THE QUESTIONS REALLY MEAN

When assessing yourself and others, you will be looking for life-damaging consequences of clinical syndromes. Specifically, you will be asked to determine the extent to which psychological problems have interfered with your family, job, friendships, and physical health. For example, divorcing your husband because of his alcohol-related spousal abuse, or withdrawing from college because of recurrent panic attacks are both clearly life-damaging consequences of disorders, and it is likely that your husband *is* an alcoholic and that you *do* have a panic disorder.

On the other hand, some life-damaging consequences are more

subtle—like passing up a trip to Hawaii because of your fear of flying, or making up an excuse to get out of a tour of the World Trade Center because of your fear of heights. These are less obvious consequences of a disorder, but they still have a negative impact on your life. Fortunately, they can be treated easily.

To help you sort out more clearly what I mean by life-damaging consequences and who is likely to have a disorder, each chapter is loaded with real-life examples of people who do and do not have the disorders.

So sit back, take a few deep breaths, relax, and muster up as much courage and honesty as you can. Because within the pages of this book you will be either relieved and reassured to realize that you or those you love are not suffering from a psychological or psychiatric disorder; or you will be inspired and motivated to get help to begin living a healthy, happy, and productive life.

CHAPTER **1**

WHAT'S NORMAL, ANYWAY?

So what's normal, anyway?

We all go through times when we feel lonely, scared, frustrated, sad, disappointed, or out-and-out angry. But how do you know when these feelings become a serious problem?

In order to understand what is normal, we need some standard or reference with which to compare ourselves. Some of us look to family, friends, teachers, doctors, pastors, or even coworkers in the hope that they can show us what is normal. But upon close acquaintance, over time, these potential role models usually let us down. Many people look for idols in the entertainment, athletic, and political arenas, hoping to find someone to *really* look up to. But when the glitz and glamour are stripped away, we realize that everyone is only human, after all.

To further complicate our search for what is normal is the fact that we live in a complex and ever-changing world. Recent historical developments like the fall of the Iron Curtain, the dissolution of the Soviet Union, and the AIDS epidemic have had a dramatic impact on what we think and do. Casual drug use and free love which were common in the mid-1960s are generally taboo in the 1990s. In 1962, the year of the Cuban missile crisis, we were much less concerned about saving whales and the South American rain forest than we were about saving ourselves from being blown off the face of the earth in a nuclear confrontation with the Soviet Union.

17

We all share a basic and fundamental need for a safe, secure, and generally predictable world. But, unfortunately, reality does not always accommodate our needs.

In order to get a better idea of what is and is not normal, let's take a broad look at our world from several different perspectives.

On April 29, 1992 a predominantly white jury acquitted four white police officers in the videotaped beating of motorist Rodney King, sparking off the most devastating riots in recent U.S. history. More than fifty people were killed and more than $500 million worth of property was destroyed. Thousands were injured and thousands were arrested. Was the jury's verdict fair? Was the rioting a normal reaction to perceived injustice?

Do people really want to go crazy, at least sometimes? At a rock concert in Salt Lake City a heavy-metal band whips the crowd into a frenzy. As a wave of humanity sweeps over the stage, several teenagers are injured seriously and three are killed. Should such an occurrence be considered an occupational hazard in the life of a rock concertgoer?

In Southern California, the opening-night's showing of a movie depicting gang violence triggers a series of bloody drive-by shootings involving the Crips and the Bloods. Is the continuing tragedy of inner-city drugs, despair, and turmoil understandable or normal?

What would have been considered crazy twenty-five or thirty years ago is becoming increasingly acceptable now.

High in the French Alps, a 22-year-old female rock climber hangs precariously by a thumb and an index finger as she pulls herself to a three-inch rocky ledge which provides momentary security. Some 2,500 feet below, a rocky plateau gravely awaits any mistake. Is this woman normal?

Above the tiny village of Albertville in the French Alps, thousands gather to watch World Cup freestyle inverted aerialist Jean Philipe LaRoche launch off a ski ramp 50 feet into the sky and execute a flawless twisting triple back flip. The beauty of his execution is unparalleled, yet not atypical, since the same trick is performed by the next three Olympic freestyle aerialists.

No, these guys aren't crazy. Freestyle aerials have just become a competitive Olympic sport.

On a bridge above a 200-foot rocky ravine, an attorney straps a bungee cord around his ankles. He pulls himself to the top of a rail, spreads his arms, and executes a 170-foot swan dive before the bungee cord pulls him back. Does this guy have a death wish, or is he just enjoying a new and exciting sport?

In perhaps no other area is the question of normality more fascinating than that of sexual behavior.

In San Francisco, gay couples stroll leisurely along a shaded boulevard and look askance at heterosexual couples, as if *they* are abnormal and don't really belong there. Do they? Homosexuality, which was considered a disorder in the 1950s, is now considered a lifestyle preference.

At a roadside tavern in Massachusetts one evening, a young woman is viciously gang-raped by three men on a pinball table while dozens of typical bar patrons watch the spectacle and do nothing to intervene. Several other men actually cheer them on. Where are the heroes? Is this typical male behavior?

In cities throughout our country, confused, pregnant teen-age girls become guilty and sometimes even suicidal when told that their plans for abortion represent murder. Should they have their babies? Should they have been on the Pill? Is premarital sex okay? What about AIDS? Is there a new emerging model for sexual normality?

In a small Midwestern Methodist church, a female pastor delivers her first sermon to mixed reviews. While many members are delighted at the novelty of her position, an old-timer comments, "It just isn't normal for a woman to be a pastor." Are changes in the clergy reflecting changes in our religious beliefs? Is there a new emerging pantheistic or universal religion?

Under a large tepee during a men's therapy group in California, members are encouraged to beat a drum and get in touch with their true male nature by speaking their minds in front of other men. In another men's therapy group in New York City, participants are encouraged and praised for revealing their most private thoughts and crying, while the strong, silent types are chastised as being rigid and overly defensive. What does it mean to be a normal male in the 1990s? Are any of these men normal?

In the late 1980s, casual drug use becomes a serious offense. Supreme Court nominee Douglas Ginsberg withdraws from contention after it is revealed that he smoked pot more than twenty years ago while in college. A top presidential aide states, "Casual cocaine users should be taken out and shot in the head." Is the presidential adviser's comment an understandable and normal reaction to the drug problem? Are you abnormal if you have ever used drugs casually?

Toward the end of the twentieth century, environmental concerns become paramount to the world. The reality of ozone depletion, global warming, and the disappearance of the South American rain forest prompt national and international protest. Environmentalists battle to save the endangered spotted owl at the cost of lost jobs for hundreds of multigenerational logging families who are forced to line up for welfare benefits when the sawmills close. Who is right? What is normal?

The debate over what is normal and abnormal could go on and on. Normalcy is relative not only to our particular time in history, but also to the particular culture, subculture, family, and peer system to which we belong.

But let's look at normal from a more personal and individual perspective. At some level we all want to know if we are psychologically normal.

Is it normal to feel nervous on that first job interview? Is it normal to feel scared when you first move away to go to college? Is it normal to get angry when your husband continues to ignore you, or your wife won't get off your back? How about feeling fear when you realize that your company is downsizing and you know that you are the first or second on the chopping block? Is the desperate confused loneliness you feel when your husband abandons you or your wife dies "normal"?

Closely related to the question of your own normality and almost as important is the question: "Who is normal?"

Is your wife depressed if she lies in bed for a week and has trouble sleeping and eating, and loses weight? Is your husband an alcoholic if he drinks two or three beers every evening after work? Is your son schizophrenic if, after cramming for two days for final exams, he thinks he hears voices without knowing where they come from? Are the occasional bouts of shortness of breath and dizziness your best friend suffers from a heart attack or a panic attack? When you notice a coworker doing a few lines of cocaine a couple of times a year at parties, does this mean that she is a drug addict? Do your boyfriend's feelings that the boss has it in for him mean that he is paranoid?

* * *

A little later, I will gently walk you through a series of psychological tests that will give you answers to all of these questions and many more. But before we begin our journey, it is important to keep one idea in mind:

All of the psychological and substance-abuse problems that I will be describing are clearly treatable, and most are curable. But, in order to get treatment for a problem, you must first know whether you have a problem.

MODELS OF NORMALITY

We already know that what is normal varies not only across a time dimension, but also from nation to nation, culture to culture, state to state, and city to city. What's perfectly normal in Reno is not okay in Cincinnati. If you don't believe me, ask Pete Rose.

Psychologist Sheldon Korchen reviewed research showing that there are five models of normality.

The first idea of normality is that of health. Here, "normal" simply means not being sick or disturbed. If no obvious emotional or behavioral problems are present, you are normal. In this model, "health" refers to a reasonable rather than an optimal state, and you can be normal without being happy.

In contrast, a second perspective describes "normal" in terms of a desirable or ideal state. In this model, normal is not thought of as not sick, but as optimal or very healthy. If you are not happy, fully functioning, or self-actualized, you are thought of as less than normal.

Statisticians and mathematicians have their own view of normality. If any human emotional or behavioral trait is measured along a continuum, most will fall near the middle of the range, with fewer and fewer cases falling farther out on either end. Within the statistical concept of normal, the average is described as normal; both extremes—positive and negative, are abnormal. The problem with viewing normality as average is that certain traits which are far from the norm are extremely desirable, yet in this model considered abnormal. For example, a person with an IQ score of 155 would not be considered brilliant, but abnormally intelligent.

A fourth, fascinating view of normality is that developed by sociologists in a concept called "cultural relativism," which states that "normal" can be judged only in terms of the social context in which it occurs. If a behavior conforms to the norms and expectations of the culture in which you are living, you are said to be normal. If it does not, you are abnormal. In the Mende tribe of Africa, paranoia was normal because tribe members routinely poisoned each other. Similarly, many inner-city gangs routinely attack other gangs, use and sell drugs, and burglarize businesses as a way of meeting their subculture's expectations, needs, and behavioral norms. A fifth, final view of normality describes "normal" as a process of adapting to situational changes over time. This concept is based on the biological idea of adaptation of the species to the environment. Essentially, it defines "normal" as "the ability to adjust."

The tests you'll be taking a little later are based on the concept of normal as an absence of symptoms or problems. These tests are not designed to assess whether you are happy, well-adjusted, powerful, effective, creative, self-actualized, or culturally accepted. They are simply a way of helping you assess whether you or the people you care about have the symptoms of a major psychological or substance-abuse problem.

ARE EMOTIONS NORMAL?

As a human being, you are entitled to a wide range of feelings. These emotions are completely normal. To simplify things, let's look at some of the basic human emotions, their purpose, and some examples of each.

SPECTRUM OF FEELINGS

	Emotion	Purpose	Example
Sadness	A feeling of sorrow, grief, or distress associated with some type of real or potential loss.	To demonstrate your feelings to others, and give them an opportunity to offer you comfort and solace.	Divorce, loss of a job, death of a loved one, loss of activity level due to a physical injury.
Fear	A feeling of distress composed of a sense of personal vulnerability, a real or potentially dangerous situation, and a sense of inability to overcome that dangerous situation.	To prevent you from being hurt, injured, or even killed. Without fear, many of us would have already been dead.	Nearly being hit by a tractor-trailer truck on the freeway, or concern over your children going to a dangerous school.
Anger	A feeling of strong displeasure turned against anyone or anything that has hurt or wronged you or someone else.	To prevent you or someone else from being hurt in the future.	Honking your horn at someone who cut you off in traffic, or shouting at your son for hitting your daughter.
Guilt/Remorse	A deep painful regret for having done a wrong in the past.	To prevent you from making the same mistake again.	Feeling bad about cheating on an exam, or feeling overwhelmed by despair over battering your spouse.
Disappointment	Failing to have your expectations met. It necessarily leaves you hoping for something you did not receive.	To prevent you from getting your hopes too high in the future. To motivate you to try harder.	Being denied your request for a raise, making a lower grade than you expected.
Anticipation	Involves looking forward to some event or occurrence in the near or distant future.	To prepare you for an actual sequence of events that are about to happen.	Looking forward to receiving a promotion or a good grade in a class you studied for.

	Emotion	Purpose	Example
Envy	A feeling of distress when you feel your personal qualities, possessions, abilities, or achievements don't measure up to those people who are important to you.	To motivate you to measure up to your standards and achieve your potential.	Using your envious feelings to make you work longer and harder to achieve the promotion your co-worker got last month.
Jealousy	Refers to the feeling that arises when an actual or a desired relationship with another person is threatened.	To motivate you to protect and improve your relationships.	Losing that extra 20 pounds or paying more attention to your spouse.
Surprise	A feeling caused by something happening suddenly or unexpectedly.	To give you a sudden recognition that something has happened, so you can possibly learn to anticipate such occurrences in the future.	Receiving a bouquet of roses from your negligent husband, receiving an unexpected bonus or promotion, or bumping into an old friend.
Acceptance	The act and feeling of taking what is offered or given to you. A favorable reception, involving approval of others.	To allow you to acknowledge in yourself the approval of others.	Being congratulated by your supervisor on doing an outstanding job. Being told you are loved by your spouse, or being complimented on how beautiful your garden is.
Optimism	The tendency to look on the bright side of things with the belief that everything will turn out for the best.	To give you hope during times of despair and to keep you going.	Holding out with hope when you have a serious physical disease and hanging in through the difficult times during your marriage.
Love	A mixture of joy and acceptance.	To give you a feeling that your behavior is acceptable not only to you but to others.	Protective love toward your children, and the romantic love towards your spouse.

Anger is a strong feeling of displeasure turned against anyone or anything that has hurt or wronged you or someone you care about. The purpose of anger is protection: to prevent you or someone you care about from being hurt in the future.

Sharon, a 42-year-old computer technician with fifteen years of experience is outraged when Will, a 26-year-old rookie with a comparable college degree, is promoted to supervising technician ahead of her. Sharon immediately schedules a meeting with the division manager in charge of personnel and expresses in no uncertain terms how she feels ignored, overlooked, and taken for granted. She strongly challenges each reason the manager gave for promoting Will and threatens to file a grievance if the decision is not reconsidered. Two weeks later, Sharon receives a phone call and is told that she would receive the promotion after she attended a three-day personnel-management seminar.

Sharon's anger, when channeled constructively, got her the promotion.

Sadness is a feeling of sorrow, grief, or distress associated with a real or potential loss. The purpose of sadness is to demonstrate your feelings to others and give them an opportunity to offer you the comfort and support you need. Sadness also motivates you to replace your loss. You will feel an emptiness inside until you reinvest your emotional energy in someone or something else.

Ted, a 40-year-old assistant manager at a grocery store, was just told by his wife of twenty-one years that she is in love with another man and wants a divorce. Ted's initial feelings of stunned confusion soon gave way to an overwhelming sense of sadness and loss. After going through all of the second-guessing and allowing the tears to flow, Ted's distress is noticed by his coworkers. Before long, several sympathetic female coworkers befriend Ted, and one attractive woman asks Ted out for lunch and eventually develops a dating relationship with him. Ted's sadness and loneliness motivated him to open up to her friendship.

Although Ted did not plan his reaction consciously, his expression of sadness clearly served the purpose of getting other people to reach out and try to fill the gap in his life.

Fear is a feeling of distress composed of a sense of personal vulnerability, a real or potential dangerous situation, and a sense of inability to overcome it. The purpose of fear is also protection: to prevent you or someone you care about from being hurt, injured, or even killed. Without fear many of us would be dead by now.

While the ultimate purpose of fear is to keep us alive, fear is also very useful in terms of maintaining our level of security and comfort.

Jack is a 47-year-old lineman for a utility company. He has been with the company for twenty-seven years, yet is surprisingly low on the seniority list. When word that cutbacks have to be made comes down from high-level management, Jack realizes that he is in a vulnerable situation and begins to feel fear. Since he is unable to change management's decision on who will be laid off and when, he directs his fear into constructive behavior to solve the problem. He enrolls in night classes at the local college, to earn a degree in engineering.

Jack's fear has served a purpose and led to goal-directed behavior to solve a problem.

Guilt is the realization that you have transgressed a moral, social, or ethical principle. It is associated with a lowering of your self-esteem and a need to make retribution for the wrong you have done. Guilt can involve either mistakes of commission, in which you did something wrong, or mistakes of omission, in which you failed to take an action. In essence, guilt is a kind of psychological jail time you give yourself for doing something wrong.

The purpose of guilt is simply to prevent you from making the same mistake again.

Roy, a 38-year-old alcoholic, is overwhelmed with guilt when he learns that his 20-year-old daughter is undergoing major surgery. Since Roy left his wife and daughter ten years ago, he has been plagued by feelings of remorse, which have kept him from achieving his potential and have dragged him down emotionally.

Roy finally realizes that his guilt is urging him to make retribution to his wife and daughter, and he begins a serious effort to help them. Although he realizes he can never make up for the damage he has done, at least Roy is on the right track.

Disgust is a strong or sickening dislike characterized by such adjectives as "loathing" and "repugnance." The purpose of disgust is to remove you from a situation which is distasteful or harmful.

Audrey, a 40-year-old heroin-addicted prostitute, is near the end of her rope. Under the influence of heroin, she has done things which she couldn't have dreamed of twenty-five years ago. Her disgust with herself is so severe that, in a last desperate attempt to escape the pain, she slashes her wrists. Fortunately for Audrey, her life is spared, and she is removed from the world of drug addiction and prostitution and placed in the healing environment of a drug-rehabilitation facility.

One of the most common distressing emotions we all experience is that of *disappointment*. Disappointment involves having an expectation that a certain outcome is going to occur and being let down when it does not happen. Your expectations are not fulfilled, and you are left with the lingering feeling of dissatisfaction.

The purpose of disappointment is to teach you to either learn to anticipate the future more accurately, or to lower your expectations and make them more realistic.

Dana, a 28-year-old legal secretary, is disappointed. Her boyfriend, Matt, has just decided that they should wait to get married. It wouldn't be so bad if it wasn't the third time Matt has backed down. Dana's disappointment serves a purpose. She begins to seriously question Matt's commitment and, within several months, decides that he really wasn't right for her after all.

Closely related to the emotion of disappointment is that of *frustration*. Frustration implies that you have a goal which you are prevented from achieving. The function of frustration is to motivate you to try even harder to reach your goals.

Any weekend tennis or golf player can tell you the enormous degree of frustration that goes with learning the basics and subtleties of these games. But without frustration, there would be no need to strive harder and improve.

If you have been following along closely, you may start to think that all human emotions are distressing and upsetting. Fortunately, there are many very enjoyable human emotions which we often take for granted.

The emotion of *acceptance* is the act and feeling of taking what is offered or given to you. A favorable reception involving approval by others is usually a good example of acceptance. The purpose of acceptance is to help you realize that others approve of what you are doing.

Sean, an 18-year-old graduating high-school senior, feels a sense of pride as he receives his diploma in front of his family and friends. He has worked hard for his degree and knows he deserves his family's respect and accepts it.

Surprise is a usually enjoyable feeling caused by something happening suddenly or unexpectedly. The purpose of surprise is to give you the sudden recognition that something favorable has happened and to give you hope in times of despair. Surprise can also teach us to predict the future more accurately. But if we could anticipate all our surprises, then there wouldn't be any, and we'd miss out on one of the most delightful of all of our emotions. And can you imagine how boring life would get without any surprises?

Ellen, a 28-year-old recent divorcée, is delightfully surprised when she receives a bouquet of roses from her estranged husband with a note saying that he would like to try to work things out.

Perhaps the most treasured emotion is *joy*. Joy is a strong feeling of pleasure, happiness, and excitement characterized by such adjectives as "bliss," "delight," "rapture," and "ecstasy." Joy lets you know that what you're doing is right. Joy is a way of reinforcing your behavior and encouraging you to continue it.

My most joyful experiences occurred the day I was married and the day each of our three children was born.

It's easy to express enjoyable feelings such as surprise, joy, and acceptance. But most of us run into problems when we have to face emotions like anger, disgust, sadness, fear, or guilt.

It is completely normal to cry if you're sad, shout if you're angry, tremble when you're afraid, feel repulsed when you're disgusted, not be able to stand yourself for a while when you're guilty, or throw up your hands when you are frustrated.

While the expression of some of these feelings is anything but fun, it is essential to realize that they serve a purpose and must be recognized and expressed in order to adjust to life's challenges and really feel alive.

BARRIERS TO FIGURING YOURSELF OUT

Before we examine some psychological defense mechanisms which are capable of distorting or blocking your feelings, it is important to look at something which has become known as the first-year-medical-school syndrome. You endorse every symptom you read about and soon find that you have every problem or disease imaginable.

In order to overcome the first-year-medical-school syndrome and not falsely diagnose yourself as having problems which you really don't have, it's useful to ask the people who know you best whether they feel you really have the particular symptoms you think you do.

If you are in touch with your feelings and are acting on them appropriately, there's a good chance you are not going to be suffering from any major emotional or substance-abuse problems. But, before taking the psychological tests to determine whether you have any of these problems, lets first look at several barriers that may prevent you from getting to know your emotions and assessing yourself accurately. These are called "psychological defense mechanisms." One of the most common of these barriers is known as denial.

Denial is the blocking out of a problem because it is distressing and unpleasant. Denial occurs at a deep level and you may not even be aware that you are doing it. Denial is the most common psychological defense mechanism used by alcoholics and drug addicts. Essentially, these people operate under the assumption that they really could kick the drug or alcohol habit if they had to, but simply choose not to. In fact, they often prove this to themselves by stopping drinking or taking drugs for weeks or even months at a time, only to fall off the wagon later. They are denying that the problem exists; and as long as they feel the problem does not exist, there is no possibility for treatment.

Although denial is a severe form of blocking out your emotions, one of the easiest ways to overcome this barrier when answering the questionnaires is again to ask the people who know and care about you if they feel your responses to the test questions are honest and consistent with their knowledge about your behavior.

Suppression can be thought of as a milder form of denial. Suppression means ignoring or trying not to think about distressing problems in your life. While denial may include a total blocking out of the problem, suppression usually means that you are aware of the problem at some level, but are trying not to think about it or focus on it.

The classic example of suppression is the businessman who has not made his quarterly tax payments, and when he is reminded about his predicament by his accountant, says, "I don't want to think about that right now." Usually the barrier of suppression can be overcome with little honest soul searching.

Another barrier to getting to know yourself is *minimization*. When you minimize your problems, you acknowledge that they are there, but you vastly underestimate their significance. Again, one of the easiest ways to overcome minimization is to check it out with your friends or people you love.

Selective inattention represents a combination of minimization and suppression. If you pay selective inattention to a problem, you distract yourself with other things and choose not to think about what's bothering you. Examples of selective inattention can include a wide range of behaviors like shopping, golf, tennis, or reading; actively pursuing something and distracting yourself to keep your mind off what's really bothering you. It's healthy to take a break from working on your problems; but if distracting behaviors interfere with solving your problems, selective inattention can make things worse.

Acting out is a defense mechanism which involves the externalization of emotional conflict through inappropriate behavior. Acting out is a behavioral representation of a blocked-off feeling.

Displacement is a shift of emotion from the person or object toward which it was originally directed on to another—often unrelated —person or object. It usually means taking out your frustration on someone or something that doesn't deserve it—like the classic example of kicking the cat after having a fight with your spouse.

The devastating riots in Los Angeles in reaction to the Rodney King police-brutality verdict represent classic examples of a combination of acting out and displacement. Thousands of people, frustrated with the jury's verdict, chose to displace and externalize their anger by rampaging through the city and destroying or stealing anything they could find.

The defense mechanism of *rationalization* involves attributing the wrong reasons to a feeling or event. An example of rationalization is Aesop's fable of the fox who wanted some grapes. Unfortunately, the grapes were too high on the vine and could not be reached. After his repeated efforts to get the grapes failed, the fox rationalized his frustration and disappointment by saying, "Oh, the grapes were probably sour anyway." In short, rationalization usually involves some type of after-the-fact excuse or explanation for why things happened the way they did. It is not valid.

Intellectualization is a defense mechanism that employs your intellect in trying to understand or explain a distressing problem so that you can avoid the emotion it evokes. In short, the feeling seems to be bombarded with intellectual bafflegab or nonsense. An example of intellectualization is a woman who goes into great detail about the anatomy and physiology of her breast cancer, but does not acknowledge her fear and anxiety.

The psychological defense mechanism of *projection* involves attributing your own distressing emotions or faults to other people. If you have found yourself reacting strongly to someone's arrogant or condescending attitude, there's a good chance that you sense these unpleasant traits in yourself.

Reaction formation is a defense mechanism that consists of counteracting an unpleasant feeling, emotion, or impulse with its opposite. For example, the person with strong homosexual impulses and underlying guilt who vigorously crusades against homosexuality.

Finally, *identification* is a defense mechanism consisting of the imitation of another person when trying to master unpleasant feelings or impulses. You may act as you feel others would if they suffered the same sequence of events. Identification is not necessarily bad if the person you are identifying with is handling his or her emotions appropriately.

In order to overcome psychological defense mechanisms, you need to be aware that you are using them. Take a retrospective look at how you have handled situations which would evoke emotional reactions in most people, and notice how you have responded. If you are healthy and in touch with your feelings, you will experience a spectrum of emotions ranging from fear and frustration to joy and surprise.

Remember that your emotions are normal. They are there to serve a purpose. They let you know that something meaningful is happening with respect to your needs and values. If you try to hide from unpleasant emotions through psychological defense mechanisms, you prevent your feelings from serving their purpose. Also, distressing feelings, no matter how thoroughly blocked out, don't disappear. In fact, they often build in intensity and manifest themselves through such things as headaches, backaches, and disturbed relationships with others.

Although your emotions are normal and serve a purpose, it is essential to realize that they are based on underlying assumptions or beliefs which may not always be healthy or useful. Look at the assumption, "I must always have the support and approval of everyone I consider important." This assumption is based on a valid need for respect and appreciation from others, but it goes way overboard.

People cannot consistently have the respect and approval of everyone that they consider important, and if you go through life with this assumption, you will set yourself up for chronic frustration. Instead, substitute a more useful, realistic assumption like, "I will work to earn the respect and approval of those I consider important, but I can't please all of the people all of the time."

Before we embark on our journey of self-discovery and assess where you stand psychologically, it is essential to take a look at the circumstances of your life and what kind of stress you have been experiencing.

CHAPTER **2**

HOW STRESSED OUT AM I?

ANY HUMAN BEING, NO MATTER HOW HEALTHY OR PSYCHOLOGICALLY WELL-ADJUSTED, will reach a psychological or physical breaking point if subjected to enough stress. Psychologists and psychiatrists actually take into account how much stress people have been under when making their diagnoses. There is a special scale—the severity of psychosocial stressor scale—which is considered a crucial part of making each diagnosis. So before we begin to assess whether you or those you love have a problem, let's look at how much stress you have been subjected to in the past year or so.

FIGHT-OR-FLIGHT RESPONSE

Most of us think of "stress" as a term used to describe the time pressures or threatening events in our lives. Medically, "stress" has been defined by pioneering researcher Hans Selye (1956) as "an organism's nonspecific response to any internal or external demand." In his pioneering work, Selye demonstrated that every demand on the body elicits not only physiological responses specific to

33

that demand, but also a nonspecific or general response. These non-specific but stereotypic responses help the body adjust and return to its normal state, called "homeostasis."

A "stressor" is the factor which produces the stress and may be as varied as the pressure to win a race, the demands of your job, or the pain of watching someone you love dying of cancer.

In 1953 psychologist Walter Cannon demonstrated an emergency reaction with which people respond when they are confronted with what might be a life-threatening situation. Cannon called this reaction the *fight-or-flight response;* the organism was ready to do whatever was necessary to survive.

While Cannon's research was important in helping us to understand how our bodies react to life-threatening stressors, Selye identified numerous stressors such as exposure to heat or cold, infection, anesthesia, injury or medication, fasting or overeating, and even sorrow or joy. Selye pursued the stress response beyond the alarm reaction and identified the later phases of the stress response cycle in which the person survives the initial reaction and the stressor continues.

THE GENERAL ADAPTATION SYNDROME

Selye's research led him to discover three basic aspects of a stress response cycle: (1) the alarm reaction, (2) resistance, and (3) exhaustion.

Similarly to Cannon, Selye found that during the alarm reaction, stress activates the sympathetic nervous system and a complex neurohormonal system called the hypothalamic-pituitary-adrenocortical axis to prepare the person to fight or run. This fight-or-flight response is very adaptive and serves to increase the heart rate to speed up blood flow to oxygen-dependent muscles. In addition, the nervous system accelerates and deepens breathing, dilates the pupils, increases perspiration, slows or retards digestion, stimulates the inner core of the adrenal gland to secrete adrenaline, and affects a number of other physiological functions in order to mobilize the energy needed for an emergency.

Emotional responses to the emergency also serve an adaptive purpose in that the hypothalamus, a center for many emotions including fear and anger, sends messages to the pituitary and adrenal glands, which in turn secrete more adrenaline into the blood. Adrenaline then causes the liver to release stored glycogen into the bloodstream to form carbohydrates, a quick source of energy. The adrenaline also prepares the blood to clot more rapidly, thus reducing bleeding time if there is injury.

Selye observed that if the stress was strong enough during the alarm reaction, death may actually occur. Even if death does not occur at the time of the alarm reaction, the person's resistance is lowered.

During the second phase of the general adaptation syndrome, physical signs of the alarm reaction are diminished and resistances to harmful stimuli such as toxins or infectious diseases increase above their normal level.

If, however, the stress response is *not* diminished, the stage of resistance is eventually followed by a third stage: exhaustion. During this final phase, exposure to the stressor has nearly depleted the person's adaptive energy, and the signs of the initial alarm reaction reappear but do not diminish. Resistance is further decreased, and illness or death may follow.

Selye's general adaptation syndrome is important to theories of disease because it helps us understand how stress and resistance play important roles in every illness.

STRESSORS OF MODERN TIMES

Clearly the fight-or-flight syndrome played a crucial role in the survival and evolution of humankind. If primitive people did not react with terror to the sight of a hungry bear in the woods, they would not have had the physical energy and resources to run for their lives and escape.

In the last half of the twentieth century, the stressors we deal with are not likely to be physical ones, but rather social or psychological ones. Rather than dealing with true threats to our physical safety, such as a hungry predator, we are now likely to face such chronic stressors as months of despair over an impending layoff or the fear of living in a crime-riddled neighborhood. Psychological conflicts—real or imagined—can trigger strong emotional reactions like anger, anxiety, fear, despair, and helplessness. These emotional responses may, in turn, lead to an overactivation of our alarm reaction. In short, we're ready to run for our lives from a hungry tiger, but the tigers have been replaced by all types of social, economic, and interpersonal stressors. To further compound the problem, we human beings have the capacity to go beyond the present and think about the past as well as anticipate the future. Anything—both past and future—can be thought of as dangerous; and this realization, in turn, is capable of eliciting the fear necessary for our fight-or-flight alarm reaction. How many times have you found yourself worrying about such things as the death of a parent, being abandoned by your lover, having your home repossessed, or developing some dreadful disease?

Television, radio, and newspapers often barrage us with dangerous messages which elicit the frightening possibilities that lead to the activation of our alarm reaction. Depletion of the ozone layer, the disappearance of the South American rain forest, global warming, and the AIDS epidemic are but a few of the stressors which can elicit a general alarm reaction in almost anyone.

STRESS, LIFE CHANGE, AND ILLNESS

In the early part of the twentieth century, psychiatrist Adolf Meyer charted the life events of his patients and found that major life events often preceded illnesses. Later, Thomas Holmes systematically applied and validated Meyer's findings by collecting and studying the medical and social histories of more than 5,000 patients.

In 1967, T. H. Holmes and R. H. Rahe developed a test called the Social Readjustment Rating Scale by having a large number of volunteers rate the extent to which various life events required a change or adjustment in lifestyle.

In order to use this scale, you need to know that during any year about 10 percent of the U.S. population requires hospitalization for physical or psychiatric care. The probability of hospitalization increases as a person accumulates points on the Social Readjustment Rating Scale. Cumulative scores between 150 and 199 increase the probability of hospitalization to 37 percent. Scores between 200 and 299 increase it to 50 percent, and scores above 300 increase the probability of hospitalization to 80 percent.

Social Readjustment Rating Scale

Directions: Read each life event and indicate next to it the number of times you have experienced the stressor within the last year. Then multiply the number of times you have experienced the stressor by the points next to it and add up the total. Ongoing difficulties should be scored only once since they have not subsided, then reappeared.

RANK	LIFE EVENT	LIFE CRISIS UNITS
1	Death of spouse	100
2	Divorce	73
3	Marital separation	65
4	Jail term	63
5	Death of close family member	63
6	Personal injury or illness	53
7	Marriage	50
8	Fired at work	47
9	Marital reconciliation	45
10	Retirement	45
11	Change in health of family member	44
12	Pregnancy	40
13	Sex difficulties	39
14	Gain new family member	39
15	Business readjustment	39

16	Change in financial state	38
17	Death of a close friend	37
18	Change in different line of work	36
19	Change in number of arguments with spouse	35
20	Mortgage over $50,000	31
21	Foreclosure of mortgage or loan	30
22	Change of responsibilities at work	29
23	Son or daughter leaving home	29
24	Trouble with in-laws	29
25	Outstanding personal achievement	28
26	Spouse begins or stops work	26
27	Begin or end school	26
28	Change in living condition	25
29	Revision in personal habits	24
30	Trouble with boss	23
31	Change in work hours or conditions	20
32	Change in residence	20
33	Change in school	20
34	Change in recreation	19
35	Change in church activities	19
36	Change in social activities	18
37	Mortgage or loan less than $50,000	17
38	Change in sleeping habits	16
39	Change in number of family get-togethers	15
40	Change in eating habits	15
41	Vacation	13
42	Christmas	12
43	Minor violations of the law	11

Total Life Crisis Units _____

Scoring: 0–150 : No significant problems (10% chance of stress-related illness)

150–200 : Mild life crisis (33% chance of stress-related illness)

200–299 : Moderate life crisis (50% chance of stress-related illness)

300 and up : Major life crisis (80% chance of stress-related illness)

Adapted from the Holmes and Rahe Social Readjustment Scale.

When examining the Holmes and Rahe scale, it is fascinating to note that interpersonal stressors such as death of spouse, divorce, or marital separation are the greatest contributors to stress-related diseases. On the other hand, positive stressors such as vacation or Christmas are usually considered enjoyable to most of us and are not really stressful. However, they, too, require some degree of temporary adjustment or adaptation.

STRESS-RELATED DISEASES

When your mind and body are constantly subjected to the demands of readjusting to acute or chronic stressors, it becomes likely that you will suffer from a stress-related disease. The more severe and chronic the stressor, the greater the probability that one of these related problems will emerge.

It has been estimated that 50 to 70 percent of all medical complaints are associated with some kind of stress. Physicians report that the majority of complaints they see are either brought on by or made worse by stress.

Research is continuing into the role of stress and disease, and the list of stress-related illnesses appears to be a long one. Stress has been determined to be a major contributor to such problems as hypertension, coronary heart disease, diabetes, migraine and tension headaches, ulcers, tics, and asthma.

Stress has been implicated as a factor in such problems as chronic backache, arthritis, allergies, hyperthyroidism, sexual dysfunctions, dysmenorrhea, vertigo, hyperkinesis, musculoskeletal pain, bruxism (teeth grinding), and even multiple sclerosis. Dermatologists have implicated stress in such disorders as hives, dermatitis, and eczema.

Gastroenterologists have noted that stress plays a strong role in the development in such disorders as irritable colon, incontinence, colitis, and gastritis.

Finally, chemical-dependency specialists have noted that the use and abuse of alcohol and drugs are strongly associated with the degree of stress the patient is experiencing.

IS ALL STRESS HARMFUL?

Toward the latter part of his career, Hans Selye wrote *Stress Without Distress,* a book in which he pointed out that what many of us would consider stress is not always harmful, but actually sometimes enjoyable. He believed that if we eliminated everything that was considered stressful, we would live in a boring, unimaginative, vegetative state.

Even beyond its usefulness in dangerous situations that call for immediate physical action, our stress response gives us much of our motivation for living. It can spur us to climb quickly up the corporate ladder, to work creatively, and can enrich the joys of living.

Thrill seekers often love the excitement of such activities as skydiving, hang gliding, or bungee jumping. These sports elicit an immediate stress response, but it dissipates quickly when the exciting or stressful action is completed.

Therefore, the phase of stress we are most concerned about eliminating is the prolonged resistance phase, which eventually leads to exhaustion.

RATING THE SEVERITY OF YOUR STRESSORS

When rating the severity of your stressors, it is important to realize that you are trying to determine the extent to which your reaction to the stressor is beyond what you would consider that of an "average person" in similar circumstances with similar cultural values. Your judgment of how stressful an event is depends greatly on: (1) the degree to which it requires a change or adjustment in your lifestyle and (2) the extent to which the change is desired and under your control.

Stressors can also be thought of in terms of a time frame. Acute stressors typically last for a period of six months or less. Chronic or enduring stressors, by definition, last six months or longer.

Acute stressors that most of us have faced include such events as taking a new job, entering a new school, or getting married. Chronic stressors include such events as long-term marital or family discord, coping with a chronic disease, or enduring job stress due to a difficult supervisor.

TYPICAL PSYCHOSOCIAL STRESSORS TO BE RATED

In order to determine the significance of psychosocial stressors in your life, step back and take a broad-based look at your life from different perspectives.

Marriage/Significant Other

Events like engagement, marriage, marital fighting, separation, divorce, death of a spouse, or breakup of a relationship are clear and obvious stressors which require a major adjustment on your part. As we know from the Holmes and Rahe Social Readjustment Rating Scale, the top three stressors you can experience are death of spouse, divorce, and marital separation. Clearly, a change in your relationship with your spouse/significant other has the greatest potential for requiring a change in your lifestyle.

Parenting

On the Psychosocial Rating Scale, which you'll be using a bit later, the birth of your first child is a great stressor. It involves a complete readjustment of your lifestyle. An enormous demand is made upon you and your spouse. Other parenting stressors include chronic friction with your child, illness of a child, and chronic sibling fighting (for over six months).

General Interpersonal Problems

This category includes readjustments and relationships with friends, neighbors, associates, or other nonfamily members. The best examples of this type of stressor are the conflicts that some workers experience with their coworkers or supervisors.

Occupational

This category of stressors involves problems which typically arise at work, school, or in the course of homemaking. Occupational stressors involve problems like difficulty making grades, a pending layoff, being fired, a change in work conditions, or an increase or decrease in workload. Anyone who has had to work a swing or double shift knows how much stress or pressure you experience, not only on the job, but also at home.

Living Circumstances

Living circumstances involve such stressors as moving, living in a crime-riddled neighborhood, emigrating to a new country, or living in poverty.

Financial

Probably the most common category of stressors Americans face at the end of the twentieth century have been financial. The possibility of a recession, inadequate finances, or bankruptcy are all clear and compelling stressors which clearly impact the quality of your life.

Legal

Arrest, trial, imprisonment, or even lawsuits represent severe and sometimes extreme psychosocial stressors. Just ask yourself how much of an adjustment it would take for you to survive a term in prison.

Natural Transitions in Life

Key developmental changes like puberty, transition to adult status, menopause, and retirement are inherently stressful because they usually require a readjustment in your lifestyle. Changing your role from that of a child to a teen-ager, or from a worker to a retiree requires an enormous psychological adjustment.

Physical Injury or Illness

In a strict biological sense of the word, injury or illness to your body requires a physiological adaptation to either repair tissue damage or fight off disease. In addition to the biological readjustment, a psychosocial readjustment usually accompanies physical injury or illness. When you are ill, you are not capable of taking on your normal duties and responsibilities, and they must be performed by other people in your life.

SEVERITY OF PSYCHOSOCIAL STRESSOR SCALE

Elaborating on the work of Cannon, Selye, Holmes, and Rahe, psychologists and psychiatrists have categorized stressors along a dimension ranging from "none" to "catastrophic." When trying to understand yourself or others, it is crucial to know the extent to which stress may be contributing to—or even causing—psychological or substance-abuse problems. Realize that when you or someone you care about is under severe stress, there is a much greater likelihood for a problem to develop. In many cases, when the stressor subsides or is eliminated, the psychological problems disappear.

Use the following scale to evaluate the severity of your problems:

Adult Stress Scale

Examples of Stressors

Severity Rating	Acute	Chronic
None	No immediate stressors that are relevant to psychological problems	No long-term circumstances that are related to psychological problems

Mild	Graduating from high school; beginning school; child leaving home; breakup of a relationship	Dissatisfaction with your job; living in a dangerous neighborhood; constant family fighting
Moderate	Getting married; getting fired or laid off; retiring; separating from your spouse; miscarriage of a pregnancy	Constant marital fighting; serious financial problems which threaten bankruptcy; constant problems with your supervisor; raising a child on your own
Severe	Birth of first child; divorce; loss of career	Living below poverty level; constant unemployment
Extreme	Death of spouse; serious physical injury or illness; victim of severe assault or rape	Serious chronic illness in self, spouse, or child; ongoing physical or sexual abuse
Catastrophic	Death of multiple family members; suicide of family member; devastating natural disaster (earthquake or hurricane in which all is lost)	Long-term incarceration; captivity as a hostage

These psychosocial stressors are relevant to adults. However, children also experience the same stress-related responses:

Stress Scale for Children and Adolescents

Examples of Stressors

Severity Rating	Acute	Chronic
None	No acute events that are related to psychological problems	No long-term circumstances that are related to psychological problems
Mild	Change to a new school; breakup with boyfriend or girlfriend	Frequent family arguments; crowded living conditions
Moderate	Birth of a sibling; expulsion from school	Chronic parental fighting; parent's disabling illness
Severe	Arrest; unwanted pregnancy; abortion; divorce of parents	Negligent or rejecting parents; multiple foster-home placements; institutionalization; parent's life-threatening illness or injury
Extreme	Sexual or physical abuse; death of a parent	Continuing sexual or physical abuse
Catastrophic	Death of both parents or multiple family members	Chronic life-threatening illness or disease

Crisis as Opportunity

How severe are your stressors? No matter how stressful or nonstressful your situation, remember that people respond to stress differently. I have known patients who respond to the most severe psychosocial stressors, like death of multiple family members, serious illness, or loss of a career, with courage and power.

These people have learned how to turn crises into opportunities and exemplify the proverb: "Pressure turns coal into diamonds."

Irene was one of those diamonds. I first saw Irene in the emergency room of a hospital after she had been beaten severely by her alcoholic husband. Irene's doctors informed me that a year earlier she had been diagnosed as having Hodgkin's lymphoma. Unbelievably, six months before her most recent hospitalization, Irene had been in a severe auto accident and had suffered mild brain damage, a broken arm, and multiple contusions. Irene had no medical insurance and, due to her injuries, was dismissed from her job.

Despite this devastating course of events, Irene refused to fold. She continued to live her life and fight her battle against cancer and the many other difficulties she was facing.

Today, nearly nine years later, Irene's cancer has gone into full remission, she has remarried, and is employed part-time as a real-estate agent.

On the other end of the spectrum is Dorene, a 36-year old social worker. When Dorene is told that her workload will be increased 20 percent, she develops tension headaches, ulcerative colitis, and mild hypertension. Despite what would probably be considered by most to be a mild stressor (moderate increase in workload) Dorene's response was maladaptive and created more problems in her life.

A SIMPLE STRESS-MANAGEMENT STRATEGY

We are all different, yet we all tend to face many of the same problems in the course of our lifetime. Clearly, some of us handle our problems better than others. In Chapter 12, "Tips on Getting and

Staying Normal," I will give you twelve established keys to psychological health and emotional well-being. But for now, let's look at a simple coping strategy that has been developed by a number of psychologists to help us cope with typical stressors.

When you are faced with any type of stressful situation try the following steps:

(1) Clarify the nature of the stressor exactly and precisely. For example, do you find your stomach tied up in knots every morning on the freeway when you are on your way to work? If so, you're likely to have severe job stress. On the other hand, do you have the same physical symptoms when you are driving home? If so, the problem is probably in your marriage, family, or living situation.

(2) Next, try to correct or fix the stressful situation. If you have constant problems with a supervisor or a coworker, go to those people directly and let them know your concerns. If this fails, take it to the next level and let upper management know what's wrong. In your marriage, first go to your spouse directly and communicate clearly and honestly what you need that you are not getting, and listen to what your partner has to say about it. If this doesn't work, seek professional help. Usually the perspective of an objective, interested third party can overcome most marital conflict.

(3) If you cannot correct or fix the stressful situation, consider leaving it. Most of the stressors we have been talking about are psychosocial. They involve situations in your environment to which you react psychologically. For environmental or psychosocial stressors like marital conflict, occupational uncertainty, or interpersonal friction, if your best efforts at fixing the stressor fail, it may be in your best interest simply to get out of the situation. For example, if you know your job situation is never going to improve, you are probably better off looking for another job. If you realize that the neighborhood you're living in has become crime infested, it is probably in the best interest of you and your loved ones to move.

(4) For situations in which leaving the stressful situation is not a reasonable alternative, learn to relax and accept the stressor—at least temporarily. For example, if you are dealing with an impossible boss who has never liked you and never will, learn to relax into upsetting thoughts or fantasies about this difficult person

while you continue to look for another job. You may find that quitting your job would create such a financial burden that it would actually cause more stress than dealing with this difficult individual.

The process of defusing stress by relaxing is based on an established clinical psychological technique called "systematic desensitization." The relaxation script similar to the one used for systematic desensitization is offered in Chapter 12.

CONCLUSIONS

It is a big mistake to think that you should be happy, well-adjusted, or satisfied under all circumstances. Research on psychosocial stressors has taught us that your problems are not entirely inside your head. Stressors in your environment are likely to have a strong effect on not only you, but anyone else who experiences them. Even the most physically and psychologically healthy and well-functioning people, if subjected to enough stress or pressure, will reach a breaking point.

Before determining whether you have any major psychological or substance-abuse problems, take a good, clear look at the amount of stress you have been under. Then either try to eliminate the stress, leave the situation, or relax and learn to tolerate it—at least temporarily.

Remember, stress can not only contribute to psychological disorders, but in some cases can actually cause them.

We will all go through a number of stressors in the course of our lifetime, and your personal response to these stressors will largely determine the quality of your life.

When you read the rest of this book, be sure to keep in mind the amount of stress you or others have been under when answering the questionnaires. Since stress can not only exacerbate but actually cause psychological problems, see whether you can eliminate the stressors before you diagnose yourself or someone else as having a psychological disorder that might require the help of a therapist.

When put under enough pressure, everyone has a breaking point. But pressure can also turn coal into diamonds. You can learn to turn stress into an opportunity for a psychological breakthrough to a new level of emotional strength and well-being.

CHAPTER 3

AM I AN ALCOHOLIC?

MIKE, A 38-YEAR-OLD STUDENT IN MY CHEMICAL-DEPENDENCY CLASS, WROTE THIS essay on his experiences with alcohol:

It was my first junior high-school boy/girl party and everybody seemed stiff and scared. The girls were on one side of the room and the boys were on the other. Cindy, head cheerleader and heartthrob for me and any guy in his right mind, was wearing worn, tight 501 denim jeans and a soft, fuzzy turquoise sweater. Whatever shampoo she had used made her hair smell irresistible.

Since the party was at Cindy's house, her mom had made Cindy and the other girls promise to keep one 150-watt lamp on in the living room. The glare from the lamp was ridiculous, and the guys felt like we were in a police lineup. After a few minutes of brainstorming, Cindy and her friends put a dark beach towel over the lamp, which made the atmosphere a little bit better.

Then someone put on the Beatles' *Abbey Road* album, and me and the other guys really began to wonder what to do. After thirty minutes of nervous pushing, laughing, and blushing, Ricky, a 9th-grader who seemed mature beyond his fifteen years, came in and told several of us, "I scored a case of cold beer."

51

The next thing I remember is being huddled in the dark behind a fence with ten other kids and tasting a cold but awfully bitter Budweiser. It took a lot of effort not to spit the beer out or make a stupid face, but before long me and the other guys began to feel different. The bitter taste had led to a tingling exhilaration. Two beers later I felt like I had high-octane fuel running through my veins.

Within thirty minutes we were all dancing and feeling like we really fit in. Then somebody brought out a Coke bottle, and about twelve of us began to play spin the bottle.

Gone were the inhibitions, fears, low self-confidence, and terror. I remember landing a spin on Cindy and the thrill of making out with her. This was terrific and I felt confidence like I never had before. That Budweiser was pretty powerful stuff.

Alcohol—my confidence builder, social facilitator, and inhibition eliminator, continued to be my friend through most of high school. The glowing orange flames of high school bonfires against the cool purple October nights provided a perfect backdrop for a few glasses of jungle juice, some close friends, a warm girlfriend, and some memorable times.

I never thought of my alcohol use on the weekends as a problem until one night driving home from a high-school party I was pulled over by a highway patrol officer for suspicion of drunken driving. Even though I was well below the .10 required for the legal definition of drunk driving, the thirty minutes I spent in a cold, dark cell was all that it took to convince me that drinking and driving don't mix and never would.

My personal relationship with alcohol continued into college, and attending the number-3 party college in the United States did little to alert me to any problem with alcohol. Weekend frat parties and Saturday-night football games were not complete without a couple of kegs of beer or a few bottles of booze. Drinking was interwoven into the culture during the 70s.

Besides, my grades in college were great, I had some

real good friends, and I was pretty happy with my girl-friend at the time.

As an adult, there are still occasions where a hot Irish coffee after a cold, crisp day of snow skiing, or a cold beer after a long day of windsurfing or rafting, really hit the spot. The delicious lasagna at that romantic little Italian restaurant my wife and I frequent doesn't really seem complete without a rich glass of Cabernet Sauvignon.

And what would an exciting week in Maui be without an occasional mai tai, piña colada, or strawberry daiquiri.

Yet there is another side to alcohol which Mike hasn't seen. A side which I didn't see myself until I became director of psychology at a drug- and alcohol-rehabilitation unit.

A side of alcohol that showed itself as the orange skin and lifeless eyes of a 35-year-old husband and father of two, dying of alcohol-related advanced liver disease. The confused, disoriented, redundant thought processes and speech patterns of an organically brain-damaged 65-year-old alcoholic whose conversation sounds like an old record which skips and repeats itself again and again. The broken homes and marriages. The sad, lonely faces of abandoned children. The skid row bum lying in the gutter in the rain, drowning in his own alcohol-saturated vomit. The successful businessman who loses his family and career due to uncontrollable drinking. The frustrated, lonely, divorcée who sucks down bloody marys in a smoke-filled bar, hoping desperately for a knight to come rescue her, only to end up later that night in a black plastic bag in the coroner's office after a late-night accident on the way home to her two teen-age children. The blue Pontiac wedged underneath the back of an 18-wheeler with the body of an 18-year-old college freshman who had far too many rum and Cokes that night.

The more subtle damage: the gradually declining memory of a brilliant writer; the lost passion of a man in love; the dull resignation of a woman who has lost hope and becomes more and more depressed with each and every vodka and tonic she downs.

But what is this magical elixir which can be both healer and slayer?

Pharmacologically, alcohol fits into two distinct categories. First, it is a sedative. There is a lot of truth to the saying, "Have a drink to settle your nerves." And, in small doses (one to three ounces), alcohol does just that.

Second, alcohol is an anesthetic. Yes, it kills pain. Unfortunately, the quantity of alcohol required to kill pain completely is very close to the lethal dose. In the old John Wayne westerns before the bullet is removed from the deputy, he takes a shot of whiskey, and then more whiskey is poured into the bullet wound. After severe pain, the nerve endings are deadened, and there is no pain.

Yet alcohol works in a gradual and insidious way on your brain, in both the short and the long term.

To understand how alcohol works, let's look at a typical partygoing man who weighs 160 pounds.

We know that one-half ounce of pure alcohol is the equivalent of 12 ounces of beer, a 4-ounce glass of wine, or 1 ounce of 86-proof whiskey.

After one drink, our partygoer will feel noticeably more relaxed, and he may loosen up a bit. Very little of his actual behavior will change, and his blood-alcohol level is now .02.

If our partygoer drinks 2½ drinks in an hour, he will have a blood-alcohol level of .05. By this time he is "high." The parts of his brain controlling judgment have been affected, and our friend may become loud, obnoxious, boisterous, and may begin making passes. By now he is doing and saying things that he might not usually do or say.

If our partygoer has five drinks within an hour, you certainly have a bona fide drunk a on your hands. His blood-alcohol level is .10, which is clearly sufficient in all states to convict him of driving while intoxicated. By this time, his judgment is severely impaired. Blurring of vision and marked problems controlling muscular coordination are apparent, so that he will probably stagger and slur his speech. Although his manual dexterity and reaction times will clearly be poorer than usual, our partygoer will insist that his perception, judgment, and movements have never been better.

If he has ten drinks within one hour, his blood-alcohol level is .20. Now much more than judgment is impaired. Our partygoer's emotions are probably extremely erratic, and he may change instantly, without reason, from laughter, to tears, to rage. He is likely to have lapses in his short-term memory and not recall where he put things. After six hours, this man will still be legally drunk.

If our partygoer consumes one pint of whiskey within an hour, he is likely to become stuporous. Although he has not passed out completely, very little that he senses actually registers. His coordination is nil, his judgment is wiped out, and his sensory perception is inaccurate. Since his liver can metabolize one ounce of alcohol per hour, it will be sixteen hours—or well into the next day—before all of the alcohol is gone from his system.

If our partygoer is foolish enough to drink a pint and a quarter of whiskey on a dare, he will probably fall into a coma and be dangerously close to death. His vital brain centers which send out instructions for his heart and breathing are partially anesthetized. At a blood-alcohol level of .40 to .50, he will be in a coma, and at .60 to .70, he will die.

Unfortunately, every year a number of alcohol-related deaths occur because people try to chug a fifth of hard liquor on a dare.

But when does alcohol abuse really become a problem?

Do we have an alcoholic if a person drinks to the point of passing out once in his or her life and never does it again? Do you have to drink every day to be called an alcoholic? Can you ever get to the point of being legally intoxicated and *not* be an alcoholic? Are you an alcoholic if you can stop drinking for six months?

Jed was new on the alcohol rehab unit. The 55-year-old aeronautical engineer shuffled down the hall with his baggy black and white checkered pants and oversized gray sweater billowing behind him. Jed and I both already knew that he had a serious problem with alcohol. His hunched posture gave him a perfect vantage point over his potbelly at the diagonal tile pattern of the floor, which he examined methodically.

Once seated, Jed looked up over his dark glasses which would have slid off his face if his big red nose weren't bent to the right from a barroom brawl.

It was visiting hour, and the one son who still occasionally spoke to him had just called to postpone the visit. "Business, you know." Of course, Jed understood.

On the other side of the country, Jed's ex-wife was informed by her oldest daughter, "Dad's back in the drunk tank again."

"A leopard can't change his spots," she retorts.

Beneath Jed's peppered gray receding hairline was a pale image of a once brilliant and lucid mind. A Stanford graduate in 1964 and a job with a national defense contractor had sent Jed's career skyward like the rockets he designed. His career and being married to a sensitive junior high-school teacher who bore him four lovely children was all Jed could ask for.

But the incessant waves of time and stress began to wear down Jed's sandcastle life. Defense budget cuts. A layoff. Financial pressures. His wife's battle against breast cancer. His oldest daughter's unwanted teen pregnancy. His youngest son's serious drug problem. And his youngest daughter's abusive husband. All have contributed to Jed's ulcers and high blood pressure.

But, at a deeper level, Jed's once-joyful spirit was slowly being eaten away by the day-to-day routine of checking the wind resistance of Japanese import cars. None of these projects would be soaring past Jupiter and out to explore the farthest reaches of the solar system and the galaxy.

In despair and frustration, Jed started to routinely stop at the local watering hole to assuage the pain of his crumbling dreams. Three, four, or five martinis later and the sympathetic ear of Nick, the local tavern owner, seemed to have made things better—at least for a while. But unlike the orange skin and yellow eyes of Jed's 35-year-old roommate who was dying of advanced liver disease, there was still a sparkle of life in Jed's blue eyes. During the interview, he cackled, "Doc, I'm really going to kick it this time. There's still a lot of hunting and fishing trips in this old boy. And besides, I've got three grandchildren that I have to spoil."

By definition, Jed is an alcoholic. He has been arrested twice for DWI, lost his marriage due to drinking, alienated his children with his alcohol-related behavior, and been in a barroom fight. His memory is declining much more rapidly than that of a man his age who does not drink, and his doctor has recently told Jed that his drinking has exacerbated his ulcers, and begun to create mild cirrhosis of the liver.

If Jed continued to drink, he would be dead within one to two years.

Sheldon, on the other hand, is an 85-year-old retired sales manager who has enjoyed two or three beers each evening after work until his retirement twenty years ago. At that point, he cut down to one or two highballs two or three times a week because he felt that daily drinking was making him a little bit slower.

Sheldon's son, Chris, said that as far back as he can remember, his dad would come home from work, plop down on the couch with a beer in one hand and the paper in the other, and frown at the headlines while the evening news droned on the television in the background.

"At dinnertime Dad was alert and conversant with Mom and me and seemed to be a bit more relaxed than when he first walked in the door from work. . . . I can't remember his ever missing work or getting into any fights with Mom that were related to alcohol. An occasional beer or two on fishing trips, watching a ball game, or potting his flowers, and he was done. Mellow, relaxed, and easy to be around."

While using alcohol regularly for sixty-four years, Sheldon is not an alcoholic.

However, the regularity and amount of alcohol consumed are not the primary criteria for diagnosing an alcohol-abuse problem.

Becky, a 42-year-old school psychologist, gets drunk only three or four times a year. But when she does, things get out of hand quickly. Becky can prove to herself and others that she is not an alcoholic by going for weeks or even months without touching the stuff. But when Becky's stress level gets too high or she begins to lose control, she goes on alcohol binges.

After her last binge, Becky's husband finally had enough and started divorce proceedings. At the school's staff Christmas party, Becky made obvious sexual advances to her vice-principal in the presence of his wife. Becky was suspended without pay two weeks later, following a one-week unexcused absence from work, and ordered to enter a thirty-day rehabilitation program if she wanted her job back.

Becky is an episodic alcoholic.

At the far end of the spectrum of alcohol use is what is known as the "alcohol-dependent individual." Such individuals have gone far beyond using alcohol to calm their nerves, kill pain, reduce inhibitions, or party hearty. An alcohol-dependent person actually needs alcohol daily to prevent going into convulsive seizures. Such individuals no longer get the high of alcohol, but use alcohol to maintain a relatively normal level of functioning and to prevent delirium tremens.

Joe, a wiry, 150-pound 35-year-old transient, arrived in the emergency room in a semiconscious stupor. His eyes rolled up into the back of his head periodically, and his body stiffened violently and arched off the bed as if jolted by a powerful electric current. Within an hour and a half, the anticonvulsive medications began to reduce Joe's seizures, and he regained some semblance of consciousness.

But almost immediately Joe reported seeing flying bugs and insects in the air and began to scream and hit himself to kill the imaginary bugs which he actually felt crawling on his skin. Joe had no idea of where he was, what month or year he was in, or what was going on around him.

Joe's sense of reality is very different. It is consumed by seeing and actually feeling these bugs which no one else perceives. His violent lunges at himself and the staff require his being tied down to the bed. Joe's vital signs are taken, and his pulse is 160, blood pressure 190/110, and fever 101.5 degrees. His arms and legs tremble involuntarily.

Joe has been a routine drinker of 1 to 1½ fifths of hard liquor a day for the past ten years and has not had a drink for two days. Joe is going through alcohol withdrawal with grand mal seizures and delirium tremens.

Certainly no one would deny that Joe has a serious alcohol problem. But sometimes recreational alcohol use and alcohol abuse become very difficult to sort out in the context of a person's life.

Blake, a 55-year-old bank CEO, has been driven to strive for perfection all of his life. In his quest to make his bank and staff the best in the county, Blake has done more than step on just a few people's toes. His meticulous compulsion to detail and lack of sensitivity have driven more than a few coworkers away.

Then one night at a company party last May, one of the company's new secretaries, an attractive 32-year-old named Jill, asked Blake to dance. A few rum and Cokes later, Blake and Jill were sharing intimacies about themselves. Two hours later, Blake offered Jill a ride home and expressed somewhat inappropriate disappointment when she chose to leave with a female coworker.

The following week, Blake is confronted at work by the vice-president and chairman of the board. His briefcase and coat are picked up by the two men, and he is escorted briskly out the door into a waiting car. He is driven to the local alcohol-rehabilitation unit. There he is greeted by an intake coordinator, program director, head counselor, and several coworkers, including the secretary who had asked him to dance. Each in turn expressed their "love and concern" for Blake to take care of his alcohol problem. When Blake's 21-year-old daughter says that she's had a suspicion that her dad may have had an alcohol problem for a number of years, Blake begins to wonder if he's crazy, or are these people really right.

Blake is assured by the chairman of the board, vice-president, and other key coworkers and board members that he is a valuable CEO, and will be gladly welcomed back to his position when he completes his alcohol-rehab program.

In an effort to break down his defenses and denial, Blake is slammed verbally by his counselors every time he expresses a concern that he may not be an alcoholic. "Sometimes I really wonder if I just had a few too many drinks and said something kind of inappropriate to Jill." Blake is informed by the head counselor that such statements represent denial of his alcohol problem, and he must fully and completely admit that his alcohol consumption is completely and totally out of control before he can be helped.

After being in this environment for thirty days, Blake did begin to accept that fact that he was an alcoholic and accepted treatment. Unfortunately, upon his return to the bank, Blake is called in by the board of directors and told that he has been fired.

Despite financial distress, Blake does not turn to the bottle to cope with his problems. It is only after three months of individual counseling and a few occasional social drinks that Blake begins to realize he is not in fact an alcoholic. He had been set up by disgruntled board members and coworkers who used an overzealous yet sincere alcohol-rehabilitation program to meet their own personal objectives.

Other than the inappropriate remark to Jill, Blake has never had an alcohol related problem in his life, and is not an alcohol abuser in any meaningful sense. His alcohol usage appeared to be coincidental with a work-related problem which was not related to alcohol at all.

Alcohol can sometimes be blamed for problems it does not create.

WHY DO PEOPLE DRINK?

In the course of my nine years as director of psychology for a drug and alcohol rehabilitation program, I have had the opportunity to ask approximately 1,400 alcoholics why they drink.

Here are some typical responses:

"It started out as a social thing, just going out with the boys after work to have a few beers to unwind."

"I drink to cope with the pain of divorce. After four children and nineteen years of marriage, my husband left me for one of my best friends."

"I drink simply to relieve the boredom. My husband is a rancher and never around, and I'm stuck on a 200-acre ranch with no neighbors within shouting distance. I get bored and lonely, and there is nothing to do, so the bottle of Jack Daniels is my friend."

"Alcohol helps me cope with pain. I injured my lower back $2^{1}/_{2}$ years ago, and a few beers or a couple of martinis really takes the edge off."

"I drink to help me meet women in bars. I'm a real shy kind of person, and I've never been dancing when I'm not under the influence of alcohol. It serves as a way of opening me up and helping me relate to others. If I had never had a drink, I don't think I would have ever had a date."

"I drink to steady my nerves. After twenty years with the phone company, my division was told that within the next three years we would be phased out."

"I guess I really drink to cope with the pain of losing my 2-year-old son nineteen years ago. It's something I've never really been able to handle, and I've had to block it out with alcohol."

"I drink because my job is the pits. It's miserable sitting there all day grading lumber. I feel like anyone could do this job and sometimes I just can't stand it anymore. Alcohol is a way of helping me escape from the job stress."

"I drink because I have to. If I don't have a drink, my body begins to shake and tremble, and I begin to feel like I'm going to go crazy."

As can be seen from the above examples, there are a variety of reasons why people drink. But the basic underlying reason people drink is that they feel some form of physical or emotional pain, in a very broad sense of the term. Although boredom isn't really pain, it certainly is a very unpleasant emotion. And people who do not know how to escape boredom and entertain themselves frequently turn to alcohol.

If you don't believe this, just ask any typical high-school weekend partygoer. These kids are basically bored out of their minds and look at alcohol as a way of escaping a very mundane reality.

As you already know, alcohol is a pain killer, and in the short run it does a very good job eliminating physical and emotional pain.

But, over the long run, alcohol tends to have a diminishing effect as your tolerance for it increases. It takes more and more alcohol to achieve the same effect. The diminishing returns lead to what is known as "alcohol dependence." When you are dependent on alcohol, you are no longer drinking to feel better or kill pain, you are drinking because you have to, to keep from going into convulsive seizures or delirium tremens.

From a broader perspective, another major reason for the 20.1 million alcoholics in the United States is that alcohol is a *legal* mind-altering drug. Every Sunday afternoon in the fall, millions of pro-football fans are inundated with a barrage of beer commercials. The basic message is drink up, you'll be happy, more relaxed, better able to bond with your male buddies.

WHO IS AN ALCOHOLIC?

Definitions of alcoholism are extremely diversified. Here are some examples:

"An alcoholic is someone who spends all his time in bars."

——Anonymous

"An alcoholic is my father-in-law."

"An alcoholic is somebody who sits on the sidewalk and asks for money to buy wine."

On a more serious level, let's look at some professional definitions of alcoholism:

Marty Mann, a founding member of the National Council on Alcoholism (NCA), defines an alcoholic as "A very sick person, who is the victim of an insidious, progressive disease, which all too often ends in fatality. An alcoholic can be recognized, diagnosed, and treated successfully."

According to Mark Keller, the former editor of the *Journal of Studies on Alcohol,* "Alcoholism is a chronic disease manifested by repeated implicative drinking so as to cause injury to the drinker's health or to his social or economic functioning."

Alcoholics Anonymous does not have an official definition of alcoholism, but the concept of Dr. William Silkworth, one of AA's supporters, is sometimes cited by AA members: "An obsession of the mind and an allergy of the body. The obsession or compulsion guarantees that the sufferer will drink against his own will and interest. The allergy guarantees that the sufferer will either die or go insane." An operative definition in AA is that "An alcoholic is a person who cannot predict with accuracy what will happen when he takes a drink."

In 1951 the alcoholism subcommittee of the World Health Organization defined alcoholism as "Any form of drinking which in extent goes beyond the tradition and customary 'dietary' use, or the ordinary compliance with the social drinking customs of the community concerned, irrespective of etiologic (causative) factors leading to such behavior, and irrespective also of the extent to which such etiological factors are dependent upon heredity, constitution, or acquired physiopathological and metabolic influences."

The American Psychiatric Association's committee on *DSM III-R* defines alcoholism: "This category is for patients whose alcohol intake is great enough to damage their physical health, or their personal or social functioning, or when it has become a prerequisite to normal functioning." Three types of alcoholism were further identified: episodic excessive drinking, habitual excessive drinking, and alcohol addiction.

According to the American Medical Association, "Alcoholism is an illness characterized by significant impairment that is directly associated with persistent and excessive use of alcohol. Impairment may involve physiological, psychological, or social dysfunction."

Implicit or explicit in all of these definitions is the concept of alcoholism as a disease.

It is crucial for alcoholics to think of themselves as having a disease. This takes the burden of responsibility off the alcoholic for having a sinful character, or being a moral weakling. If alcoholism is a disease, by definition the patient is not responsible for it. The accepted idea is that a sick or diseased person does not choose to be this way and that a sick patient should receive sympathy.

With very little thought, anyone can see that this disease notion could be vastly abused by alcoholics.

Therefore, the disease concept has been modified and described as a chronic disease which requires the *active participation* on the part of the alcoholic in order to *manage* the disease.

Certainly alcoholism is not a disease in the sense of the flu or strep throat. But, most importantly, the disease concept of alcoholism has lowered the sin or moral-failing barrier and allowed millions of alcoholics to receive treatment they otherwise would have rejected.

But, disease or not, let's take a close look at the actual questions used to help professional clinicians determine whether their patients are suffering from alcohol abuse or dependency.

The *DSM III-R,* a professional manual used to diagnose all emotional and substance-abuse problems defines alcohol abuse as:

> "(a) A pattern of pathological alcohol use; need for daily use of alcohol for adequate functioning; inability to cut down or stop drinking; repeated efforts to control or reduce excess drinking by 'going on the wagon' (period of temporary abstinence) or restricting drinking to certain times of the day; binges (remaining intoxicated throughout the day for at least two days); occasional consumption of a fifth of spirits (or its equivalent in wine or beer); amnesic periods for events occurring while intoxicated (blackouts); continuation of drinking despite a serious physical disorder that the individual knows is exacerbated by the alcohol use; drinking of nonbeverage alcohol.
>
> (b) Impairment in social or occupational functioning due to alcohol use; e.g., violence while intoxicated, absence from work, loss of job, legal difficulties (e.g., arrest for intoxicated behavior, traffic accidents while intoxicated), arguments or difficulties with family or friends because of excessive alcohol use.
>
> (c) Duration of disturbance at least one month."

The *DSM III-R* diagnostic criteria for alcohol dependence includes all of the criteria necessary for alcohol abuse plus tolerance and withdrawal.

"Tolerance" describes a need for markedly increased amounts of alcohol to achieve the desired effects, or markedly diminished effect with regular use of the same amount.

"Withdrawal" means the development of serious alcohol-withdrawal symptoms (e.g., morning "shakes" and malaise relieved by drinking) after cessation of or reduction in drinking.

With these definitions in mind, let's take a close look at alcohol and see whether it really is a problem in your life.

Remember, denial is the primary defense mechanism of the alcoholic, so check your answers with those who care about and know you.

Alcoholism Questionnaire

Directions: Answer the following questions as honestly as possible. Try not to minimize or deny questions which apply to you. Similarly, do not exaggerate or answer yes to responses which are not descriptive of your drinking habits.

1. Has drinking alcohol ever caused you any noticeable problems in your life? (If yes, has heavy drinking of alcohol been a problem for you over a period of at least one month?)

Interpersonal Significance Questions:

2. Has drinking alcohol ever interfered with your education, your occupation, or your work around your home?
3. Has drinking alcohol caused you problems with your family or caused your family to worry about you?
4. Has drinking alcohol ever interfered with your friendships or social life?
5. Have you ever gotten into trouble with authorities because of your alcohol consumption?
6. As far as you know, has your health ever suffered because of your alcohol consumption?
7. Have you ever received medication or treatment for an alcohol problem?

8. (If yes on question 7) Have you ever been hospitalized because of alcohol or its effects?
9. How old were you when alcohol caused you the most trouble in your life?

Adjunctive Questions:

Group I

10. Have you ever had the shakes very badly when you stopped drinking alcohol? (If yes) Has this happened more than one time?
11. Have you ever had convulsions, visions, or delirium tremens when you stopped drinking alcohol?
12. Have you ever kept drinking alcohol even though a doctor said it was harming your physical health?
13. Have you ever had any medical problems due to alcohol such as cirrhosis of the liver, gastritis, pancreatitis, muscle pains, or burning in your hands or feet?
14. Have there ever been times when you blacked out and could not remember what you did while you were drinking alcohol?
15. Have you ever drunk alcohol continually or regularly for at least two days in a row? (If yes) Have you done this more than once?
16. Have there ever been times when you drank a fifth or more of whiskey in one day, one or more gallon of wine in one day, or one or more cases of beer in one day?
17. Over a period of months, did you ever notice that it took more alcohol to make you feel good or get you high?

Group II

18. Have you ever noticed that you could not control or limit your alcohol consumption once you took one or two drinks?
19. Have you ever really wanted to cut down on your alcohol consumption but found that you could not?
20. Have you ever tried to keep your drinking under control by limiting yourself to drinking only at certain times of the day or days of the week?
21. Have you ever felt that you needed an alcoholic drink when you

first woke up in the morning to help you get going? (If no) Have you ever felt you could not get through the whole day without an alcoholic drink?
22. Have you ever drunk alcohol substitutes like mouthwash or shaving lotion?

Group III

23. Have you ever been arrested because of alcohol-related behavior?
24. Have you ever gotten into trouble at work, missed work, or been fired because of drinking or being hung over?
25. Has anyone ever accused you of driving while intoxicated?
26. Have you ever gotten into physical fights while you were drinking alcohol?

Group IV

27. Has your family tried to get you to cut down or stop drinking alcohol?
28. Have your friends or other people tried to get you to cut down or stop drinking alcohol?
29. Did you ever feel guilty or ashamed about your drinking habits?

Scoring: In order to be diagnosed as having an alcohol-abuse problem you must have answered:
*Yes to question 1
*Yes to at least one question in 2–8
*Yes to at least one question in any three of the groups I–IV.

In order to meet the criteria for alcohol dependence, in addition to meeting the alcohol-abuse criteria, you must also have answered yes to question 10 or 11.

Remember that the major psychological defense mechanism of the alcoholic is denial. Alcoholics will tend to ignore, block out, or lie about their drinking even though it is very apparent to everyone who knows them.

FAST FACTS REGARDING ALCOHOL

Personal, Economic, and Social Costs

- It is estimated that 77 percent of the men and 60 percent of the women in our country drink alcohol. This comprises 67 percent of the adult population. But, since 1978, the consumption of alcohol has dropped in our country by 5 percent.
- During the year 1984, a statistically normal American consumed the equivalent of 2.69 gallons of pure ethanol. The average American drinks 2.34 gallons of liquor, 2.77 gallons of wine, and 30.4 gallons of beer per year.
- While in 1967 the United States per capita alcohol consumption was second only to the country of France, by 1990 it had dropped to twenty-fourth compared to other countries.
- Of the approximate 67 percent of our population who drinks alcohol, 70 percent of this drinking population consumes only 20 percent of all the alcohol. The remaining 30 percent of the alcohol consumers drink 80 percent of the alcohol. Most importantly, 33 percent of that heavy-drinking 30 percent, or about 10 percent of the total population, consumes 50 percent of all alcohol.
- Approximately 10 percent of the total adult population (over 20 million people) are problem drinkers.
- Approximately 2.8 million teen-agers (14–17-year-olds) have an alcohol problem.
- Therefore, in the United States, over 20 million people have serious drinking problems.
- If family members who are directly affected by alcohol are included, approximately 82 million people (one-third of the population) suffer the effects of alcohol problems.
- The projected costs for 1983 based on direct and indirect alcohol-related losses for our country are $116.7 billion.
- In 1984 it was estimated that alcohol-related deaths may run as high as 10 percent of all deaths each year. The alcoholic's average life expectancy is reduced by 15 years.
- Alcohol is believed to be involved in approximately 50 percent of all home accidents and about 70 percent of all drownings.

- Studies indicate that in 4 out of 5 suicide attempts, the individual had been drinking.
- Alcohol is implicated in over half of all homicides. It is also an important factor in assaults in general, and alcohol played a role in the crime in an estimated 72 percent of the perpetrators and 79 percent of the victims.
- Statistical studies have consistently shown that a minimum of 20 percent of all hospitalized persons have a significant alcohol problem, whatever the presenting medical problem or admitting diagnosis.
- As of 1987, the National Institute of Alcohol Abuse and Alcoholism estimated that approximately 85 percent of our nation's alcoholics and problem drinkers are not receiving any formal treatment.

Facts About Alcohol and Your Body

- Your body can metabolize about 1 ounce of 86-proof whiskey, 12 ounces of beer, or 4 ounces of wine per hour.
- 20 ounces of whiskey consumed within one hour will place an average individual in a coma and dangerously close to death.
- With repeated exposure to alcohol, your central nervous system adapts to its presence. You learn to tolerate more and more alcohol and still maintain a normal level of functioning. This property makes alcohol an addictive drug, and over the long run your body requires larger dosages to induce the effects which you could receive earlier with smaller levels of alcohol.
- Alcohol is an irritant. That is why you have a burning sensation in your stomach when the alcohol goes down. Alcohol in your stomach will promote the flow of gastric juices. Increasing quantities of alcohol actually impede or stop the digestive process entirely.
- Alcohol has only slight effects on the circulatory system and affects your heartbeat and blood pressure minimally. However, recent research has shown that moderate alcohol consumption (3–4 ounces a day) can lead to enlarged hearts in middle-aged men.
- Alcohol interferes with your liver's ability to maintain stable blood

sugar, and over time is implicated in the vast majority of cases of irreversible cirrhosis of the liver, which is often fatal.
- With prolonged use, alcohol can lead to dementia, disorganization, confusion, and irreversible organic brain damage.
- Alcohol is the third leading cause of death in the United States.

HOW TO CALCULATE YOUR BLOOD-ALCOHOL LEVEL (BAL)

Although people vary in the extent to which alcohol affects their bodies, the three primary predictors of your blood alcohol level are:

(1) the amount of alcohol consumed
(2) your body weight
(3) the length of time since your last drink

It is important to realize that your liver can metabolize about one ounce of alcohol per hour. Two ounces of alcohol require two hours, three ounces three hours, and so on. So, when you calculate how much time it will take you to get over the effects of alcohol, figure about one hour for each ounce you have consumed.

Your body weight and the quantity of alcohol you consume directly affects your blood-alcohol level. To be considered legally intoxicated in most states requires a blood-alcohol level of .10 percent. Other states, such as California, have lowered the blood-alcohol level required for legal intoxication to .08 percent.

Use the following table to help you calculate your estimated blood-alcohol levels within one hour of consumption of the alcohol on an empty stomach. Remember that it takes your liver about one hour to metabolize or neutralize one ounce of alcohol.

How to calculate your blood-alcohol level (BAL):

1. Find the number of ounces of alcohol you have consumed in the last hour, using the bottom row.

2. Find your estimated body weight using the column on the far left.

3. Read across the row of your weight until you are above the number in the bottom row that represents the number of ounces of alcohol consumed in the last hour.

4. The resulting number is your BAL. For example, a 140-pound woman who had 2 ounces of alcohol in an hour would have an estimated BAL of 0.44.

Blood-Alcohol Levels

	1	2	3	4	5	6	7	8	9	10	11	12
260	.02	.024	.036	.048	.06	.072	.084	.096	.11	.12	.13	.14
250	.02	.025	.038	.05	.063	.075	.086	.10	.119	.123	.135	.145
240	.02	.026	.04	.052	.066	.08	.09	.105	.12	.13	.142	.155
230	.02	.027	.041	.054	.068	.082	.094	.109	.122	.135	.15	.16
220	.02	.028	.042	.058	.072	.085	.10	.115	.13	.14	.155	.17
210	.02	.029	.044	.06	.074	.09	.105	.12	.135	.145	.16	.175
200	.02	.03	.046	.064	.078	.096	.11	.122	.14	.155	.17	.185
190	.02	.032	.05	.066	.082	.099	.115	.13	.145	.16	.175	.195
180	.02	.034	.052	.07	.088	.105	.12	.14	.15	.175	.19	.21
170	.02	.036	.055	.074	.092	.11	.13	.15	.165	.18	.20	.22
160	.02	.038	.06	.078	.10	.12	.14	.155	.175	.188	.21	.25
150	.021	.041	.063	.084	.105	.125	.145	.165	.185	.21	.23	.255
140	.022	.044	.068	.09	.11	.138	.16	.18	.20	.23	.25	.26
130	.024	.047	.072	.098	.12	.145	.17	.19	.22	.24	.26	.27
120	.026	.05	.078	.11	.13	.16	.18	.21	.24	.26	.29	.31
110	.028	.056	.086	.112	.145	.17	.19	.23	.25	.27	.31	.34
100	.03	.06	.095	.122	.155	.19	.24	.25	.28	.31	.34	.37
90	.034	.068	.125	.14	.175	.21	.24	.28	.30	.34	.37	.40
0	1	2	3	4	5	6	7	8	9	10	11	12

Number of Ounces of Alcohol per Hour

EFFECTS

.02% —Drivers show mild change, may seem slightly elated.
.05% —Drivers hesitant; alternate from "Who cares?" to impulsive aggression. The driver is in a danger zone. Try not to drive. If you *must* drive, be extremely cautious.
.10% —Judgment seriously affected. Coordination impaired. Legally considered "under the influence." Simply stated—DON'T DRIVE.
.15% —Unmistakably drunk. All faculties seriously affected.
.30% —Stuporous.
.40% —Unconscious. Possibly in coma and on verge of death.

NOTE: This table is only a guide and is not sufficiently accurate to be considered legal evidence.

ALCOHOL TREATMENT TECHNIQUES AND APPROACHES

Traditionally, individual counseling has been one method of treating alcoholism. Unfortunately, many times this method fails because alcoholics see the counselor only once or twice a week and spend the rest of their time in a situation which may be conducive to drinking.

Recently, inpatient alcohol-rehabilitation units have become more available. Typically, patients are admitted to these programs for anywhere from one to four weeks and then followed up with outpatient group and individual therapy.

During this time, alcoholics are initially detoxed over a period of one to three days, and then involved in structured group programs, many of which include a twelve-step recovery program, discussed on the following pages.

Alcohol treatment programs try to break down the alcoholic's denial that he or she has an alcohol problem. Many times strong and repeated confrontation is necessary to break down this barrier.

The family is included in any comprehensive alcoholic-treatment program. The alcoholic is given information from all family members to help break down the denial and learn to cope with the problem.

Many times, members of the alcoholic's family develop what is known as codependence: their behavior revolves around that of the alcoholic. They typically find themselves making excuses for their spouse's or parent's behavior, covering up for them, or doing things to keep other people from realizing that they are alcoholics. Although trying to help, these people are actually *promoting* the alcoholic's problem by helping them avoid the consequences of their behavior, a phenomenon known as "enabling."

Disulfiram or Antabuse has long been used to help alcoholics overcome the urge to drink. This drug, when consumed and combined with alcohol, causes a violent physical reaction characterized by throbbing of the head and neck, flushing, breathing difficulties, nausea, vomiting, sweating, rapid heartbeat, weakness, and vertigo. The intensity of the reaction to disulfiram varies from person to person, but it takes up to four to five days to get the drug out of the system so it does not cause a reaction with alcohol.

Unfortunately, the effectiveness of disulfiram is dependent on the alcoholic's taking the drug in the first place.

By far the most prevalent of all treatment approaches to alcohol in the United States at this time is the Alcoholics Anonymous twelve-step model. This is a spiritually based program which began as recovering alcoholics helping each other.

Although it is far beyond this text to go into detail on how the twelve steps work, a framework of the basic structure of the twelve steps is certainly worth reviewing:

> Step 1. "We admitted we were powerless over alcohol and that our lives had become unmanageable."
> Step 2. "We came to believe that a power greater than ourselves could restore us to sanity."
> Step 3. "We made a decision to turn our will and our lives over to the care of God as we understood Him."

The first three steps point up the necessity of giving up previous attempts at controlling drinking and making a leap of faith that there is a higher power within you that can help you control it.

Step 4. "We made a searching and fearless moral inventory of ourselves."

Step 5. "We admitted to God, to ourselves, and to one other human being the exact nature of our wrongs."

Steps four and five are often very difficult for the alcoholic. They essentially involve taking yourself to task for all of the things you've done wrong in life or all of the people you've hurt. These steps require honest soul searching to root out and release the guilt and shame which have accumulated over your lifetime. Honest soul searching for guilt and shame is easier said than done. But you've got to know what you have done and are doing wrong before you can change it.

Step 6. "We were entirely ready to have God remove all these defects of our character."

Step 7. "We humbly ask God to remove our shortcomings."

Steps six and seven illustrate the power of forgiving yourself. Having God or your higher power forgive you comes directly from the Lord's Prayer, "And forgive us our trespasses." If you continue to carry around guilt and shame, at a deep level you won't feel that you deserve anything really good, and you will continue to sabotage your own life and to set yourself up for failure.

Step 8. "We made a list of all persons we had harmed and became willing to make amends to them all."

Step 9. "We made direct amends to such people wherever possible, except when to do so would injure them or others."

Steps eight and nine center on the idea of actively trying to correct your mistakes. You've admitted whom you have hurt and how, and now you try actively to repair as much of the damage as possible.

Step 10. "We continued to take personal inventory and when we were wrong promptly admitted it."

Step ten points out the necessity of continuing to be honest with yourself and allowing your conscience to guide you.

> Step 11. "We sought through prayer and meditation to improve our conscious contact with God as we understood Him, praying only for knowledge of His will for us and the power to carry that out."
> Step 12. "Having had a spiritual awakening as a result of these steps, we tried to carry this message to alcoholics and to practice these principles in all our affairs."

Steps eleven and twelve come back full circle to the spiritual or higher-power source, yet add a directive or prescription not only to continue to use these principles in your life, but to carry the message of healing to other alcoholics.

The Twelve Steps of the Alcoholics Anonymous (or Narcotics Anonymous) model are not a one-time quick cure, but an ongoing life process or program.

Recently, cognitive psychology has come on the scene in the treatment of alcoholism. Many psychologists have begun experimenting with teaching alcoholics to engage in what is known as controlled or social drinking. Valiant and his colleagues have run a number of experiments indicating that it may be possible to teach alcoholics to drink socially without full-blown alcoholic relapses, although definitive results are not yet in.

Although the results of these programs appear to be quite variable, it is promising to realize that cognitive psychology may be valuable in the fight against alcoholism.

Most recently, an innovative approach to the treatment of alcohol and drug abuse has involved a mixture of different therapies in an eclectic framework. In the comprehensive alcohol and drug abuse program in which I acted as director of psychology, patients were encouraged not only to use the twelve steps, but also to engage in recreational therapy, relaxation training, cognitive therapy, biofeedback, assertiveness training, art therapy, refusal-skills training, emotional-ventilation techniques, situational engineering, and replacement activities and pastimes to take the place of alcohol.

Such integrated eclectic approaches are springing up all over the country. It is not uncommon for a comprehensive alcohol-rehabilitation unit to have the following professional staff: medical director, psychiatrist, clinical psychologist, marriage/family/child counselors, recreational therapist, and even biofeedback technicians.

Although such extensive treatment programs are very intense and diversified, most focus on four basic principals of intervention:

1. Detoxification of the alcoholic
2. Removal of the alcoholic from the situation which facilitates drinking
3. The immersion of the alcoholic in a strong and pervasive support network involving other recovering alcoholics and staff
4. The substitution of activities, pastimes, and relationships which alcoholics lose when they give up alcohol

A very promising and open-minded approach to the treatment of alcoholism has come from the employers of alcoholics. Alcoholism cost businesses billions of dollars each year in lost time and productivity. Until recently, alcoholics could be sure of being fired if their employers found out about their heavy drinking. With the advent of employee assistance programs (EAPs), alcoholic employees are being given help where once they would have been fired.

Such programs involve educating employers of the signs of alcoholism in their workers, and instructing them on steps to help their employees correct the problem.

In a number of cases I've been involved with, after repeated problems with alcohol, employees are informed that they must either participate in a comprehensive rehabilitation program and follow-up care, or be dismissed from their jobs.

Such individuals are often highly motivated to recover and appreciate the fact that their employers are recognizing their problems and trying to help them. In fact, a number of company policies have been developed which prohibit an individual from being fired from a job unless some attempt at rehabilitation has been made. Yes, alcohol is a very manageable and treatable disorder. But in order to get help, first you have to realize that you have a problem with alcohol. Unfortunately, like many of the other emotional problems discussed in this book, alcoholism is usually protected by the very strong defense mechanism of denial. Part of your brain will desperately want to hold on to the alcohol and not give it up. In order to break through this denial, you need not only to answer the questionnaire as honestly as possible, but also to ask your family and friends whether they feel your responses are honest and fair.

If you are an alcoholic, there is a world of hope and help out there for you.

Gone is the stigma of the alcoholic as a disordered character, moral weakling, or sinful person. Alcoholism is generally recognized as a chronic disease which, with effort, can be managed successfully.

And in the course of managing this disease, you will be exposed to the caring, nurturing, loving, and helpful group of people who comprise the national community and family of recovering alcoholics.

CHAPTER 4

AM I A DRUG ADDICT?

Chris and Charlene marched up the narrow stony trail toward the jagged granite summit with the youthful exuberance of two young lovers. It was a cold, crisp November morning, and a few islands of white clouds floated in the sea of blue.

The northern California wilderness was everything Chris hoped it would be, and the enthusiasm of a beautiful 22-year-old guide gave Chris a sense of excitement that he hadn't felt since his first high-school date.

Chris was astonished by the transition in scenery. A trailhead surrounded by towering sequoias had soon yielded to a narrow, sandy path along a babbling stream. Lush green trees, vines, and vegetation were everywhere. To his left, Chris noticed the whispering of a seasonal waterfall trickling down the soft green moss-covered face of granite rock.

They next came out onto a rocky trail with a wall of sheer granite on the left and a panoramic view of the tree-covered mountains and valleys on the right. As they continued hiking, the trail widened, yet groups of gnarly red-barked manzanita bushes cluttered the path to the summit. Charlene encouraged Chris to follow her to the top of a rocky mound, and as Chris pulled himself over the top, he could see a 14,500-foot snow-covered mountain looming like a giant.

They continued their journey upward and finally came to a series of jagged gray granite crags, towering hundreds of feet into the sky.

To the right was a domed rock with what seemed to be a winding path somehow faintly sketched into the granite. Charlene bolted up the granite dome like a billy goat, while Chris measured his steps and holds carefully. About three-fourths of the way up, Chris's sense of self-preservation overcame his desire for excitement, and he returned to the foot of the dome.

After a delectable lunch of red grapes, Monterey Jack cheese, Wheat Thins, and a bottle of grape juice, Charlene pulled out a white vial and said, "Do you want to do a line?"

Chris watched Charlene put a scoop of the white powder onto a small pink spoon and snort it up her right nostril before repeating the procedure with her left.

The next thing Chris knew, he was sitting there with his left index finger pinched over his left nostril and a pinch of cocaine directly beneath his right nostril.

> "I remember the first thing I felt was an incredible tingling sensation in my nostrils, sinuses, and down the back of my throat. It's kind of like the feeling you get when you spray 24-hour Relief Dristan into your sinuses, yet a lot more powerful. . . . Then, a few seconds later, I felt an exhilarated alertness of consciousness and my perceptions started to change.
>
> Charlene then jumped up, and we both bolted down the trail running and jumping over rocks like a couple of little kids. My inhibitions, which were already barely existent, had now completely disappeared. I felt like a squirrel, I was so energetic, bouncing from rock to rock and leaping over fallen tree trunks. The intensity of the already beautiful situation was magnified threefold. The sky seemed to be an electric blue, and the rocks and trees seemed to exude a life force that I had never been aware of."

Two and a half hours later, Chris and Charlene snorted another line of coke and tumbled into Charlene's waterbed to get to know each other even better.

Chris, now a successful 37-year-old account executive, has continued to use cocaine occasionally over the years. A line or two here or there with a friend, or at a party, and Chris receives a more gentle reminder of the once-intense high he first experienced. But Chris recognizes the potential addictive danger of cocaine and limits himself to minimal usage only three or four times a year. Chris cannot be diagnosed as having a cocaine abuse or dependency problem because he has had no life-damaging consequences due to cocaine.

Jimmy, a 29-year-old heir to a multimillion-dollar northeastern estate, sat back and smiled smugly as he negotiated a reduced fee for his sessions with me. Jimmy had been required by the court to receive six months of psychological counseling after pleading guilty to a charge of cocaine possession.

I was soon contacted by Jimmy's lawyer, who told me that Jimmy had just been found innocent of a charge of murdering his father the year before. An icy chill went through my veins when the attorney told me, "Well, he was found innocent. But after you get to know him, see what you believe."

During my sessions with Jimmy, it soon became apparent that I was dealing with a conscienceless creature who felt no sense of guilt or remorse over any of his actions. He had, in fact, successfully completed numerous thefts and burglaries, and had only recently been caught on a possession charge. Furthermore, he had actively been involved in dealing cocaine.

In our fourth session, Jimmy confided to me that once when he was on cocaine, he "saw the face of the devil," and felt as if his soul had been stolen from him. He described craving cocaine so badly that he only reluctantly refrained from smashing a brick through a jewelry store window when a police patrol car drove within twenty feet of him.

Jimmy's father, a wealthy man from an old-money family, had drawn the line and told Jimmy that if he didn't get some help for his cocaine problem he would be disinherited. Jimmy's allowance was $50,000 a year, and he stood to inherit over $20 million on his thirtieth birthday.

Faced with the prospect of losing his multimillion-dollar inheritance and the overwhelming compulsion to satisfy his needs for cocaine, Jimmy's thinking and judgment became maniacal.

In our eighth session, Jimmy admitted giving a twelve-year-old cocaine-addicted runner a semiautomatic rifle and instructing him on how and when to murder Jimmy's dad.

I'll never forget his expressionless dark eyes as Jimmy smiled and told me how the twelve-year-old runner described his father screaming Jimmy's name as bullet after bullet was pumped into his dying body.

Jimmy's justification was that he felt he had simply become an apparition of the drug. Everything he thought, felt, and did revolved around maintaining his supply of cocaine. And Jimmy would stop at nothing to get his supply of coke.

After going through the motions of six months of counseling, it became apparent that Jimmy had no intention whatsoever of trying to kick his cocaine habit. He refused a referral to an inpatient treatment program. Jimmy is still heavily involved in cocaine abuse.

Jimmy is a cocaine addict.

PROPERTIES OF COCAINE

Cocaine has long been used by Colombian indian tribes who routinely chew the coca leaf to obtain energy and a sense of well-being. Reports of chewing the coca leaf did not reach Europe until the sixteenth century. A German scientist isolated a pure form of cocaine from the coca leaf in 1855. In 1884, Sigmund Freud began to experiment with cocaine on himself and his psychiatric patients. Predominantly through Freud's efforts, cocaine became so popular in Europe that a song was even written about it. Later, however, Freud discontinued all use of cocaine both personally and professionally as he became aware of its effects on the mind and body of the user.

Pharmacologically, cocaine may best be described as a stimulant and a local anesthetic.

Recently, the free-base form of cocaine, also known as crack, has become available for smoking. Crack is made by mixing baking soda and water with cocaine to make an insoluble form which is rocklike in appearance, can be broken into pieces, ignited, and the smoke inhaled.

As mentioned earlier, cocaine is a powerful central nervous system stimulant, and it is also a very effective local anesthetic, with its own vasoconstrictor action.

When inhaled, 25–100 mg. of pure cocaine produces maximum

central nervous system effects for about 15–30 minutes. These effects have been described by cocaine users as a mixture of exhilaration, euphoria, self-control, confidence, greater energy and endurance, and complete elimination of the needs for food and sleep.

It is believed that cocaine works within the cells of your body by stimulating the release of and blocking the brain's uptake of neurotransmitters (brain messenger chemicals) called dopamine and norepinephrine.

Cocaine is one of the most powerful pharmacological reinforcers known to man. Once cocaine has been used, the urge to continue is powerful. Cocaine helps induce a pleasurable, seldom-achieved state of ecstatic experiences, which can be magnified dramatically through intravenous usage or smoking crack, its free-base form.

To get an idea of the reinforcement properties of cocaine, you need to know that it is the only drug that laboratory animals will prefer over food, water, and even sex. Laboratory mice will self-administer cocaine until they overdose and die.

As usage of cocaine increases, signs of toxicity begin to appear. The initial effects of cocaine and crack involve vasoconstriction, dilation of the pupils, increased blood pressure, breathing rate, heart rate, and body temperature. Heavy cocaine users typically lose their appetite and have difficulty sleeping, and those who snort cocaine on a daily basis often have a runny nose. As the dosage of cocaine increases, convulsions and respiratory failure are possible, as well as liver damage and complete cardiovascular collapse. Such a cardiovascular accident is believed to be the cause of death in basketball star Len Bias, who died after taking some cocaine at a party.

The heavy cocaine abuser may hallucinate such things as insects crawling on his skin and may become involved in violent and aggressive behavior. Often the nasal septum, which separates the two nostrils, is perforated or ulcerated in chronic cocaine sniffers. Loss of weight, poor nutrition, and irritability are often seen in chronic users. In extremely high doses, depression and paranoia are apparent, with the paranoia bordering on severe delusional behavior in which the cocaine addict does not trust anyone.

In terms of prevalence, 25 million Americans indicate that they have tried cocaine at some point in their lives. About 12 million have used it in the past year, 5.7 million in the past month.

Cocaine Abuse and Addiction Questionnaire

Directions: Answer the following questions as honestly as possible. Do not deny or minimize your responses, but do not answer yes to questions that do not apply to you.

1. Have you ever used cocaine more than once in a one-month period?
2. Has cocaine ever caused you any problems or discomfort in your life?
3. Has cocaine interfered with your schoolwork, your employment, or your work around your home?
4. Has cocaine caused you problems with your family or caused your family to worry about you?
5. Has cocaine ever interfered with your friendships or social life?
6. Have you ever gotten into trouble with the police or authorities because of cocaine usage?
7. Have you ever received medication or treatment for a cocaine habit?
8. Have you ever been hospitalized because of cocaine or its effects?
9. Did you ever notice that it took more and more cocaine to get you high or make you feel good?
10. Did you ever notice that when you stopped taking cocaine you soon became more depressed and irritable than before, or became tired easily and had trouble sleeping?

Scoring: If you answered yes to question 1 and to any two questions 2–10, there is a clear likelihood that you have a cocaine-abuse problem. If you answered yes to questions 9 or 10, you not only have an abuse problem, but you are probably addicted to cocaine.

MARIJUANA

John is a 40-year-old city planner who has enjoyed getting stoned two or three times a week for the past twenty years. John finds that the mellow comfort he gets from pot enhances the natural highs he gets from his hobbies like snow skiing, whitewater rafting, and hiking.

John recently married a woman who shares his philosophical views on pot. John's wife has been smoking pot for over thirty years and sees nothing especially wrong with it. She is a real-estate agent and has been moderately successful in her career.

Despite a couple of close calls in high school, John has never been busted for possession of marijuana and has never engaged in marijuana sales.

Although John is not exactly a ball of fire on his job, his boss feels that his performance is adequate and has never given him a warning for not getting his work done.

John's parents don't approve of his frequent pot usage, but they don't let it get in the way of their relationship with him. They are comfortable talking to John on a weekly basis and enjoy visiting him three or four times a year.

John, while being a moderately heavy pot user, is not, by definition, a pot abuser.

Eric, a 16-year-old high-school junior, has always loved to play the guitar. He recently joined a rock band, and they landed several local club acts. Eric was introduced to pot by the bass player of the band, and soon found himself getting stoned at nearly every practice session.

Soon Eric's musical talent began to decline, and he found that he could not keep up with the other musicians. Eric's grades also began to slide. The former B student was barely getting by with Ds.

Perhaps more importantly, Eric didn't really seem to care.

"Well, it's not really that big of a deal. I like to go and jam with the guys, but if they don't think I'm good enough, that's fine with me. And my grades are good enough to get by. Why should I make Bs or As? Ds will pass me just as well."

When Eric is unable to secure his weekly supply of pot, he becomes irritated and edgy, but does not go through any withdrawal syndrome. Eric is psychologically but not physically dependent on pot.

The *amotivational syndrome* (not really caring about anything) of pot is not the only side effect this drug has had on Mindy, a 22-year-old fifth-year college senior. After an extra year in college she will still not receive her bachelor's degree this summer. Mindy has had a long history of pot usage, dating back to the age of twelve. She was introduced to pot by her older brother's friend and soon found that she was routinely smoking pot so that she could hang out with the people she thought were "cool."

Mindy's mother and father split up when she was fifteen, and Mindy's pot usage became even heavier. Both of her parents strongly criticized her for not living up to her potential.

Although not doing her best, Mindy could always come back at her strongest critics and remark, "Well, I'm still in college, and I'm about to receive my degree."

The turning point for Mindy came two Saturdays ago, when after smoking more pot than usual, she found herself being sexually victimized by three men who took advantage of her drug-induced lack of inhibitions.

Two days later, Mindy found out that she had contracted herpes, and felt disgusted and ashamed of herself.

Although Mindy could have been considered a borderline pot abuser for a number of years, the most recent life-damaging consequences of her pot-induced behavior clearly pushed her over the line into the pot-abuse category.

PROPERTIES OF MARIJUANA

By far the most popular illicit drug in the United States is marijuana. The active ingredient of marijuana, tetrahydrocannabinol (THC) is found in both the leaves and the stems of the marijuana plant.

Scientific estimates indicate that more than 62 million Americans have tried marijuana at least once in their lives, 29 million have used it at least once in the past year, and 18 million in the past month.

While marijuana is clearly the most popular illicit drug, there has been a downward shift in the number of overall users and teen-age users of pot. From a peak in 1979, rates of pot usage among the 18–25-year-olds has dropped steadily. The usage for 12–17-year-olds, after dropping significantly between 1979 and 1982, has leveled off. Usage among adults over the age of 26 has remained relatively constant since 1979.

While THC, the active ingredient in marijuana, has shown some promise as an antiemetic (a drug which reduces nausea) in cancer chemotherapy patients and as an adjunct to the treatment of glaucoma, the medicinal uses of marijuana have been largely overlooked in favor of vigorous criminal prosecution of marijuana users, growers, and sellers.

Although possession of pot was nearly legalized in the 1970s, pot dealing has become a major criminal offense in many states. In a stunning 6-to-3 reversal of two lower courts, the U.S. Supreme Court recently upheld the constitutionality of a forty-year sentence given to a Virginia man for selling four ounces of marijuana to an undercover informant and for his possession of six additional ounces. The defendant received a twenty-year sentence for each offense, to be served consecutively.

California spent hundreds of thousands of dollars in the late 1980s and early 1990s locating and destroying pot plantations in the remote California wilderness areas. The sentencing of these pot growers seems severe, considering that about 10 percent of the population are regular marijuana smokers.

On the pro-pot side of the controversy is a group called the National Organization for the Reform of Marijuana Laws (NORML). With active political lobbying, between 1973 and 1978 NORML was able to get marijuana decriminalized in eleven states. In addition to state decriminalization, several additional states passed laws permitting local options for decriminalization. Such decriminalization has occurred in Seattle, Washington and Ann Arbor, Michigan. Alaska, the state with the most lenient pot laws, permits personal possession of up to 4 ounces of marijuana.

Decriminalization is not to be confused with legalization. Decriminalization has had two effects:

(1) small amounts of pot are considered a misdemeanor not a felony

(2) penalties are generally reduced to simple fines that usually don't exceed $200

In contrast to other drugs, marijuana usage, no matter how heavy, does not lead to physical dependence and withdrawal effects. In short, it is impossible to become *physically* addicted to pot.

Psychological dependence, on the other hand, is quite possible and even likely with increasing usage.

Marijuana Abuse Questionnaire

Directions: Answer the following questions as honestly as possible. Do not deny or minimize your responses, but don't exaggerate or answer yes to questions that do not apply to you.

1. Have you ever used marijuana more than once within a one-month period?
2. Has marijuana ever caused you any problems in your life?
3. Has marijuana ever interfered with your education, your occupation, or your work around your home?
4. Has marijuana ever caused you problems with your family or caused your family to worry about you?
5. Has marijuana ever interfered with your friendships or social life?
6. Have you ever gotten into trouble with police or authorities because of marijuana?
7. Have you ever received treatment or medication for a marijuana problem?
8. Have you ever been hospitalized because of marijuana or its effects?
9. Did you ever notice that you needed more and more marijuana to get high or make yourself feel good?

Scoring: If you answered yes to question 1 and yes to any one question 2–9, you have met the criteria for having a marijuana-abuse problem. If you answered yes to question 9, there is also some indication that you are developing a tolerance for this drug and possibly becoming psychologically dependent.

AMPHETAMINES (SPEED, CRANK, UPPERS)

Andy, an 18-year-old, is just completing his freshman year of college. After coming to a major state university from a small town, Andy found himself spending a lot of time partying on the weekends and not keeping up with his classes during the week.

As the panic of final examinations begins to hit Andy, one of his fraternity brothers offers him a drug which he says will help him cram better for finals. The drug is called "white cross" (dexedrine) and is commonly used by many of the fraternity members.

Trusting his fraternity brothers, Andy buys a bottle of fifty dexedrine tablets and begins taking them.

He notices immediately after taking the small white pill that he feels much more alert and aware. He talks more quickly, thinks more sharply, and has a lot more energy. He notices a quicker step to his walk and feels that his arms and legs are moving much more rapidly than usual.

When Andy sits down to focus on mastering his zoology material, he finds that his understanding is easy and effortless. He feels that his reading pace is about double what it normally is and develops a sense of confidence and security.

Andy finds that instead of the usual one to one-and-a-half hours of reading per block of time, he can sit for three to four hours at a time and become absorbed in the material.

After cramming for two days, Andy memorizes many of the crucial facts of a 500-page zoology textbook and is able to scrape by with a C– on the final examination.

Andy has used a drug that many college students have taken to help prepare for final examinations. Does this mean that he is a drug addict? Does the fact that he is arrested six months later for amphetamine possession change his diagnosis?

Ted, a 54-year-old long-distance truck driver has been awake for eighteen hours and has another four hours of driving ahead of him. Ted is working his way across country, and his eyes begin to get very heavy as the hours go by. Ted intermittently shifts his radio to songs which he thinks will keep him awake, rolls down the window to get some fresh air, and stops for a couple of cups of black coffee. But nothing seems to be working.

Ted is required by his employer to get his load to St. Louis on a tight schedule to meet his deadline. Ted begins to drive unsafely and finally pulls over into a rest area and takes an amphetamine tablet.

Within twenty minutes, Ted is clear, alert, and aware. He has the perceptual vigilance and motor reactions necessary to successfully avoid an erratic driver who swerves in front of him.

Three hours later, Ted delivers his cargo safe and sound. Is Ted a drug addict? Would he be a drug addict if he had been involved in an accident or been arrested?

Stimulants comprise a vast category of drugs that involve activation of the central nervous system. Stimulants may include everything from caffeine and nicotine to methamphetamines and crank, the street name for amphetamines.

April is a 21-year-old college junior whose amphetamine use has gone far beyond just helping her study for final exams. The occasional dexedrine tablets which she took to help her study eventually found their way into her social life. But soon the dexedrine high was not even noticeable, and April was introduced to intravenous amphetamines.

Within six months, April lost 25 pounds and began to think that people were constantly watching her and talking about her. When she tried to stop using the drugs, she immediately became depressed and irritable. She overreacted in an argument with her father, and threw an ashtray at him because he wouldn't lend her any money.

April is suffering from an amphetamine addiction and amphetamine-induced delusions.

After 3½ days of detoxification in a rehab unit, April's paranoid beliefs disappear, and she finds herself needing a lot more sleep than usual. After sleeping for nearly a day and a half, April's cravings for speed are gone, and she is nearly back to normal.

Sometimes the use of amphetamines can seem very well justified.

Mark is a 26-year-old papermill worker whose wife is pregnant with their second child. Mark and his wife have just bought a new home and, due to her pregnancy, his wife had to give up her job. Faced with the increasing pressures of bills pouring in, Mark is forced to take on extra work. He routinely works sixteen-hour shifts for six to seven days in a row, and sometimes more.

Mark's work is potentially hazardous, and any lapse of concentration could result in a tragic injury. In order to meet the physical and mental demands of his job, Mark begins to take amphetamines.

Here are Mark's own words:

"It got to the point where I was just getting so run down I had to have something to get me through the swing shift. About half the guys in the mill are on crank, and it didn't really seem to be hurting them. The only guys who aren't on it are the ones who don't work the swing shifts or extended hours. At first it really seemed to be helping me a lot in terms of getting things done. The work was a lot easier, I was clear and focused on what I was doing, and I could actually accomplish more than I ever had before. . . . But eventually the effect of the crank seemed to be wearing off. I had to take more and more to get that same level of energy that I first got when I took it. And finally, when I didn't take it, I noticed that I was way below my average level of work output before I started crank. In fact, I got so slowed down and drained that I couldn't work at all and had to call in sick three times. . . . I did hear that crank was addictive, so I promised myself and my wife that I would never use it except when I was working at the mill. I still found that I had to take more crank to keep my energy level up. My work output became so low that my employer finally forced me to take a urine screening. The urine screening showed that I had been using amphetamines, and I was required to either get into a drug-rehab program or lose my job."

Although Mark experienced a clear tolerance for amphetamines, he did not go through the withdrawal syndrome when he quit taking them.

By definition, Mark's amphetamine use resulted in significant impairment on the job. Based on this factor alone, he meets the criteria for the diagnosis of an amphetamine-abuse problem.

So how do you know when you actually have an amphetamine problem?

Amphetamines, just like most drugs, are harmless in and of themselves. The problem with amphetamines lies in the pattern of their use or abuse.

In one of the chemical-dependency classes I was teaching at our local college, one of my students was a veteran pilot of the Vietnam War. He told the class that pilots would routinely be given amphetamines to help them think more clearly after repeated sorties on enemy targets. Is this amphetamine abuse?

In order to determine whether you have an amphetamine problem, you must look at the overall effect that amphetamines have on your life.

Amphetamine Abuse/Dependence Questionnaire

Directions: Answer the following questions as honestly as possible. Try not to minimize or deny facts that apply to you, but don't answer yes to questions that do not apply to your pattern of use/abuse.

1. Have you ever used amphetamines (speed, uppers, crank) more than once in a one-month period?
2. Have amphetamines ever caused you any problems in your life?
3. Have amphetamines ever interfered with your education, your occupation, or your work around your home?
4. Have amphetamines caused you problems with your family, or caused your family to worry about you?
5. Have amphetamines interfered with your interpersonal relationships or friendships?
6. Have you ever gotten into trouble with police or authorities because of amphetamines?
7. Have you ever received treatment or medication for an amphetamine problem?
8. Have you ever been hospitalized because of amphetamines or their effects?
9. Did you ever notice it took more and more amphetamines or speed to get you high or make you feel good?
10. When you stopped taking amphetamines or speed, did you notice any of the following symptoms: irritability, despondency, fatigue, trouble sleeping, or dreaming more than usual?

Scoring: If you answered yes to questions 1 and 2, and yes to any one question 3–10, you have met the criteria necessary for the diagnosis of an amphetamine-abuse problem. If you answered yes to questions 9 and 10, you are likely to have an amphetamine-dependency problem.

PROPERTIES OF AMPHETAMINES

Amphetamines (often called "uppers" or "speed") represent a large category of central nervous system stimulants. While cocaine is clearly a stimulant, it is also a local anesthetic and possesses some distinct properties which distinguish it from amphetamines.

Common amphetamines—crank, "cross tabs," "white cross," dexedrine, Preludin, biphetamine, "black beauties," and "crystal speed" are all used widely.

In the early part of the twentieth century, chemists began to understand the chemical structure of epinephrine, a naturally occurring chemical which prepares the body to meet life-threatening situations. They developed a group of drugs known as amphetamines, which mimic the effects of epinephrine.

Amphetamines were legal until 1965, when Congress passed the drug abuse control amendments that gave the FDA the authority to regulate the manufacturing and distribution of dangerous drugs.

Amphetamines were designed to be chemically similar to adrenaline (epinephrine). In low to moderate dosages, 1–50 mg., amphetamines generally have the following effects:

(1) stimulation of the central nervous system
(2) elevation of mood
(3) improved concentration, thinking, and coordination
(4) physiological signs of arousal
(5) delay the onset of fatigue and reduce the need for sleep
(6) moderately increase blood pressure
(7) moderately increase respiration rate
(8) raise blood-sugar levels
(9) dilate the bronchi
(10) divert blood flow from internal organs to skeletal muscles

(11) constrict the nasal mucous membranes
(12) suppress the appetite
(13) improve athletic performance

Medicinally, amphetamines have been used with significant success in the treatment of narcolepsy and hyperactivity in children. Although the alerting effects in combating narcolepsy are obvious, the paradoxical effect in the use of amphetamines for hyperactive children is that these stimulants actually reduce hyperactive behavior and calm the children.

Although amphetamines have been used extensively for weight reduction, physicians are usually critical of their use for the following reasons:

(1) After a few weeks, the dieter develops tolerance to the amphetamine and may have to take larger dosages to obtain the same effect. This can lead to psychological dependence on the drug.
(2) The benefits of amphetamines for weight control are short-term. Unless diet and exercise are also included, the weight loss will be trivial, and the lost weight will return.
(3) About 25 percent of the prescription amphetamines for weight reduction find their way into the illegal market.
(4) Some physicians who ran "fat clinics" abuse their prescription privileges, and the DEA has information on physicians who have ordered and received more than 3 million amphetamine dosage units in one year.
(5) Amphetamines taken for weight loss usually cause nervousness, central nervous system excitation, and users may have to take sedatives or barbiturates to help them sleep.
(6) Obesity is considered a chronic problem which requires a comprehensive, multifaceted lifestyle change.

NARCOTICS (CODEINE, MORPHINE, HEROIN)

One of the most prescribed groups of medication in the world are narcotic analgesics. Narcotics depress the central nervous system, leading to analgesia (pain removal), drowsiness, alteration of mood, mental clouding, apathy, and lethargy. In large enough doses, narcotics produce unconsciousness, but narcotics are most often prescribed for their pain-killing effects without the loss of consciousness.

Morphine in 5–20-mg. doses every four hours can ease or completely eliminate the pain of fractures, trauma, surgery, kidney stones, or terminal illness.

Codeine, while only 8 percent as powerful as morphine, has found its niche as a narcotic cough suppressant.

Percodan and methadone are also effective pain killers, but are only about 11 percent as powerful as morphine.

Despite its bad press, heroin is an excellent pain reliever. Many people consider heroin to be a more effective pain reliever than morphine. Although legalized as a pain killer in thirty countries, heroin is outlawed in the United States because of its potential for addiction. Some lawmakers believe that heroin should be available to terminally ill patients.

In 1975 Drs. John Hughes and Hans Kosterlitz discovered naturally occurring morphinelike substances which they termed endorphins. Although there are an estimated eighteen different pain-killing chemicals that occur naturally in your brain, the endogenous opiate known as dynorphin is estimated to be 200 times more potent than morphine in relieving pain.

Endorphin activity increases during pregnancy and reaches its peak just before and during labor. One explanation for postpartum depression is the huge drop from the peak level of endogenous opiates within twenty-four hours after delivery.

Endorphins have also been associated with long-distance-runners' high, and recent research from Scandinavia involving chemical assays of animal brains support this idea. It has been found that after 90 minutes of running on a treadmill, there is a significant increase in endorphins in dogs' brains.

OPIATE ADDICTION

While opiates—both manmade and endogenous—play a vital role in pain control, the biggest problem with these chemicals is obviously their addiction potential.

Although no rigorous studies are available regarding casual users of narcotics, many people who experiment with heroin and other opiates enjoy the euphoric rush and become addicted. Some of the factors that determine whether an individual will become addicted include:

(1) *The specific individual.* People differ greatly in their ability to respond to drugs, stress, and peer pressure.
(2) *The specific opiate used.* Heroin is much more addictive than codeine. Methadone maintenance is based on the idea that methadone, while an addictive opiate, is far less addictive than heroin.
(3) *Dosage size.* Hospital doses of 15 mg. of morphine three times a day are not likely to produce addiction, while larger doses can easily do so.
(4) *Frequency of use.* The more often an opiate is administered, the greater the likelihood of addiction.
(5) *Method of administration.* Intravenous or intramuscular injection of narcotics is much more addictive than oral ingestion.

When people become addicted to a narcotic, they have become physically dependent on the drug and require an adequate level on a daily basis in order to function. The opiate-addicted individual's need for narcotics is similar to the insulin-dependent diabetic's need for insulin. At this stage, narcotic dependence can clearly be considered a disease.

Let's look at some cases to see the difference between use, abuse, and dependence.

Sal, a 37-year-old Vietnam veteran reports that while he was in Vietnam, he used heroin regularly.

> "When I went over there I was eighteen years old and full of piss and vinegar. I guess all of us young guys who just got there thought we could lick the world. I got put on night patrol in the Mekong Delta, and being stupid as I was, volunteered for point. Once the bullets started flying,

reality set in, and it was all about pure instinctual survival. To say that I was scared shitless would be an understatement. But the fear wasn't really the worst part. I responded to fear with adrenaline, channeling energy into fighting Charlie. When we got back, there was first a sense of relief, and then a realization of impending doom knowing that we'd have to go out and do it again the next night.

My sergeant, Vic, turned me and the other guys onto heroin about the second week. All I can remember is thinking how wonderful it was. Here I was in this hellhole with nothing to do but kill or be killed, and here was this miracle drug that made me feel on top of the world—at least for awhile. In 1973 my tour of duty ended, and I returned back to the States. I left war, death, fear, and heroin all back there in the Mekong Delta."

Sal is a man who used heroin on a regular basis for nearly two years. While it may be argued that he abused heroin, since it could have diminished his performance as a soldier, a reasonable counterargument would be that heroin helped him cope with a nightmarish situation. Nonetheless, with the situational change and removal from the battle zone, Sal quickly and easily gave up heroin.

Kerry, a 32-year-old unemployed mother, used narcotics to cope with a different kind of pain. When Kerry was 28 years old, she had an argument with her father and stormed out of the house, refusing to speak with him again. Three days later, her father was killed in an automobile accident, and Kerry has been unable to forgive herself ever since. Kerry became involved with a man who introduced her to heroin, and she found that this effectively killed the emotional pain of the loss of her father and her guilt.

Upon physical detox, Kerry became aware not only of the pain of withdrawal, but the emergence of a tremendous amount of emotional hurt regarding her father's death.

Kerry told me that she would have never come into the rehabilitation unit if she hadn't been threatened by Child Protective Services with the removal of her child, due to her negligent behavior when on heroin. Since her addiction was interfering with the care of her child and virtually every other area of her life, Kerry certainly could be diagnosed as a heroin-dependent individual.

Kerry went through the double agony of physical withdrawal from heroin and the emergence of tremendous sadness and guilt from her blocked emotional feelings. When Kerry expressed and ventilated these feelings fully, she felt much better, yet still felt occasional cravings for heroin.

Kerry's successful recovery from heroin was established when she developed a new set of friends, a new boyfriend, and took up marathon running.

Kerry went through physical withdrawal from the heroin to reduce her required physical dependence on it, confronted and ventilated the emotional pain which the heroin had been masking, removed herself from the social situation which had encouraged her heroin use, and substituted a naturally occurring endogenous opiate high (marathon running) in place of the heroin.

An entirely different group of narcotics addicts are those who actually get permission from their physicians to use pain killers regularly.

Bill, a 53-year-old victim of multiple sclerosis has been taking Percodan for nearly two years. Bill's doctor, a well-intentioned internist, has agreed to continue to prescribe Percodan for Bill and has allowed gradually increasing dosages.

Unfortunately, Bill continues to need more and more of this drug that provides diminishing pain-killing effects.

Upon initial evaluation, Bill told me that the Percodan he's taking now has barely any effect on his pain. The other critical problem for Bill is that his consciousness is cloudy, he feels depressed, and is beginning to consider suicide.

Withdrawing Bill from Percodan was extremely difficult, and the physicians, nursing staff, and counselors often felt we were making a mistake in taking away the narcotic which was tempering the pain of Bill's illness.

But fortunately, after three days off the Percodan, Bill's pain decreased dramatically, indicating that most of his pain was due to narcotic withdrawal.

Bill, with the assistance of a well-intentioned doctor, had become a prescription narcotic addict.

Let's see whether you or someone you care about may be suffering from a narcotic abuse or addiction.

Narcotic Abuse/Addiction Questionnaire

Directions: Answer the following questions as honestly as possible. Try not to minimize or deny facts that apply to you, but don't answer yes to questions that do not apply to your pattern of use/abuse.

1. Have you ever used heroin, morphine, codeine, or any other narcotic more than once in a one-month period?
2. Have narcotics ever caused you any discomfort or distress in your life?
3. Have narcotics ever interfered with your education, your occupation, or your work around your home?
4. Have narcotics caused you problems with your family or caused your family to worry about you?
5. Have narcotics interfered with your interpersonal relationships, friendships, or social life?
6. Have you ever gotten into trouble with the police or authorities because of narcotics?
7. Have you ever received treatment or medication for a narcotic habit?
8. Have you ever been hospitalized because of narcotics or their effects?
9. Did you ever notice that you needed to take more and more narcotics such as heroin, morphine, codeine, or Percodan to make yourself feel good?
10. When you stopped taking these narcotics, within a week or two did you notice any of the following symptoms: (1) feel as if you had the flu, (2) become teary-eyed, (3) have a runny nose, (4) yawn a lot, (5) have trouble sleeping, (6) sweat more than usual, (7) have diarrhea, (8) have your hair standing up on end, or (9) have dilated pupils?

Scoring: If you answered yes to question 1 and yes to any one question 2–10, you are likely to have or have had a narcotic-abuse problem. If you answered yes to question 1 and yes to questions 9 and 10, you are likely to have or have had a narcotic addiction.

SEDATIVES (VALIUM, LIBRIUM, ZANAX, AND OTHER TRANQUILIZERS)

In the 1960s, a group of minor tranquilizers called benzodiazepans was introduced to the American public for the treatment of anxiety, muscle spasms, and sleeping disorders. These new drugs were much safer than barbiturates and quickly became one of the most popular prescriptions given by physicians to their patients. In fact, at some time during this year 11 percent of all Americans will take a minor tranquilizer.

It took more than fifteen years after the Controlled Substance Act of 1970 for physicians to realize that while the short-term effects of minor tranquilizers (up to one month) are often beneficial, their long-term use can lead to addiction (tolerance and withdrawal). In fact, withdrawal from minor tranquilizers can be worse than heroin withdrawal and has actually been documented to be life-threatening.

Liska (1990) cited studies showing an unexpectedly high rate of minor tranquilizer use among housewives, retired people, and people who are not employed full-time. While unemployed women make up only 26 percent of the general population, they account for over 46 percent of minor-tranquilizer usage.

The movie *I'm Dancing as Fast as I Can* brought attention to the plight of women who become addicted to these minor tranquilizers by their well-meaning physicians.

More recently, a new benzodiazepan called Zanax was introduced as a safe, nonaddictive tranquilizer. It quickly gained acceptance among the medical community and today is the fourth most popularly prescribed new drug.

With all the stress we face at the end of the twentieth century, Zanax seemed to be a godsend, without the addiction potential of Valium or Librium. One of the reasons Zanax was thought to be safer was its shorter half-life in the human body. Half-life refers to how long it takes for one-half of the dosage of the drug to be eliminated from your system. Therefore, the longer the half-life, the longer the drug will be in your system and effect your consciousness. Compared to Librium, Valium, and Dalmane which, in typical dosages, have a half-life of 24–72 hours, Zanax has a half-life of only 4–20 hours.

But, unfortunately, Zanax proved to be not only as addictive, but possibly even more addictive in the long run than its predecessors.

To get some idea of the sedating effects of benzodiazepans, consider that in an average person, a 5 mg. dose of Valium causes driving impairment comparable to that of a person with a blood-alcohol level of .07%, or 3 ounces of alcohol in one hour for a 140-pound person.

Withdrawal from significant doses of benzodiazepans are characterized by anxiety, tremors, nausea, cramps, diarrhea, muscle spasms, tics, restlessness, confusion, disorganized thinking, racing thoughts, moodiness, bizarre dreams, violence, depression and, in some cases, even paranoia and hallucinations.

Unlike the 72-hour period of acute withdrawal from alcohol, acute withdrawal from benzodiazepans can take 21–28 days. Many people have actually died from going off sedatives "cold turkey." Reduction from significant doses of benzodiazepans over a long period of time should be done only under medical supervision, with the usual withdrawal schedule being 2 mg. or less per week. Zanax requires an especially gradual withdrawal schedule of ¼ to ½ mg. per week.

Secondary withdrawal from minor tranquilizers (less severe symptoms) may continue to occur up to two years after all minor tranquilizer use has stopped.

APPROPRIATE SEDATIVE USE

By now you may have gotten the idea that minor tranquilizers are harmful and should be avoided at all cost. But tranquilizers, when used for their designated purposes, are a very useful tool in the armory of the physician to combat such problems as occasional sleeplessness, muscle spasms, coping with severe trauma, presurgical preparation, severe anxiety management, and even helping the alcoholic get through the acute phase of withdrawal.

There are two key points to keep in mind:

(1) Most—if not all—tranquilizers are designed for short-term usage: less than one month, and often as little as two or three days.

(2) Some tension and stress are normal and should be looked at as an opportunity to develop strength of character in coping with life.

Remember, if you require more of a minor tranquilizer to obtain their designated effect (tolerance), or if you notice withdrawal symptoms when you stop taking the drug, you are beginning to enter the downward spiral of sedative addiction.

EXAMPLES OF SEDATIVE USE, ABUSE, AND DEPENDENCE

Rhonda, a 32-year-old licensed vocational nurse, wife, and mother of two, has been suffering from increasing bouts of anxiety and panic. Rhonda's physician initially prescribed Valium, but quickly became aware that her condition was not improving. He referred her to a clinical psychologist, who attempted to help Rhonda explore the underlying causes of her anxiety. In the course of this discovery, Rhonda's anxiety and distress actually increased as she became closer to the core of her problems. In fact, at one point her anxiety became so incapacitating that her psychologist sent her back to her physician for a temporary trial of the minor tranquilizer Zanax to calm Rhonda down enough so that she could continue to work at uncovering her problems gradually. After a month of taking ½ mg. of Zanax per day, Rhonda's physician, with the encouragement of her psychologist, began to withdraw Rhonda from the tranquilizer. During this time, Rhonda had made significant progress in facing the source of her problems: severe neglect from her mother.

Eventually Rhonda came to realize that her panic and anxiety attacks were a desperate bid for the attention which she never received from her mother. Once Rhonda learned this, she was able to develop alternative behaviors which got her a lot of positive attention, like becoming actively involved in a food-for-the-poor project and becoming an aerobics instructor.

Louise, a 66-year-old widow, was prescribed 20 mg. of Librium a day by her well-meaning family physician of twenty-five years. The shock of losing a husband of forty-one years was devastating, and Louise's doctor felt a compelling need to help Louise cope with her pain.

Unfortunately, the Librium blocked the natural grieving process that Louise had to go through, and she became stuck in the phase of denial. Much of Louise's behavior seemed to be characterized by simply waiting around for her husband to come back home.

After two years, Louise could no longer escape her pain, and her grief began to emerge. After a brief stint of increasing tranquilizer usage, Louise's physician finally became aware that her problems needed a more human and compassionate solution.

Louise was gradually withdrawn from Librium and simultaneously taught biofeedback and relaxation techniques to cope with anxiety. She was then encouraged to fully express and ventilate the grief and loss she was blocking out. Within two months, Louise's life was back on course.

Sharon, a 42-year-old school-bus driver complained to her physician that she was having chronic low back pain and intermittent anxiety attacks.

Her physician prescribed Zanax. Sharon felt that her lower back pain began to improve and also noticed her anxiety attacks were not nearly as frequent. On the other hand, Sharon's daughter noticed a distinct change in her mother's personality. Sharon's usually ebullient mood seemed to be getting more and more subdued with each passing week.

As the months stretched on, Sharon's anxiety reemerged.

About two years had passed when, on a trip with her daughter and son-in-law to Colorado, she forgot to take her Zanax with her. Two days later, Sharon found herself in the emergency room of a Boulder, Colorado hospital, suffering from sedative-withdrawal seizures. Sharon went through extensive detoxification, which took over a month. During this time Sharon was confused and often disoriented.

After detoxification, Sharon continued to have strong urges to take Zanax or other sedatives for more than a year and a half.

Sharon is a classic example of an unwitting victim of a well-intentioned physician who negligently led his patient into a near-life-threatening sedative addiction.

BARBITURATES

Unlike minor tranquilizers, barbiturates have long been recognized as having the potential for abuse, dependence, and addiction. The great German organic chemist Adolf Baeyer is credited with the discovery of barbiturates.

Historically, barbiturates were used to help patients overcome insomnia, and in the short run they work very well for this purpose. Unfortunately, barbiturates are some of the most addictive of all prescribed drugs.

Commonly used barbiturates such as Seconal or Nembutal have a pronounced sedative effect. Although these drugs quickly and effectively put patients to sleep, they unfortunately decrease the amount of time the insomniac spends in rapid eye movement (REM) sleep. For most users of barbiturates, this decrease in REM sleep corresponds to dreamless sleep, which is a psychological abnormality. The result of dreamless sleeping often results in increased irritability and anxiety.

Just like sedatives, barbiturates are often useful for an occasional bout of sleeplessness, but continuous use can lead quickly to trouble.

Another problem with barbiturates is that they act in a synergistic fashion with alcohol: both drugs tend to enhance each other's effects. In fact, the sedation effects of barbiturates are so increased by alcohol that the combination often leads to suppression of breathing and death.

Liska (1990) also cited sleep-research-laboratory results showing that barbiturates lose their effectiveness within three to fourteen days of continuous use.

When a barbiturate dose is near 400 mg. a day for several weeks, symptoms of physical dependence begin to develop. When barbiturates are discontinued abruptly, withdrawal syndromes include convulsions, insomnia, hallucinations, tremors, and sometimes death. Paradoxically, with all the bad press that kicking the heroin habit receives, little attention is given to barbiturate withdrawal, which is far more life-threatening and difficult.

Perhaps the most dangerous effect of barbiturates are the intentional and unintentional suicides which they cause. Liska cites studies showing estimates ranged from 1,000 to 3,000 deaths annually that involved barbiturates. Many other barbiturate-related deaths and near-deaths are probably due to an accidental combination of alcohol and barbiturates.

Barbiturates are often also involved in polydrug-dependency problems. In these cases, it's not only barbiturates, but other sedatives and prescribed medications which create addiction.

Maureen, a 41-year-old account executive for a major advertising company told her doctor that she was having difficulty sleeping. Her physician prescribed 50 mg. of Seconal at bedtime and assured her that Seconal had a high margin of safety and would not create addiction. After one week on Seconal, Maureen began to experience a pounding heart, a dry mouth, and became extremely anxious and fearful about any event or news or story that was even remotely upsetting. Her physician then decided to treat her anxiety by prescribing Zanax, a minor tranquilizer.

By this time, sleep was impossible without the Seconal, and anxiety was unbearable without the Zanax. For the first time in her life, Maureen considered suicide. At this point, her physician decided a third drug was necessary and prescribed Mellaril, a major tranquilizer to be taken once or twice a day.

Maureen continued to deteriorate. She lost 20 pounds and became manifestly depressed. Her physician then prescribed a fourth drug, Elavil, an antidepressant.

Maureen was now taking four psychoactive drugs simultaneously: Seconal (a barbiturate), Zanax (a minor tranquilizer), Mellaril (a major tranquilizer), and Elavil (an antidepressant), but was getting worse. At this point, Maureen was brought into a drug-rehabilitation center, and within two weeks had detoxed from all of her medications. At that point, she felt as if she had returned to normal and realized her life had been given back to her.

Minor Tranquilizer (Sedative) and Barbiturate Abuse Questionnaire

Directions: Answer the following questions as honestly as possible. Try not to minimize or deny facts that apply to you, but don't answer yes to questions that do not apply to your pattern of use/abuse.

1. Have you ever used minor tranquilizers (sedatives) or barbiturates more than once in a one-month period?
2. Have barbiturates or tranquilizers ever caused you any problems in your life?
3. Have barbiturates or tranquilizers interfered with your education, your occupation, or your work around the home?
4. Have barbiturates or tranquilizers caused you problems with your family or caused your family to worry about you?
5. Have barbiturates or tranquilizers ever interfered with your interpersonal relationships or friendships?
6. Have barbiturates or tranquilizers ever gotten you into trouble with authorities or the police?
7. Have you ever received any treatment or medication for your tranquilizer or barbiturate habit?
8. Have you ever been hospitalized because of barbiturates or sedatives or their effects?
9. Did you ever notice that you needed to take more and more tranquilizers or barbiturates to calm yourself down or make yourself feel good?
10. When you stopped taking tranquilizers or barbiturates, did you notice any of the following symptoms almost immediately: (1) becoming more anxious or fearful than before, (2) becoming more depressed or irritable than before, (3) feeling weak, tired, and unmotivated to do your normal activities, (4) experiencing nausea, dizziness, or vomiting, (5) sweating a lot more than usual, (6) having trouble breathing or finding your heart was racing or fluttering, (7) finding that you could not keep your eyelids, tongue, or hands from trembling?

Scoring: If you answered yes to question 1, and yes to any two questions 2–10, you are likely to have a minor-tranquilizer- or barbiturate-abuse problem. If you answered yes to question 1 and yes to questions 9 and 10, you are likely to have a minor-tranquilizer or barbiturate addiction.

HALLUCINOGENS (LSD, ACID, MUSHROOMS, AND MESCALINE)

On April 16, 1943 Dr. Albert Hoffman, a chemist who worked for Sandoz Pharmaceutical Company was experimenting with a derivative of nicotinic acid, a B vitamin. In handling the material, Hoffman apparently accidentally swallowed some lysergic acid diethylamide.
    He then described what occurred:

> "Last Friday, the 16th of April, I was forced to interrupt my work in the laboratory in the middle of the afternoon and go home to seek care, since I was overcome by a remarkable uneasiness combined with a slight dizziness. At home I lay down and fell into a not unpleasant, intoxicated-like state which was characterized by an extremely exciting fantasy. In a twilight condition with closed eyes (I found the daylight to be annoyingly bright) there crowded before me without interruption, fantastic pictures of extraordinary plasticity, with an intensive, kaleidoscopic play of colors. After about two hours the condition disappeared."

Dr. Hoffman had just experienced the first LSD trip.
    A dedicated research scientist, Hoffman decided to experiment more with LSD and described a subsequent trip:

> "The visual disturbances were still pronounced. Everything appeared to waiver, and proportions were distorted, similar to a reflection in moving water. In addition, everything was drenched with changing colors of disagreeable predominantly green and blue hues. Colorful, very plastic and fantastic images passed before my closed eyes. It was especially noteworthy that all acoustical perceptions, perchance the noise of a passing car, were translated into optical sensations, so that through each tone and noise, a corresponding colored picture, kaleidoscopically changing form and color, was elicited."

In 1949 the first LSD was shipped from Europe to the United States, where researchers had the opportunity to begin studying it scientifically.

Researchers found that in a typical LSD trip, which lasted for about eight to twelve hours, there was an odd mixture and blend of visual and auditory hallucinations, unusual patterns, and synesthesia, in which smells are "felt," sounds are "seen," and the user experiences sensations of being able to step outside of himself and look at his body (depersonalization).

During these scientific trials, it became apparent that sometimes the subjects would experience unpleasant hallucinatory experiences, or "bad trips." It was determined that the mental set of the user's mind and the setting in which the LSD trip is taken strongly influence the entire experience. In experimentation with animals, it was found that a 11,000-pound elephant died shortly after receiving a minuscule 0.297 gram dose of LSD. The elephant, as well as some other animals who were experimented on, died of respiratory arrest in reaction to the LSD.

In the 1950s the U.S. Army conducted a series of drug experiments by giving LSD to soldiers without their knowledge. Some of the men experienced frightening visions and developed fears of losing their minds, which led to nervous breakdowns. In one case, a well-adjusted family man committed suicide by leaping from a window.

The army did not acknowledge that the trials had taken place until fifteen years after the actual experiments were finished.

At a neurochemical level, researchers discovered that LSD interferes with—or blocks—serotonin receptors, thus limiting the natural amount of serotonin occurring in the brain. It was also found that LSD enhances the norepinephrine systems, which are activated in states of high arousal and excitement.

In the early 1960s, Harvard psychologist Timothy Leary began to experiment with LSD in hope of finding self-knowledge and insight. Other psychologists and psychiatrists throughout the country began to experiment with the idea that through ingestion of LSD the patients could discover self-evident truths and resolutions to conflicts within themselves.

Prior to 1966, the Sandoz Pharmaceutical Company had been supplying LSD free to researchers seeking to explore possible benefits of the drug. During this time it was common to see individuals called "acid heads," who frequently could receive 50–80 microgram doses of acid for $1–$4 a dose.

Many of these users suffered bad LSD trips, and some overdosed.

Treatment consisted of having friends "talk the user down" in familiar and safe surroundings. Minor tranquilizers or barbiturates were often given by injection to bring the user out of a bad trip.

The deaths of rock stars Jimi Hendrix and Jim Morrison have been attributed partially to their extensive use of LSD.

PCP is considered by many pharmacology experts to be the single most dangerous drug on the illegal market today. In one expert's view, PCP can change people so that they are never the same again.

PCP was originally introduced as an anesthetic, but its potential for serious side effects became known quite quickly. It was then reintroduced in 1967 by the Parke-Davis Company as an anesthetic called Sernylan, for veterinary use only. It first hit the streets at the 1967 Monterey Pop Festival and was mixed with a mixture of mint leaves, parsley, and low-grade marijuana and was called "angel dust." Since it looked like marijuana, it was often smoked unknowingly.

The trouble with PCP is its unpredictability. The PCP-intoxicated person is often described as having incredible strength and being totally oblivious to pain. Depersonalization, hallucinations, apathy, drowsiness, self-injurious behavior, and severe violence are common, unpredictable, and frightening symptoms of this drug.

Psilocybin and psilocin are hallucinogenic substances obtained from mushrooms of North and Central America. The use of mushrooms by Mexican and Guatemalan indians dates back to 1,000 B.C.

The hallucinatory experience produced by psilocybin and its derivatives is comparable to that produced by LSD, but the psilocybin trips last only about half as long.

Another hallucinogen, mescaline is derived from peyote (the buttons of certain species of cacti), and has a chemical structure similar to that of amphetamines. While mescaline remains popular among the indian tribes of Central America, its use in the United States has declined significantly due to illegal laboratories' abilities to manufacture synthetic hallucinogens.

One of the most common problems with all hallucinogens is the phenomenon of flashbacks. Although a very small percentage of people who take hallucinogens experience flashbacks, when they do appear the sudden and vivid hallucinatory experiences can occur weeks or even months after users stop taking the drug. In some documented cases, the acid users' inability to escape the recurrent panic from flashbacks has made them commit suicide.

The issue of flashbacks brings up a fascinating problem. If a single dose of LSD or other hallucinogen can produce recurrent flashbacks for months or even years, and these flashback experiences interfere with an individual's life, it certainly is reasonable to assume that even a single dose of a hallucinogen could create a chronic abuse problem.

But let's take a closer look at hallucinogens and see just what constitutes use, abuse, and dependence.

Hallucinogen Use/Abuse Questionnaire

Directions: Answer the following questions as honestly as possible. Try not to deny or minimize your responses, but do not answer yes to questions that do not apply to you.

1. Have you ever used LSD, mescaline, psilocybin, PCP, or other hallucinogens once or more in a one-month period?
2. Have hallucinogens ever caused you any problems, discomfort, or distress in your life?
3. Have hallucinogens ever interfered with your education, your occupation, or your work around your home?
4. Have hallucinogens caused you problems with your family or caused your family to worry about you?
5. Have hallucinogens ever interfered with your friendships or social life?
6. Have you ever gotten into trouble with the police or authorities because of hallucinogens?
7. Have you ever received treatment or medication for a hallucinogen problem?
8. Have you ever been hospitalized because of the effects of taking hallucinogens?
9. Have you ever had difficulty reducing or stopping your usage of hallucinogens?
10. Has your life been disrupted by one or more occurrences of hallucinogen-based flashbacks over a period of several months?

Scoring: If you answered yes to question 1, and yes to any two questions 2–10, it's likely that you have a hallucinogen problem.

The *DSM III-R* does not specify a hallucinogen dependency because withdrawal syndromes are typically not seen. LSD users, however, quickly develop a tolerance for the drug and often need increasing dosages to achieve the same effect.

FACTS ABOUT TEEN-AGERS AND DRUG ABUSE

- A study concluded in July of 1991 by the National Survey on Drug Abuse yielded some interesting findings for adolescents age 12 through 17:
- More than 4 million (20 percent) adolescents have tried an illicit drug at least once in their lifetime; nearly 3 million (14.8 percent) have used drugs within the past year; and approximately 1.4 million (6.8 percent) reported using drugs within the past month.
- Approximately 2.2 million (21 percent) of the males and 2 million (19 percent) of the females in this age range have used an illicit drug at least once.
- With respect to marijuana, 2.6 million (13 percent) reported trying it at least once; 2 million (10 percent) used it in the last year; and nearly 900,000 (4.3 percent) say they've gotten stoned in the past month. Marijuana usage by race shows a nearly identical pattern; 4.5 percent for blacks, 4.6 percent for hispanics, and 4.4 percent for whites.
- Over 490,000 of the adolescents in this age range reported trying cocaine at least once. Of the 311,000 who said that they used cocaine in the past year, 83,000 used it in the past month, and 51,000 reported using it once a week or more.
- By comparison, the reported use of alcohol in the 12 through 17 age range was more than twice as much as that of all illicit drugs combined.

The following table gives an idea of the developmental trends with respect to drug and alchohol use over the past 11 years.

National Household Survey on Drug Abuse Lifetime Prevalence of Drug Use Among 12–17 Year Olds (Percentages)

	1979	1982	1985	1988	1990	1991
Any Illicit Drug Use	34.3	27.6	29.5	24.7	22.7	20.1
Marijuana	30.9	26.7	23.6	17.4	14.8	13.0
Cocaine	5.4	6.5	4.9	3.4	2.6	2.4
Alcohol	70.3	65.2	55.5	50.2	48.2	46.4
Cigarettes	54.1	49.9	45.2	42.3	40.2	37.9

A quick glance at the above table gives us good cause for optimism since reported alcohol and drug usage among adolescents has been steadily declining since 1985. But how can you tell if your child is one of the above statistics?

HOW TO TELL WHETHER YOUR CHILD IS ON DRUGS

Schlaadt and Schannon list the following possible warning signals which may suggest that your child is on drugs:

1. A change in friends or secrecy about new friends and activities
2. Withdrawal from family, old friends, and school
3. Lots of time spent in unusual places
4. Mood swings; eg., excessive anger and irritability
5. Change in appearance (drug subculture styles or sloppiness)
6. Increased discipline problems
7. Dropping grades or other performance
8. Stealing or borrowing lots of money

9. Decrease in energy and endurance
10. Weight loss or gain; increased or decreased hunger
11. Changes in timing and duration of sleep
12. Frequent use of eye drops and breath mints

HOPE FOR THE FUTURE

Despite our country's recent "war on drugs," the single best way to reduce and eventually eliminate the drug-abuse problem in our society will come through education.

A new policy adopted by some schools utilizes peer leaders to educate and inform high-school and junior-high students about the potential problems and dangers of drugs. The dramatic success in reducing the abuse of cigarettes did not come from making cigarette smoking a crime, but by using a strategy in which information is given out at a certain level and is filtered down from friend to friend and acquaintance to acquaintance.

But until the education takes hold, legal efforts to reduce the quantity and quality of drugs available to the general public appears to be having some beneficial impact. If suppliers of cocaine or other illicit drugs are targeted by law enforcement efforts, the odds are that these drugs will not be as available as before, or their availability will be priced at a range which is out of reach for many potential abusers.

The traditional Twelve Steps of the Narcotics Anonymous model (comparable to the AA Twelve Steps) has long been a stalwart of drug rehabilitation treatment programs.

Inpatient drug rehabilitation treatment approaches, in addition to the twelve-step model, typically use a three-pronged approach;

First, medically detoxing the drug dependent patient from the substance to which they are addicted.

Second, removing the drug abuser from the situation or subculture in which the drug abuse is occurring.

And finally, developing alternative natural highs to replace the mood altering effects of the drugs. For instance, thrill seeking or adrenaline highs, large muscle aerobic activities, enjoyable event scheduling, relaxation training, and even meditation all have clear consciousness-altering and mood-enhancing effects while having few if any life-damaging consequences.

CHAPTER 5

AM I ANXIOUS?

LOGAN ALWAYS WONDERED WHAT IT WOULD BE LIKE TO DIE. BEING ONLY 27 YEARS old, he figured he'd have a lot of time to prepare for it. But on that Monday night, he could have sworn the curtain was coming down on his life.

In our first session, he recalled:

> "I remember the sense of independence I felt as I stretched out in a brown beanbag chair and surveyed my new one-bedroom apartment. There wasn't a lot to look at. I picked up an old olive-green couch at a flea market the day before, borrowed a brown dropleaf table and desk chair from a friend, and brought my stereo and television with me from New York.
>
> It was the first week of my residency in psychiatry, and the 9-to-5 hours were fine. I was busy with training seminars, supervision, and working with people who really needed help. It was refreshing to look out my office window and see majestic turquoise mountains covered with towering pine and fir trees instead of a twenty-story block or red-brick apartments on the West Side of Manhattan.
>
> The problem started after I left work. There was a real dead time that started just after the evening news. During

this time my sense of independence yielded to a feeling of insecurity.

Then—one Monday night—something terrifying happened.

I was stretched out in my beanbag chair reading the paper and sipping a glass of orange juice. The smell of turkey and dressing began to fill the apartment, and I looked forward to the loud buzz of my oven timer to let me know it was dinnertime. Then it started.

The first thing I noticed was that I was having trouble catching my breath. I sat up quickly and took three deep breaths, but it seemed to be getting worse. Soon I started to feel like I was being choked or smothered. It felt like my throat was closing up, and my mouth was getting dry. I was definitely having trouble swallowing. I quickly gulped down some more orange juice, figuring that my blood sugar might be low. But the shortness of breath continued, and along with it I began to feel dizzy and light-headed. A numb, tingling feeling began to develop in my hands and feet like a thousand pinpricks. Then I noticed my palms were starting to sweat and realized I was losing control. My heart was pounding, and it felt like my throat was getting even tighter.

The crippling, incapacitating fear of death soon led to a nearly paralyzing trauma. I felt like I was either dying or losing my mind. For a while I could not move.

My sense of time slowed down and seemed to stop. What couldn't have been more than 30 minutes seemed liked 3 or 4 hours.

I didn't know if I was having a heart attack. Had I suffered some kind of food poisoning? Was it some type of acute allergic reaction? Certainly it just couldn't be psychological. I knew it wasn't in my head. The pounding of my heart, sweatiness of my palms, shortness of breath, and dizziness let me know something very real and very physical was wrong with me. I didn't know if I should dial 911 or if I could drive myself to the emergency room. Finally, as the symptoms continued to escalate, I was able to drive myself to the emergency room.

Within 30 minutes, I was informed by a nurse that my

physical examination and EKG showed nothing wrong with my heart or my health. She smiled condescendingly and said, "You must have just had a panic attack."

I knew what panic attacks were because I had treated dozens of patients for panic and other anxiety disorders during my internship and training. I always looked at people who had panic attacks as nervous people who really couldn't control their emotions. How embarrassing for this to happen to me, a budding young psychiatrist. How could I ever hope to treat people with anxiety disorders when I fell victim to one myself."

But it really did help Logan to know what was happening. He could predict with some certainty that he wasn't going to die from a panic attack, and began to use a number of psychological techniques I taught him, such as relaxation and positive self-talk to help him get through the attacks. Over time, Logan learned to control the panic attacks and eventually completely eliminated them from his life.

Yet panic disorders represent only one type of anxiety disorder.

This month in the United States, 8.3 million women and 4.2 million men will suffer from a treatable anxiety disorder. Yet three out of four people will never get the help they need, leaving over 9 million people suffering needlessly.

Are you one of these people?

To answer this question, let's look at the five basic types of anxiety disorders, some examples of each, and some quizzes to let you know whether you are suffering needlessly.

PHOBIAS (UNREALISTIC FEARS)

A phobia is a persistent and irrational fear of a specific object, activity, or situation that results in a compelling need to avoid or escape the source of the fear. If you are phobic, you realize that your reactions to the fearful object or situation are unreasonable and out of proportion to its actual danger.

Theoretically, any object, situation, or activity could serve as a possible candidate for a phobia. But, realistically, there are several types of phobias that are the most common:

Acrophobia —the fear of heights or high places.

Agoraphobia —the unrealistic fear of being alone or being in public places from which escape might be difficult or help not available: such as crowds, bridges, tunnels, or large, crowded stores.

Claustrophobia —the unrealistic fear of small or enclosed places.

Social phobia —the persistent unrealistic fear of situations in which you may be exposed to scrutiny by others—for example, speaking in public, or being the object of observation by others.

Sometimes it is difficult to sort out realistic from unrealistic fears.

Derek, a 56-year-old businessman described what happened on a flight to New Zealand in the early 1980s:

> "The first thing I remember was a loud thump that shook the cabin. Then I heard a deafening, roaring hiss and looked in front of me to see that five feet ahead was a gaping hole into nothingness where an emergency exit had been a few seconds before.
>
> My food tray and cups flew up as if lifted by some supernatural force and disappeared into the vortex.
>
> As the plane lurched violently to the right, I instinctively leaned to the left and clutched the armrests. I could see directly out the hole and felt the suction. If I wasn't buckled in, I know I would have been pulled out. The air was brutally cold.
>
> My breath appeared in hot white puffs as the ice-cold air at 36,000 feet filled the cabin. Oxygen masks sprang down from the panels above, as desperate men, women, and children struggled to place the masks over their faces. We all knew that depressurization at 36,000 feet meant certain death.
>
> As the cabin depressurized, an icy realization came over all of the passengers. The shrieks and moans of impending doom had turned into a deadly silence after 30 seconds of initial panic.
>
> It felt like we were being sucked down a giant whirl-

pool. The circles were getting ever tighter and tighter, with less and less control.

Later I learned that behind the controls of the aircraft a gutsy ex-Vietnam pilot and his crew refused to surrender or panic, yet continued in a valiant struggle to save the nearly hopeless situation.

It seemed like the seconds turned into minutes and the minutes into hours. After the eternity of a 30,000-foot spiraling dive toward doom, the plane leveled off and it felt like we were pulled up by a giant tether. I felt my stomach sink to the soles of my feet.

Then the crusty voice of the captain announced, 'Ladies and gentlemen, we have regained control at 6,000 feet and we'll be able to land this aircraft.' "

Derek sits in my office, sips a cup of coffee, and shakes his head, "I don't think I'll ever get over it, Doc," he comments. It has been eight weeks since the near-disaster, and his business is starting to suffer.

Is Derek's fear of flying normal?

Being a VFR pilot and a passenger on numerous flights myself, I can't help but wonder whether if I had been through Derek's experience, I would ever set foot on an airplane again.

Because the odds of Derek's being killed in a major airline disaster are less than 1 in 4 million and the fact that his business is suffering due to his fear of flying, Derek meets the criteria for having an unrealistic fear or phobic disorder.

Ellen, a 28-year-old wife and mother of two, finds herself panicking when grocery shopping. She feels anxiety when stopped in heavy traffic and a compulsive need to have medical help nearby should she become incapacitated. She frequently feels as if she is going to faint or have a seizure even though doctors reassure her that there is nothing medically wrong.

Rarely does Ellen ever travel beyond a 3-mile radius of her home, and several times a year she becomes so frightened that she will not leave the house for three or four days at a time.

Ellen told me that when she and her husband went to see *Dances with Wolves,* sitting in her usual aisle seat did not subdue her anxiety as it usually did. She got up in the middle of the movie and insisted that her husband take her home.

Ellen felt dizzy and frightened in a crowded high-school gym as she tried to watch her son's basketball game and had to leave before half time.

Ellen has classic agoraphobia with panic attacks.

But just because you are afraid or uncomfortable doesn't mean that you have a phobia.

Jarod is a 36-year-old X-ray technician. He works on the first floor, yet frequently has to make trips to the fifth and sixth floors of the hospital. Jarod would prefer not to ride in elevators since being trapped in one for about twenty minutes last year. On the other hand, when it's important for him to get business done as quickly as possible, he doesn't hesitate for a moment to jump into a crowded elevator.

Despite feeling some anxiety and discomfort in closed-in or crowded situations, Jarod's distress does not interfere with his family, job, friendships, or the overall quality of his life.

Jarod is not, in fact, claustrophobic.

Let's see whether you suffer from any of the major unrealistic fears or phobias.

Phobic Disorder Questionnaire

Directions: Answer the following questions as honestly as possible. Do not deny or minimize your responses, but do not answer yes to questions that do not apply to you.

1. Have you ever been unusually afraid of things a normal person is not afraid of? For instance: heights, small places, lightning, snakes are things most people are not afraid of.
2. Have you ever been so afraid of leaving home by yourself that you would not go out of the house even though you knew it was safe? (agoraphobia)
3. Have you been afraid to go into places like airplanes, elevators, tunnels, or markets for fear of being trapped and not being able to get out? (claustrophobia)
4. Have you ever been so afraid of embarrassing yourself in public that you would not do certain things that most people do? For

example: eating in a restaurant, speaking to a group of people, or using a public restroom. (social phobia)

5. When your fears were the strongest, did you try to stay away from the fearful situation, object, or activity whenever you could?
6. Did these fears interfere with your family, social life, job, school, chores around your home, or overall quality of your life?

Scoring: If you answered yes to any of the questions 1– 4, and yes to questions 5 and 6 there is a clear likelihood that you have an unrealistic fear or phobic disorder.

GENERALIZED ANXIETY DISORDER

Richard, a silver-haired, bespectacled, 56-year-old civil engineer, has been nervous all of his life. He never really wanted to see a psychologist, and sitting in my office makes him even more nervous.

Ever since Richard was a child, he has had trouble relaxing and enjoying things. He feels he is always on guard. Even when he is safe and secure at home with nothing to do but putter around the garden and watch TV, Richard still has a lingering feeling of uneasiness.

Although Richard's nervousness has not forced him to give up his job, his production in the workplace has been compromised. He often catches himself worrying about things that have nothing to do with the job at hand.

At social gatherings he often feels preoccupied about what other people think about him, and he is often worried about work which is not completed. His nervousness interferes with his ability to relate to his family and friends, and he often finds that he has to have one or two drinks just to loosen up enough to talk to people.

When real stressors like his daughter's divorce and his wife's hysterectomy do occur, Richard starts to tremble and shake and often gets panicky feelings. He doesn't do the things he should to take care of the ones he loves, but withdraws and suffers in silence.

Richard is suffering from a generalized anxiety disorder (GAD).

The frustration of working in a chronically stressful situation does not necessarily mean you have a generalized anxiety disorder, but it can contribute to one.

Patricia is a 52-year-old Child Protective Services worker for the county. Her job is to investigate and intervene in cases of child abuse and neglect. Patricia gets a firsthand look at physical abuse, neglect, ravages of drugs, and child-molestation cases. Her job description requires that she be hypervigilant. She has a heavy caseload and the welfare of dozens of children each day depends on her decisions.

On the job, Patricia finds herself tense, restless, and unable to relax. She often carries these feelings home and finds that sometimes for two or three hours after her job is over she is still wound up.

Despite her job stress, Patricia has a good marriage. She has a large number of friends and acquaintances and goes jogging each morning and plays bridge every Thursday night. Her performance on the job has been consistently good, and her boss routinely compliments her on handling an extremely difficult job.

Patricia does not have a generalized anxiety disorder. She has understandable feelings of nervousness, stress, pressure, and frustration, which go along with a very difficult and demanding position.

When Patricia takes a two-week vacation to the Virgin Islands, her symptoms disappear, and she's the happy-go-lucky, relaxed person she was before she ever knew about Child Protective Services.

In order to have a generalized anxiety disorder, the symptoms have to be present for at least six months, and any clearly identifiable psychosocial stressors, such as severe job or marital unhappiness, must be absent.

Sometimes generalized anxiety disorder can be confused with the typical feelings we all go through during certain phases of life.

Shanta is an 18-year-old high-school senior who is about to take her SATs. She is very nervous about her performance on the test and worries about which colleges she will qualify for. She's been a star on her high-school basketball team, yet questions whether her athletic ability is great enough to land her a scholarship at an NCAA Division One university. She doesn't really know what she wants to do with her life yet, and is disappointed because she doesn't have a boyfriend. She wonders if and when she'll get married, and what her life is going to be like.

Shanta is a typical adolescent. She is going through what has been described as an identity crisis, which is not at all unusual for young people making the transition from childhood to adulthood.

All of us go through times when we feel nervous and anxious. Anxiety and nervousness often serve the purpose of telling us that there is a problem that needs to be worked on or corrected.

Shanta's anxiety over her SAT examination gets her to focus her concentration on performing as well as she can on this test. Her anxiety over landing an athletic scholarship spurs her to perform to the best of her ability when she's being watched by scouts from major universities.

Although anxious feelings are likely to serve a purpose, just when do these anxious feelings become a generalized anxiety disorder?

Generalized Anxiety Disorder Questionnaire

Directions: Answer the following questions as honestly as you possibly can. Do not minimize or deny your responses, but do not answer yes to questions that do not apply to how you feel.

1. Have there ever been days when you have felt much too tense, nervous, or anxious about ordinary things or things in general, even though you are safe at home with nothing to do?
2. Have these nervous or anxious feelings caused you a significant amount of discomfort off and on for six months or longer at a time?
3. Have these nervous or anxious feelings interfered with your education, your occupation, or your work around your home?
4. Have these nervous or anxious feelings caused you problems with your family or friends?
5. When you are feeling your most nervous or anxious, do you also feel tense, restless, and unable to relax?
6. Do you notice that you are much more jittery and jumpy than usual?
7. Do you shake or tremble at times for no apparent reason?

8. During these anxious times, do you sweat a lot more than usual or notice that you feel cold or clammy?
9. During these anxious times, do you experience physical problems such as an upset stomach, the need to urinate more than usual, hot or cold flashes, dizziness, shortness of breath, or a racing or fluttering heart?
10. During these anxious times, do you feel overwhelmed by fear that something very bad is about to happen, but you don't know what?

Scoring: If you answered yes to questions 1 and 2, and yes to any two questions 3–10, you are likely to have a generalized anxiety disorder.

OBSESSIVE-COMPULSIVE DISORDER

Pam is an emotional invalid. The 42-year-old single, unemployed woman is living in a board-and-care facility.

Pam's mind is riddled with overwhelming thoughts of cleanliness and personal hygiene. These obsessions have cost Pam her job, career, and husband.

Pam feels driven to wash her hands and face continuously. When she does leave her room, she usually wears a surgeon's mask to keep germs from entering her body. She has scratches and scars all over her body from picking at herself incessantly. She spends sleepless hours pacing her 8-by-10-foot bedroom trying to figure out how to get herself clean.

Pam is a severely regressed obsessive-compulsive.

An obsessive-compulsive disorder is characterized by embarrassing, frightening, or ridiculous thoughts that keep intruding into your mind over and over, and irresistible desires to perform certain embarrassing, silly, repetitive, or even stupid actions.

Although Pam's case represents one end of the spectrum, millions of other individuals are able to struggle through their job and family responsibilities with milder forms of obsessive-compulsive disorder (OCD).

Somewhat related to—yet distinct from—the obsessive-compulsive disorder is the compulsive personality. Workaholics fit into this category.

Bill is a compulsive personality. The 34-year-old orthopedic surgeon finds little time in life for anything to do but focus on his profession. He ignores his family, friends, and relatives, and is clearly a workaholic. Although Bill spends about 50 hours a week at the hospital and his office, his wife reports that he puts in an extra 20–30 hours a week bringing his job home. Although Bill realizes that his wife and children feel neglected, he just can't seem to pull himself out of his professional role.

On the job, Bill is at the top of his game. He's the most competent orthopedic surgeon in the county and is routinely consulted regarding difficult cases. He is highly respected by his peers and heads several major committees at the hospital.

But is Bill's one-dimensional life satisfying?

Just like an obsessive-compulsive disorder, compulsive personalities show up in different degrees along a continuum.

Psychologists describe people with mild compulsive personality problems as having *compulsive features*. Somewhere in the middle of the continuum, with moderate disturbance in life, are those with *compulsive personality traits*. Finally, the *compulsive personality disorder* represents a major disturbance in one or more crucial areas of life.

A compulsive personality disorder is not an anxiety disorder. It represents a way of life which the person has developed since early childhood. The compulsive personality is often the straight-A student who has developed an inordinate need to succeed, beginning in grade school. Usually compulsive personalities are able to get by in life, and millions go untreated. In fact, the ideal of the overachieving superperson is based on a compulsive personality disorder. The tireless physician, the driving CEO, and the obsessed research scientist all contribute greatly to society and mankind, but pay enormous personal costs in their own lives.

We certainly need some compulsive behavior within our personality and culture. Without it businesses would fall apart, people would never receive their college degrees, and households would disintegrate. To be successful at whatever you do, you have to put energy and hours into your career or personal life.

Keep balance in mind determining whether you have a compulsive personality. In short, don't let your life become one-dimensional. If you put all your emotional energy in one area, even though you might be successful there, the rest of your life will probably suffer.

Now let's return to obsessive-compulsive disorders and see whether you are a candidate.

Obsessive-Compulsive Disorder Questionnaire

Directions: Answer the following questions as honestly as you possibly can. Do not minimize or deny your responses, but do not answer yes to questions that do not apply to you.

1. Have you ever been bothered by certain embarrassing, scary, or ridiculous thoughts that keep coming into your mind over and over again, even though you try to stop them?
2. Have you ever felt that you had to repeat a certain act over and over again, even though it was embarrassing, silly, repetitive, or didn't make much sense? For instance: washing your hands, counting something over and over, checking something again and again, or flipping light switches repetitively.
3. Have these thoughts/behaviors ever caused you any discomfort or distress in your life?
4. Have they ever interfered with your education, your occupation, or your work around your home?
5. Have these thoughts/behaviors caused you any family conflict or caused your family to worry about you?
6. Have they interfered with your friendships or social activities?
7. Have you ever received treatment, medication, or hospitalization because of these thoughts/behaviors?
8. Did you feel that these thoughts/behaviors were really silly and didn't make much sense?
9. Did people close to you feel that these thoughts/behaviors were silly and did not make much sense?

10. Did you ever feel that you had almost no control over these thoughts/behaviors?

Scoring: If you answered yes to questions 1 or 2 and yes to any one question 3–10, you may be suffering from an obsessive-compulsive disorder.

POST TRAUMATIC STRESS DISORDER

A post traumatic stress disorder is an emotional problem based on a traumatic psychological event that actually happened to you. Stressors which create a post traumatic stress disorder include serious accident or injury, rape, assault, near-death experience, death or serious injury of someone you love, prolonged combat duty, or severe natural disaster.

Ron, a muscular, moustached 24-year-old wood grader, with no history whatsoever of psychological problems, described what happened on Labor Day 1990:

"Me, my wife, and 2-year-old daughter, Stacy, went over to Jan and Alice's house. We had just got there, and Jan and I popped open a beer. Alice took my wife to show her a new addition to the house. Jan told Brad, his 14-year-old son, to turn off the Nintendo and let us watch the baseball game. Stacy was wearing her bright pink dress with blue ribbons and was sitting on the floor off to my left playing with a puzzle.

After we flicked on the baseball game, a few minutes passed. Then my wife came down and asked where Stacy was. I looked over and she was gone. I found the door from the kitchen to the patio had been left open when Brad went to his friend's house. My whole body went numb when I looked out off the patio and saw Stacy floating face down in the swimming pool. . . . I didn't think, I just reacted. . . . The next thing I remember was coming up under Stacy and noticing that she was completely blue. I pushed her head out of the water and swam desperately to the side. Alice had started screaming and gone inside, and before I could say anything, Jan was headed for the phone. My wife and I immediately began tandem CPR. I didn't have time to say it, but I was desperately praying, 'God please don't let her die.' Her body was cool and lifeless, but we refused to give up. It seemed like only minutes before the EMTs and firemen arrived.

When they took over, the desperate fear began to set in. As I watched them continue to try to resuscitate her lifeless body, I began to panic and pray even harder. . . .

The first 48 hours were critical, and the doctors didn't know if Stacy would make it or not. They told us that even if she did live she might have irreversible brain damage, which would prevent her from leading a normal life. We stood a vigil at her side for two days. Wednesday at 8:25 A.M. I heard her move. I looked over and saw the familiar twinkle in her blue eyes. As she whined, 'Mommy,' my wife and I realized that there must be a compassionate God."

Days of seemingly endless medical, neurological, and psychological tests revealed that Stacy had few if any problems, but the scars still remained in Ron's mind. Although relieved and thankful that things were back to normal, Ron was plagued by recurrent nightmares of Stacy's near-drowning and felt chills whenever he saw a swimming pool. He developed an overprotective obsession about Stacy and found that he could not concentrate on his work for fear that something might happen to her. He continued to replay again and again the sequence of events which happened in the swimming pool on Labor Day.

Ron was suffering from a post traumatic stress disorder.

Rosemary, a 29-year-old, auburn-haired account executive, described a different kind of trauma:

"The 32-ounce Diet Pepsi that I had two hours ago at McDonald's to wake me up had served its purpose. Now I was left with a compelling need to go to the bathroom. But a roadside sign on the long deserted stretch of Interstate 5 said next services 28 miles. . . . I came to a rest area in a secluded group of tall oak trees. It was about 10 o'clock at night, yet the heat from the August day lingered on, with temperatures in the low 90s. . . . I saw a few 18-wheelers and felt reassured knowing there were other people around.

As I opened the stall in the restroom, I felt a large hand close over my mouth. I tried to get away, but his large frame forced me into the stall and I heard the door latch behind him. I then felt a cold steel knife next to the right side of my neck and heard him whisper in a hoarse, coarse voice, 'Scream and you die.' He was a big, ugly man, with a coarse black, unkempt beard. He was wearing a brown plaid shirt and old blue jeans with grease stains on them. I could smell the stench of whiskey on his breath as he lifted up my skirt and raped me.

Time went by really slowly, and a few minutes dragged on and on. I've never felt so helpless, hopeless, and out of control. Should I scream? Did he have AIDS? Would he kill me anyway?

When he was finally finished, he slapped me in the mouth and said if I screamed, he would come back and cut my throat. . . . I felt dazed, stunned, and everything seemed unreal.

Rosemary drove herself to the nearest town and reported the rape to the police officials. They contacted county officials, and Rosemary went through the routine medical and legal procedures of a devastating and violent act. Rosemary had been a victim of aggravated rape.

Although the rape had occurred four months prior to her visit with me, Rosemary's life was not bouncing back. She had recurrent nightmares of the bearded man and found that she was unable to continue her sexual relationship with her fiancé. Her business was suffering, and Rosemary feared that the man would try to get her again even though he had no way of identifying her and did not know where she lived or worked.

Rosemary, too, was suffering from a post traumatic stress disorder;

a very natural and understandable reaction to a terrible personal and psychological assault.

Near the other end of the spectrum is the case of Patty, 26-year-old mother of two. Patty trembles, shakes, and sobs uncontrollably as she describes witnessing an accident in which she saw her husband and cousin broadsided as they backed out of their driveway. Although Patty's husband and the cousin were not seriously injured, Patty cannot help replaying the accident in her mind. She continues to think she hears the sound of the crash, and whenever a sudden or unexpected noise occurs, she finds herself nearly jumping through the ceiling. Patty has been reassured by her friends and family that the feelings will go away; still she has had them for over six weeks.

Although many of us might not respond as severely as Patty did, she, too, has all the symptoms necessary for the diagnosis of a post traumatic stress disorder.

A post traumatic stress disorder depends not only on the severity of the stressor, but on the individual who has experienced the stressor. Some people handle the most severe stressors quite well.

Mandy, a 16-year-old high-school junior, was riding back from a concert with her older sister one night when a pair of headlights suddenly appeared out of nowhere on a one-way stretch of freeway. Her sister instinctively swerved to protect Mandy and took the brunt of the collision.

The next morning, Mandy woke up in the hospital with a broken collarbone and numerous bruises. Her sister would never wake up, the victim of a drunk driver.

Mandy feels shaky, insecure, and devastated when she hears that her sister has died. She mourns the loss of her sister and accepts and gives support to her mother during their time of grieving. Despite feeling shaken, Mandy's wounds do heal, and within a few weeks she's back at school. She is able to concentrate on her grades and accepts the support and comfort of her friends. Her headaches gradually disappear.

Although Mandy feels a deep sense of loss and anger over the death of her sister, she doesn't let it ruin her life. Within a few months, she's going out with friends, and within a year she has a new boyfriend. Her grades continue to be good. The following year she tries out and makes the high-school swim team and becomes a cheerleader.

Despite undergoing a horrible psychological and physical trauma,

Mandy's personality structure is resilient, and she bounces back quickly.

Mandy does not have a post traumatic stress disorder.

Now let's see whether any traumatic experiences are locked in your mind.

Post Traumatic Stress Disorder Questionnaire

Directions: Answer the following questions as honestly as possible. Do not deny or minimize your responses, but do not answer yes to questions that do not apply to you.

1. Have you ever had nightmares or flashbacks in which you found yourself reliving some terrible real-life experience over and over again? For example: assault, accident, natural disaster, serious injury, or anything you would consider a severe psychological trauma.
2. Did your *reactions* to this trauma ever interfere with your education, occupation, or work around your home?
3. Did your *reactions* to the trauma cause you problems with your family or friends?
4. Did you ever find that you could not stop the memory of this trauma from popping into your head no matter how hard you tried?
5. Have you had frequent nightmares about the trauma?
6. Have you ever noticed that certain situations would trigger unpleasant reactions and memories of the trauma?
7. Even after the trauma was over, did you find yourself feeling weak, helpless, and withdrawn?
8. After the trauma was over, did you find yourself feeling emotionally distant and separate from people you are usually close to, or did you feel emotionally numb inside?
9. After the trauma was over, did you have trouble getting a good night's sleep?
10. Did you tend to avoid anything that would remind you of the trauma?

Scoring: If you answered yes to question 1 and yes to any two questions 2–10, you may be suffering from a post traumatic stress disorder.

If your symptoms began more than six months after the occurrence of the trauma, it's a *post traumatic stress disorder of delayed onset.*

PANIC DISORDER

Donna is a 44-year-old schoolteacher who has been through a lot in the past year. Her 16-year-old son was arrested for drug possession with intent to sell and had to spend 60 days in juvenile hall. Her husband, a city policeman of 23 years, developed a bleeding ulcer after becoming the focus of an internal affairs investigation and was forced into early retirement.

Donna feels pressured to take care of her son and husband, and to meet the needs of her family.

Within six months, Donna starts to experience what she thinks are heart problems. She has difficulty breathing and feels she's smothering. Her stomach is often upset, and she finds herself going to the bathroom a lot more than usual. Once or twice a week she gets dizzy and light-headed and feels as if things are closing in around her. She usually gets right to the point of almost fainting before her fear starts to subside.

After an episode that nearly caused her to crash her car on the way home from class one night, Donna sets up a visit with her doctor, who refers her to a cardiologist.

"EKG, treadmill, and physical examination are all normal. There's nothing wrong with your heart," her cardiologist reports.

"I know I'm not crazy. My chest really hurts, and I do have trouble catching my breath," she exclaimed in our first visit.

No, Donna's problems are not all inside of her head. She is suffering from a panic disorder.

Beside being one of the most terrifying experiences you can go through, panic disorders are unusual in that they are psychological in origin, yet have a clear neurological and physiological basis.

Donna's body has responded with what I call a "false alarm" syndrome. To understand this, let's look at what your body does when it is faced with a life-threatening situation.

Just imagine for a moment that you are on your way home from the grocery store at night when your car breaks down. The road you have routinely taken so many times during the daytime becomes something very different at night on foot. While making your way home along the sidewalk, a general sense of uneasiness begins to come over you. Suddenly, a tall, slender, bearded man wearing an old green army jacket jumps in front of you and flicks out a switchblade knife. He demands your money. You quickly hand over your wallet, but the man screams "Forty dollars! That's not enough. I'm going to have to cut you up!"

You plead for your life, yet his drugged, glazed eyes tell you that nothing is getting through. You notice your body is trembling; your hands and feet are ice-cold. Your eyes are wide open, your breathing is shallow, you feel a distinct shortness of breath. Everything seems unreal. As he moves to lift the knife, you instinctively kick him in the groin as hard as you can, turn, and run faster then you've ever run before.

Within twenty minutes, you are back home. Your heart is pounding. Your breathing is fast and shallow. You lock the door and dial 911. You look out the window to see if the man has followed you home. Realizing that he is nowhere in sight, gradually your body starts to calm down.

This sequence of events describes what occurs when your body is faced with a life-threatening situation.

Instinctively, your body responded with the fight-or-flight syndrome. Fortunately, you did both and survived.

But, unfortunately, many people experience this fight-or-flight syndrome for no apparent reason (a false alarm). The same natural chemicals and sensations which can save your life become a devastating enemy when there is no actual threat.

Almost all of us have felt nervous or anxious in difficult situations without having an anxiety disorder.

Paula, a 52-year-old widow, has recently taken a promotional job with a television station. One of her first assignments is to present an advertising package to a group of thirty-five to forty perspective clients. Though Paula knows her material well, she feels tense and anxious before the presentation. When she actually begins to talk, she notices that her mouth is dry, her hands are shaking, and she's obsessed with what other people are thinking about her. At a couple of points Paula begins to hyperventilate, but manages to stay in control. She worries that the other people realize that she is terrified. Despite some feelings of dizziness, Paula fights her way through the presentation and feels a tremendous sense of relief when it's over.

Paula did not have an anxiety attack, just understandable feelings of anxiety in a high-pressure situation.

Let's get down to the bare bones of panic attacks. Take this test based on one psychologists give their patients to see if you may be actually suffering from a panic disorder.

Panic Disorder Questionnaire

Directions: Answer the following questions as honestly as you possibly can. Do not minimize or deny your responses, but do not answer yes to questions which do not apply to you.

1. Have you ever had sudden spells or attacks of nervousness, strong fear, or panic that come over you for no apparent reason, seemingly out of the blue?
2. Did you have these panic attacks even though a doctor said there was nothing wrong with your heart?
3. Did you have these feelings even though nothing was threatening your life at the time, or you had not been vigorously exercising?
4. Have these panic attacks ever interfered with your education, your occupation, or your work around your home?
5. Have these panic attacks caused you problems with your family or friends, or caused them to worry about you?
6. When you suffered from your worst panic attacks, did you sometimes feel that you might be having a heart attack, or that you were suffocating, or totally overwhelmed by fear?
7. During your panic attack did you feel choked, smothered, or have trouble catching your breath?

8. Did you feel as if everything was becoming unreal or strange?
9. Did you feel as if you might be going crazy, losing your mind, or dying?
10. Have you had four separate panic attacks within any four-week period? Or has one panic attack been followed by a persistent fear lasting at least one month about having another panic attack?

Scoring: If you answered yes to questions 1, 2, and 3, yes to any two questions 4–9, and yes to question 10, you are indeed likely to be suffering from a panic disorder.

By now, with a little honesty and a lot of courage, you have figured out whether you have an anxiety disorder. Let's look at some interesting facts about anxiety disorders before seeing what can be done about them.

FAST FACTS ABOUT ANXIETY DISORDERS

- The probability of developing an anxiety disorder over the course of your lifetime is 15 percent.
- In any one-month period, 6 out of every 100 adults experience some type of phobic disorder.
- Women are more than twice as likely as men to experience anxiety disorders.
- Men are more likely to be drug or alcohol dependent or to have antisocial personality disorders rather than anxiety disorders.
- Only 25 percent of the people with anxiety-related disorders ever receive appropriate treatment.
- By the time the anxiety-riddled patient is referred to an appropriate psychologist or psychiatrist, he or she may well have seen dozens of other doctors, including neurologists, cardiologists, gastroenterologists, and respiratory specialists.

- In one study, 90 percent of the patients diagnosed as having anxiety disorders resisted psychiatric referral and believed that such a diagnosis labeled them as "crazy" or denied the reality of their symptoms.
- When untreated, panic disorders are likely to increase alcohol and substance abuse, depression, suicide, sexual disorders, and other medical illnesses. Jones (1989)
- People suffering from panic disorders are more likely to have difficulty getting along with their spouses and have more trouble communicating with them.
- Patients with anxiety disorders are seven times likely to visit a physician or health-care provider than the general population.
- Weissman (1989) found that adults with panic disorders were 18 times more likely to have attempted or considered suicide, compared with the general population with no psychiatric disorder.
- Most importantly, over 90 percent of the patients with panic disorders respond favorably to appropriate professional treatment.

HOPE FOR THE FUTURE

Panic attacks, phobias, generalized anxiety disorders, post traumatic stress disorders, and obsessive-compulsive disorders are all frightening and distressing, yet very treatable disorders.

All of the individual cases discussed earlier in this chapter responded quite favorably to appropriate psychological and psychiatric intervention strategies. Yes, even Derek continues to fly, although he's not happy about it.

While recent research in psychiatry has demonstrated that low dosages of antidepressant medication such as Imipramine may be effective in the long-term management of anxiety, the classic tranquilizers often offer more disadvantages than benefits.

Classic tranquilizers (benzodiazepans) such as Librium, Valium, Meprobamate, and Zanax often prove to be highly addictive.

While acting as director of psychology at a drug- and alcohol-rehabilitation unit, I discovered that approximately 10 percent of the new admissions come in with a prescription medication problem. Three times out of four, the medication they are addicted to is a minor tranquilizer, such as Valium. Such patients have become victims of well-intentioned physicians who have prescribed tranquilizers for the management of anxiety.

Unfortunately, most minor tranquilizers provide diminishing results over time, which requires increasing dosages to achieve the same effect, a phenomenon called *tolerance*. When the patient attempts to withdraw from the tranquilizer, serious side effects often occur. Two of my recent patients had seizures when trying to withdraw from the minor tranquilizer Zanax.

In addition to such drugs as Imipramine, the minor tranquilizer Buspar has, so far, looked like a candidate for the management of chronic anxiety, with little addiction potential.

The behavioral treatment of simple phobias has one of the highest success rates of all psychological interventions. Using a technique developed by Joseph Wolpe called "reciprocal inhibition," patients are taught to relax into structured thoughts or exposures to phobic situations, objects, or activities. Briefly, patients are taught a technique in which they arrange the fearful object, activity, or situation in a hierarchial fashion, with the least-anxiety-producing object at the bottom and the most-anxiety-producing situation at the top.

Patients are then taught the self-help skill of deep relaxation training.

Next, they are asked to begin imagining the least-distressing phobic object, situation, or activity while remaining deeply relaxed.

If patients notice any anxiety, they signal a therapist by lifting a finger, at which time the therapist suggests that they remove the phobic object, activity, or situation from their mind and reintroduce a relaxed state. The procedure is continued until the patient can imagine or even experience the dreaded phobic object, activity, or situation with no anxiety whatsoever.

The patients are then encouraged to imagine or perceive the next phobic object, situation, or activity in the hierarchy. The process goes on and on, until the patients are able to imagine or even experience the most dreaded phobic object, activity, or situation in a state of complete calm and equanimity.

At that point, the phobia is said to have been desensitized.

Recently, Ellen Shapiro may have developed a briefer technique called *rapid eye movement desensitization reprocessing*. Apparently,

this technique works by short-circuiting the fear response and immediately pairing up a deeply relaxed state with a fearful thought or
memory by having patients focus on the phobia or trauma while
rapidly swinging their eyes from side to side, diagonally, or up and
down. This is done only under qualified professional supervision.

Recent developments in cognitive-therapy techniques help patients to minimize distressing thoughts when they are experiencing
anxiety attacks.

Usually, the physical symptoms you have with an anxiety attack
cause you to become extremely upset. This, in turn, releases more
adrenaline, and creates more subjective distress. You're likely to say
things to yourself like, "Oh, God! I might be dying," "I think I'm
having a heart attack," or "I think I'm losing my mind." It's a snow-
ball effect. The worse you feel, the more frightening things you say
to yourself, and in turn the worse this makes you feel.

According to the cognitive therapist, the key is to learn to recognize that your body is having a "false alarm," and to not let distressing thoughts or fearful self-talk make your problems any worse.

Patients are taught to say such things as "I'm just having an anxiety
attack, and it will be over in an hour or two," "This is just a panic
attack and it's not going to kill me," or "The more I relax into my
anxiety, the more comfortable I will feel and the sooner it will go
away."

Cognitive-behavior therapists also teach patients to schedule large-
muscle aerobic activities and regularly practice relaxation in order to
cope with, minimize, and eventually eliminate anxiety.

Biofeedback training is often a very useful adjunctive treatment for
the management of anxiety disorders. Using immediate feedback regarding various states of muscle tension or indicators of anxiety
throughout your body, you can actually learn to reduce your body's
level of arousal, and thereby diminish anxiety.

Fortunately, anxiety disorders are one of the most treatable of all
psychological problems. And, if you have recognized yourself in any
of the categories, it's time to get help. Sure, you could probably stick
it out on your own and get by in life. But life is too short, and now
we have the psychological technology necessary to help you overcome these problems and to enjoy life fully.

Just like the other disorders discussed, usually community or
county mental-health centers will have a list of therapists who specialize in different types of anxiety disorders.

Finally, you will probably be relieved to realize that most treatment strategies for anxiety are short-term. Typically, you will be able to be treated successfully for almost all anxiety disorders within three to four months, and should begin to improve noticeably shortly after your treatment begins.

CHAPTER 6

AM I DEPRESSED?

KEVIN'S NICKNAME WAS "GOLDEN BOY." THE TALL, 26-YEAR-OLD FORMER MODEL turned assistant manager looked as if he had everything to live for.

In high school he seemed so cool and never let anything get to him. He always had girlfriends and was on the varsity basketball and track teams. Kevin's teachers thought of him as a model student: serious and self-disciplined.

Kevin had just bought a home in a neighborhood with other young, upwardly mobile adults and, with his wife and two children, seemed to be on the fast tract of achieving the American dream.

On the job, Kevin's supervisor thought of him as responsible far beyond his age. He had already received two promotions and was expecting a third.

But when I talked with Kevin, there seemed to be something missing. When I looked closely into his eyes, there was an emptiness; but Kevin convinced me that everything was okay.

I questioned Kevin carefully about depression, and he gave thoughtful answers indicating that he was not depressed. But my gut-level feeling told me that something was wrong. Kevin had learned to hide his depressed feelings from others and was suffering from what is known as an "atypical" or "masked" depressive disorder. Six weeks after my interview with Kevin—and for reasons unknown to anyone—he put a gun to his head and ended his own life.

It's painfully obvious that Kevin—and most people who commit suicide—are desperately unhappy. Mental-health professionals believe that the majority of people who commit suicide are suffering from clinical depression. A reported 40 percent to 70 percent or more of people who kill themselves have had a history of serious depression, and many more are probably like Kevin and have an actual depressive disorder which they hide or mask.

But how can tragedies like Kevin's be prevented?

Suicide's warning signs are often clear and worth noting.

People who have previously attempted suicide are the most likely to take their own lives. The suicide rate for repeated attempters is 600 times higher than the overall rate in the general population. Up to half of the people who actually commit suicide had previously made attempts.

People who commit suicide often talk about it before they attempt it. Statements like "People would be better off without me," or "No one is going to have to worry about me any longer," are often giveaways for an upcoming suicide attempt.

Suicide attempters often take steps to put their affairs in order before they act. Reports from survivors have indicated that they often alter their wills, give away prized possessions, or make arrangements for pets as if they were preparing for a long trip. They may even talk vaguely about going away.

A change in personality or behavior is often a tip-off for an impending suicide attempt. A normally buoyant person may seem withdrawn for no apparent reason. A regular churchgoer may stop attending services, and an avid jogger may quit running. Such behavioral change, especially if accompanied by expressions of worthlessness and hopelessness, can be a sign of desperation if the person is suffering from clinical depression.

While 85 percent of depressed people are not suicidal, most suicide-prone people are depressed. But suicide is not the only consequence of depression.

This year in the United States an estimated 25 to 35 million people will suffer from a serious depressive illness. Many will be incapacitated for weeks or even months. The cost to the United States in 1989 was more than $27 billion, over $17 billion of which was due to lost time from work.

In addition to the enormous financial cost to the economy, depression causes immense suffering not only for depressed patients, but also for their loved ones and families.

While depression is a very treatable disorder, current scientific evidence indicates that many people suffer needlessly since only one-third ever seek treatment.

The prevalence of depression throughout the rest of the world is also remarkable. In the European Community, it is estimated that over 17 million people will suffer from a depressive disorder within any one-year period. The Eastern European countries and Scandinavia have even higher levels per capita.

WHAT IS DEPRESSION?

To understand depression, we must recognize the distinction between the adjective "depressed" and the clinical syndrome "depression."

When you say you are depressed, you may be referring to such feelings as being bored, tired, upset, distressed, or frustrated.

Clinical depression, on the other hand, is a multifaceted disorder that affects not only your body, but your thoughts, moods, and behaviors.

In contrast to the descriptive adjective "depressed," clinical depression consists of several or all of the following symptoms:

1) A persistent sad, empty, or anxious mood
2) Loss of interest or pleasure in ordinary activities
3) A diminished or decreased desire for sexual activity
4) A loss of energy and a feeling of being fatigued or slowed down
5) Sleep disturbances, including insomnia, early-morning wakening, oversleeping, or duration insomnia (difficulty staying asleep).
6) Eating disturbances such as loss of appetite and weight loss, or increase in appetite and weight gain
7) Difficulty in concentrating, remembering, and making decisions
8) A feeling of pessimism, hopelessness, and despair
9) Feelings of personal worthlessness, helplessness, and guilt
10) Recurrent thoughts of suicide, death, or actual suicide attempts
11) Chronic irritability

12) Excessive crying
13) Chronic bodily aches and pains that don't respond to medical treatment

Depression represents a very broad category of disorders and can include numerous subtypes.

Depression can also be thought of from a perspective of time. Many people will suffer from a single depressive episode which lasts anywhere from a few weeks to a few months, while others may suffer from a recurrent depressive disorder which may last for years.

Qualitatively, depression may divided into four basic categories:

1) Dysthymic disorder
2) Major depressive disorder
3) Psychotic depressive disorder
4) Manic-depressive illness

Dysthymic Disorder

The essential feature of a dysthymic disorder is a chronic disturbance of mood, involving feelings of despair or loss of interest or pleasure in formerly enjoyable activities and pastimes. The distinction between a dysthymic disorder and a major depressive disorder is usually one of severity and duration.

For adults, two years of more-or-less consistent unhappiness is required; for children and adolescents, one year is sufficient for this diagnosis.

Louise, a 56-year-old secondary-school teacher has been feeling sad, blue, down in the dumps, and low for as long as she can remember. Her depressed moods lead to a loss of interest and pleasure in things she used to enjoy. Louise's moods are often interrupted by periods of a normal interest and activity level and feeling relatively good. These normal periods last anywhere from a few days to a few weeks, and Louise often thinks she's over the depression when they occur. But then, for no apparent reason, she becomes despondent again, and Louise finds herself with little or no energy. She is able to get by at her job and functions at a marginal level around her home and in her social circle. But Louise is not happy.

Louise is suffering from a dysthymic disorder.

Dysthymic Disorder Questionnaire

Directions: Answer the following questions as honestly as possible. Do not minimize or deny problems if they exist, but do not exaggerate your responses or answer yes to questions that do not apply to you.

1. Do you feel unusually down, empty, sad, or hopeless for several days or weeks at a time?
2. Are these depressed periods interrupted by normal moods and feelings, which last only for a few days or weeks at a time, and never more than a few months?
3. During these depressed periods, is there a significant decrease in previously enjoyable activities, interests, and pastimes?
4. During these depressive periods, have you experienced at least three of the following symptoms:
   a. difficulty falling or staying asleep
   b. low energy level or chronic fatigue
   c. feeling of inadequacy, and loss of self-esteem
   d. decreased effectiveness or productivity at school, work, or around your home
   e. decreased ability to concentrate, pay attention, or think clearly
   f. withdrawal from friends and family
   g. loss of interest and enjoyment in pleasurable activities
   h. irritability or excessive anger; or in children, excessive anger towards parents or caretakers
   i. inability to respond with pleasure or enjoyment to rewarding and enjoyable activities
   j. feeling slowed down or restless, with a lowered activity level and less sociability
   k. a pessimistic attitude toward the future and brooding over the past

l. crying, tearfulness, and a pervasively sad mood
m. recurrent ideas of death, morbidity, or suicide

Scoring: If you answered yes to questions 1, 2, and 3, and yes to any three symptoms under question 4, you have the symptoms necessary for the diagnosis of a dysthymic disorder.

Major Depressive Disorders

Mary, a tall, slender, 29-year-old computer technician has been only occasionally happy throughout her life. Mary's mother was a workaholic and was seldom around for her. Her father was a perfectionist, a compulsive man who tried to answer all of Mary's questions logically and reasonably. He encouraged her to hold back her feelings and insisted that she could "think" things through. Mary's father let her know at a very early age that it was never okay to cry or be upset, that she should hold her anger in, and that the solutions to life's problems come strictly through applied intellect.

Although Mary has an IQ of 130 (very superior), she has taken a job far below her level of intellectual ability. She is afraid to take risks and is constantly second-guessing herself.

In school, Mary always felt as if she was on the edge of social groups. She never felt as if she really fit in because she did not feel good about herself. She described herself as a relatively passive person who didn't get very involved in physical or social activities, not only during her school years, but throughout the rest of her life.

The breaking point for Mary occurred when Ed, her boyfriend of two-and-a-half years, told her that he could no longer tolerate her depressed moods and ended the relationship.

Mary was devastated. Her already poor appetite became nonexistent. She refused to get out of bed and go to work. She was unable to sleep at night and tossed about in frustration. She felt hopeless about the future and saw no real point in continuing to live. Mary's already marginal existence had become intolerable. She wished that she were dead, but didn't have the courage or energy to attempt suicide.

Mary is severely depressed.

Mary's friend Laura came over every morning for a week to make sure Mary had something to eat. Although Mary didn't want to leave her house, Laura persuaded her to come to my office for an evaluation.

After talking with Mary for a few minutes, it became obvious that her already significant depression had become critical. Since Mary was not suffering from hallucinations (hearing voices or seeing things no one else can see or hear) or delusions (faulty or unrealistic beliefs), she is not psychotically depressed. But she is greatly impaired to the point of not being able to meet her basic needs and requires immediate treatment. After a brief two-week stay in a psychiatric unit, Mary's condition stabilizes, and she returns home and goes back to work.

Angela, on the other hand, is an 18-year-old high-school senior who recently suffered kidney and other internal injuries in an auto accident. Prior to the injury, Angela had not only maintained above-average grades, but had worked 20 hours a week at McDonald's, and had numerous friends and acquaintances. Her mood typically had been very upbeat, and Angela was thought of as the life of the party.

During our history taking, Angela reported that she had been sexually molested by a teen-age boy when she was between the ages of seven and nine. She was open and expressive with her feelings of anger, shame, rage, and disgust regarding what happened. She appeared to get over this incident quickly. At the age of ten, Angela's mother and father divorced. Although Angela thought that she may be one of the causes of the divorce, her mother and father quickly put this concern to rest. While Angela was upset that her mother had left, she did not take it personally, and came to realize that her mother's problems were not her own.

After Angela's accident, her doctor ordered her to stay home from work and school for one week. After her next physical examination, Angela was told by her doctor that she was doing fine, and he encouraged her to return to school and her job. But Angela felt very lethargic and distressed. She told her dad that she wasn't ready to go back to school or work and asked her employer for some extra time off. She began sleeping more than usual and noticed that her appetite was not normal.

After one week of lying around and feeling bad, Angela's mood began to pick up, and she soon returned to school and her job. Her normal, resilient ego bounced back, and her friends reported that she was back to the Angela they once knew.

Despite a history which would predispose her to depression and an accident which may have triggered reactive depression, Angela is not clinically depressed. She is bouncing back from a stressor (accident) at her own pace and in her own way.

Let's see whether if you or someone you love is suffering from a major depressive disorder.

Major Depressive Disorder Questionnaire

Directions: Answer the following questions as honestly as possible. Do not deny or minimize your responses, but do not exaggerate or answer yes to questions that do not apply to you.

1. Have you ever had times when you felt unusually down, empty, sad, or hopeless for several days or weeks at a time?
2. Have you ever experienced times when you felt very tired or irritable most of the time for almost no reason at all?
3. Have these depressed, tired, or irritable feelings stayed with you most of the time for two weeks or longer?
4. Did these depressed feelings ever cause you significant problems or discomfort in your life?
5. Did these depressed feelings ever interfere with your education, your occupation, or your work around the home?
6. Did these depressed feelings cause you problems with your family or cause your family to worry about you?
7. Did these depressed feelings interfere with your friendships, social life, or overall level of social activity?
8. Have you ever received treatment or medication for depression?
9. Were you ever hospitalized for depression?

When you were your most depressed, did you ever:

10. Have a significant increase or decrease in your appetite or weight?
11. Have trouble sleeping, including difficulty falling asleep, staying

asleep, waking up early and finding you could not go back to sleep, or sleeping a lot more than usual?

12. Felt run-down and drained without the energy to do the things you normally do?
13. Felt so slowed down that you found it was hard to get going and had a hard time getting things done?
14. Tend to lose interest in things that you usually enjoy?
15. Withdraw from other people?
16. Have less interest in sex than usual?
17. Feel hopeless about the future?
18. Have trouble concentrating and remembering things?
19. Have morbid thoughts about death or dying, including wishing you were dead, or considering suicide?
20. Have you ever actually attempted suicide?

Scoring: The following scoring pattern indicates a major depressive disorder: yes to questions 1 or 2 and 3, yes to any one question 4–9, and yes to any five questions 10–20.

PSYCHOTIC DEPRESSIVE DISORDER

A psychotic depressive disorder is a more serious form of a major depressive disorder. The hallmark features of a psychotic depressive disorder include hallucinations, in which you see, hear, or feel things around you that other people cannot sense; or delusions, in which you believe things that are entirely inconsistent with reality.

Psychotic depressive disorders are often characterized by delusions of personal inadequacy, guilt, disease, death, undeserved punishment, or destruction.

Delusional depressive content often includes such beliefs as "My body is slowly being eaten away," "I am worthless, or no good," or "I have committed unpardonable sins and am assured of damnation."

Depressive hallucinations are often consistent with hearing voices telling you that you're worthless, no good, stupid, or inadequate. Depressive hallucinations are quite different from the normal self-talk we all engage in. Typically, auditory hallucinations appear to have a life of their own, and the patient does not know where the voices are coming from.

Another feature often associated with psychotic depressive disorders is psychomotor retardation. This means feeling as if you were in a stupor in which your thoughts and actions are extremely slowed down. You may even become mute and unresponsive to the people around you, or feel as if you're living in slow motion.

James is a 21-year-old college sophomore who appeared to be slipping away from reality. James's father left his mother when James was quite young, and his mother became obsessed with protecting and possessing him. She used James for comfort and support. In her own desperate attempts to get her needs met, she encouraged James to be a social misfit and to take care of her all of the time. James told me he had virtually no friends as a child and had had his first date only in his second year of college.

As I escorted James from the waiting room to my office, I looked back and noticed that he was about 8 feet behind me and moving at the pace of a snail. His head drooped, and his facial expression was hopeless. When James finally sat down in the chair, he slouched his head and shoulders and showed almost no movement for the next 45 minutes.

Besides telling me that he had suffered a decrease in his appetite, lost 15 pounds, had disturbed sleep, and withdrew from his usual activities, James was most disturbed by the fact that he was constantly hearing voices telling him that he was worthless. James said that these voices seemed to have a life of their own and were not the normal self-talk sentences which most people have when they think to themselves. He told me that the voices seemed to be broadcast into his head as if he had a radio receiver inside his skull.

James tried to make sense of these auditory hallucinations by developing delusions, in which he thought that demons or devils were trying to destroy his soul. He felt as if his mind, body, and spirit were gradually being eaten away by these demons.

James was suffering from a psychotic depressive episode.

One of the key points to keep in mind when diagnosing psychotic depressive disorders is whether there is gross impairment in reality testing, characterized by the inability to meet basic needs, hallucinations (hearing voices, seeing things, or feeling things that other people do not experience), and delusions (unrealistic beliefs involving death, destruction, disease, or personal inadequacy).

In short, in order to meet the criteria for a psychotic depressive disorder, you must meet the scoring standards for a major depressive disorder *and* experience hallucinations or delusions for at least several days or weeks.

MANIC-DEPRESSIVE DISORDER

What did Abraham Lincoln, Winston Churchill, and Theodore Roosevelt have in common? They—and many other powerful and creative people—suffered from manic-depressive disorders.

A recent change in the diagnostic nomenclature has relabeled manic-depressive disorders as bipolar disorders. Such disorders involve a rapid and dramatic shift in mood from one of despair and depression to one of elation and jubilation for no apparent reason. The bipolar disorder may involve rapidly or slowly fluctuating shifts of mood, a predominantly depressed mood, or a predominantly manic or elated mood.

It's very important to distinguish typical mood swings which react to events that happen in your life from a bipolar disorder. One of the key indicators of the bipolar disorder is dramatic mood swings which have no firm basis in reality, or which represent obviously excessive reactions to minor stressors.

Kay is a 37-year-old married woman who does volunteer work for the Red Cross. Kay's childhood was characterized by physical and sexual abuse by her older brother and her brother's friends. Kay reported that she was always described by her parents and teachers as a hyperactive child. She had excessive physical and mental energy and often found herself getting into trouble. She recalled that she often needed hardly any sleep and could easily get by on two or three hours of sleep per night. She denied any history of abuse of amphetamines or other drugs, and only rarely used alcohol.

Kay told me that her high energy and activity levels frequently made her do things she really didn't want to. She said that even in grade school her nervousness and fidgeting in the classroom got her into trouble, and she was frequently sent to the principal for arguing and fighting with other classmates.

Kay's friendship patterns tended to be intense and erratic. She would frequently find herself bored with her best friends and drift into relationships with people who were often described as dangerous or even criminal. Twice in her late adolescence she was arrested for being an accomplice to a burglary.

Kay's husband was at the end of his rope. Kay would frequently go on spending sprees and run up bills that they could not pay.

Kay loved to dance, and although her husband was tolerant of her going out dancing, he became angry when she frequently came home between 5:00 and 6:00 the next morning. Kay confided that she had been involved in numerous sexual affairs with a variety of men whom she hardly knew.

Despite her obvious problems, Kay did not feel that she was in need of treatment. She was simply coming in because her husband, sister, brother, and mother told her that she needed help. Kay continued to insist that her mood was fine and that there was nothing wrong with her behavior.

The time frame for Kay's manic episodes lasted anywhere from a few weeks to three or four months. After that, Kay appeared to settle down and be quite comfortable going through her typical daily routine. Her husband and friends described her during these normal times as an excellent wife and a person who was a joy to be around. But no one could ever predict when Kay was going to go off on one of her sprees.

Kay was suffering from a bipolar disorder, manic type.

Marjorie, a 51-year-old housewife and mother of six grown children described her upbringing as solid. She described her parents as conscientious, hard-working people who were attentive to their children's needs. Marjorie felt loved and respected as a child and felt that she could communicate anything to her mom and dad.

But Marjorie did remember that on two or three occasions her mother appeared to go kind of "crazy," and twice had to be sent to a mental hospital for a few weeks. Marjorie said that her mother's unusual mood swings were effectively controlled with the drug lithium carbonate. For most of her childhood, her mother appeared to have no problems at all.

Marjorie's husband told me that he tried to do everything he could to meet Marjorie's needs. She loved outdoor activities, and he would frequently take her camping and fishing. Twice a year they would go deer hunting together. He found out what Marjorie liked to do and tried to make good things happen for her. Marjorie had a fair number of friends and acquaintances and was relatively well thought of within her community. She especially enjoyed gardening and playing with her grandchildren.

Marjorie told me that several times a year she became extremely depressed, unhappy, and sad for no real reason. During these times, she would withdraw into her room and spend most of her time in bed. She lost interest in almost all activities she typically enjoyed, and her husband had to force her to eat. Marjorie slept a lot more than usual during these times. Although she never attempted suicide, she would occasionally wish she were dead.

On two separate occasions, Marjorie scared herself. Once, about a year ago, she was picked up by the police at 3:30 A.M. standing on a freeway in her bathrobe and slippers preaching to passing motorists. She was convinced that the world was about to come to an end and she was a special messenger of God who had to warn people of impending doom.

On another occasion, Marjorie had an impulsive urge to take all of her family's money and go to Reno. She felt certain that she could make her family millionaires overnight, but ended up losing $10,000 gambling foolishly.

Marjorie has a bipolar disorder, mixed type.

In order to meet the criteria for a bipolar or manic-depressive disorder, you must consider two basic groups of questions: the major depressive disorder questionnaire, which you have already taken, the manic-disorder questionnaire, which follows.

Manic Disorder Questionnaire

Directions: Answer the following questions as honestly as possible. Do not deny or minimize problems that exist, but do not to exaggerate or answer yes to questions that do not apply to you.

1. Have you ever had times when you felt unusually hyper, restless, excited, or charged up for several days or weeks at a time?
2. Since you were fifteen years old, have you ever been told by other people that you were much too hyper, charged up, talkative, or excited?
3. Have these excitable, hyper, or talkative moods ever stayed with you for at least one week?
4. Have these hyper, restless moods caused you distress or discomfort in your life?
5. Have these elevated moods ever interfered with your education, your occupation, or your work around the home?
6. Have these moods ever caused you problems with your family or caused your family to worry about you?
7. Have these elated moods ever interfered with your friendships, social life, or social activities?
8. Have you ever gotten into trouble with authorities or police due to these moods?
9. Have you ever received treatment or medication for these hyper moods?
10. Were you ever put into a hospital because of behaviors associated with these moods?

When you felt your most excited, restless, hyper, or charged up, did you ever:

11. Feel elated, ecstatic, or high-spirited, as if you were on top of the world?
12. Get easily irritated and fly off the handle at the slightest thing?
13. Feel so full of energy that you did not know what to do with yourself?
14. Work longer hours than you normally do or work much harder than usual?
15. Feel that you were constantly on the go, or try to start many things at once?

16. Feel an inability to sit still?
17. Notice a great deal more interest in sex than usual?
18. Go on spending sprees or make foolish investments?
19. Feel that your ideas raced from one thing to another and that other people had difficulty keeping up with you?
20. Feel that you were a very important, special, or unusual person who could do impossible things, or who had powers that no one else had?
21. Find that you needed much less sleep than usual?
22. Have trouble concentrating?
23. Get involved in so many things at once that you could not finish most of them?
24. When you were at your most excited, did you also have times lasting a week or more in which you felt unusually blue, depressed, or sad?

Scoring: The pattern for meeting the criteria for a manic-depressive or bipolar disorder is as follows: yes to questions 1 or 2 and yes to question 3, yes to any one question 4–9, and yes to any three questions 10–24.

Just like depressive disorders, bipolar disorders may be psychotic or nonpsychotic.

To determine whether the disorder is psychotic, the basic question to ask is whether or not there is

1) gross impairment in reality testing

2) the experience of auditory, visual, or tactile hallucinations (sensations that other people do not share with you)

3) delusions (faulty beliefs that are grossly inconsistent with reality)

Psychotic features typically involve grave impairment in reality testing or the inability to get basic needs met. If you are functioning on the job, able to maintain your household, and taking care of your basic needs, it's quite unlikely that you're suffering from a *psychotic* bipolar disorder.

Many of the brightest and most creative people throughout history are suspected to have suffered from bipolar or manic-depressive disorders. They apparently learned to channel their excessive energy into socially or culturally constructive areas.

FAST FACTS REGARDING DEPRESSIVE AND BIPOLAR DISORDERS

- Research in Europe and the United States indicates that approximately 18–23 percent of women and 8–11 percent of men have experienced a major depressive episode at some time.
- It is estimated that 6 percent of women and 3 percent of men have had a depressive episode severe enough to require hospitalization.
- Only 0.4–1.2 percent of the adult population have had a bipolar or manic-depressive disorder.
- Women are more than twice as likely as men to be depressed.
- Including the United States and Europe, 27 million people this year will suffer from clinical depression.
- Most cases of clinical depression, including the most serious kinds, usually improve significantly with treatment in a matter of weeks.
- Depression is much more than sadness or distress.
- Depressive disorders rarely require extensive inpatient psychiatric hospitalization.
- Over 80 percent of all depressive and bipolar disorders are clearly treatable.
- Less than 33 percent of the people who have a clinically significant depressive disorder will ever seek treatment.
- Some depressive episodes occur suddenly and for no apparent reason.
- Some depressive episodes are triggered by stressful life experiences, such as divorce, separation, loss of job, or loss of a loved one.
- Some people will have one episode of depression in a lifetime; others will have recurrent episodes.
- Some people's depressive symptoms are so severe that they are unable to meet their basic needs.
- Others have ongoing chronic depressive symptoms that do not prevent their functioning in life, but keep them from enjoying it.
- Depression is not due to personal weakness or lack of strength.
- At times depression can be so disabling that people who suffer from it are not able to reach out for help.
- Suicide is a common result of depression.

- Suicide cuts across all age, racial, occupational, religious, and social groups.
- Although suicide rates generally increase with age, current rates for young people age 25–34 rival those in older groups.
- While the overall suicide rate has remained the same, the rate has soared for adolescents and young adults, and surprisingly declined somewhat among the elderly.
- Almost 3,500 white U.S. men over the age 65 killed themselves in 1982.
- Suicide is the second most common cause of death for college students.
- Reports of suicide among very young children are rare, but suicidal behavior is not. As many as 12,000 children between the ages of 5 and 14 may be hospitalized in this country for such deliberate self-destructive acts as stabbing or cutting themselves, or deliberately overdosing on drugs.
- The overwhelming majority of successful suicides are men. They comprise approximately 75 percent of the total number.
- Men tend to use the deadliest weapons in suicide attempts; well over half shoot themselves.
- Four times more women than men attempt suicide, usually using such potentially less lethal means as drugs or wrist slashing.
- Those at the greatest risk for suicide are the widowed, separated, divorced, and those who live alone.
- Sharp increases in suicides among young black men have in some urban areas outdistanced rates for white men in the same age group.
- Overall, the suicide rates for blacks is about half that for whites.

HOPE FOR THE FUTURE

When diagnosed early in the course of the illness, depression can usually be treated on an outpatient basis and be improved quite rapidly. Improvement usually occurs within a matter of a few weeks and greatly reduces the cost of lost productivity, work time, and the often-unnecessary costs for prolonged treatment or hospitalization for other illnesses which are confused with depression.

The very nature of depression can interfere with your ability to want to receive help. Because depression saps your energy and lowers your self-esteem, it makes you feel exhausted, worthless, helpless, and hopeless. You feel so run down that you give up hope and don't want help, even when it's available.

Therefore, seriously depressed people need strong encouragement from family and friends to seek treatment to ease their problem.

Often, people may be so depressed that they must actually be coerced or taken in for treatment by friends or family members.

A variety of mental-health specialists can treat depression.

Clinical psychologists are mental-health professionals who have received their doctorate of philosophy degree in the study of human behavior and experience. They are qualified to diagnose and treat depressive disorders.

Psychiatrists are physicians who specialize in the treatment of mental illness. They diagnose and treat depressive disorders and can prescribe medication for the treatment of depression.

Marriage, family, and child counselors (MFCCs) are mental-health professionals with a master's degree who have done internship training. They focus on the family and interpersonal relationships as a source of the depressive disorder. They develop strategies to treat not only the individual but also the whole family.

TREATMENT APPROACHES

One of the most effective ways to treat depression is called cognitive behavioral therapy. Cognitive refers to what we think. Behavioral refers to what we do.

Cognitive behavioral therapy is based on a model called social learning theory, which holds that most of our depressive behavior is learned and therefore can can be unlearned. Some of the typical ways we learn behavior include being rewarded when certain behaviors occur, being punished or ignored when other behaviors occur, or learning behavior through imitating others.

An example of how depressive behavior could be learned through reinforcement is illustrated by Lew, a 52-year-old contractor.

While at work one day, Lew twisted his back. He was told by his doctor to take some muscle relaxants and to rest for a week.

During this time, Lew was relieved of all of his job pressures. He received a disability payment and was catered to by his wife. All of the work Lew had to do around his house was taken up by his wife and children, and all that was left for Lew to do was sit back and relax.

Whenever Lew complained of distress, pain, or depression, his wife was immediately at his side asking him if she could do anything to help.

Over the course of the week, at an unconscious level, Lew learned that being distressed and depressed had many positive benefits to it: he didn't have to go to his difficult job, he didn't have to do the hard work around the house and the yard, and he had complete relief from responsibilities.

Long after Lew's back had healed, he continued to exhibit depressive symptoms because they had been rewarded or reinforced.

Reinforced depressive behavior is important in understanding the treatment of depression.

Punishment—or negative consequences of behavior—is also another way in which depression can be learned.

Dale, a 32-year-old junior executive for a medical corporation continues to be admonished, castigated, and ignored by his overly punitive supervisor. It seems as if no matter what he does, he cannot win his boss's approval. Instead of focusing on Dale's contributions, his boss will look for reasons to find a flaw in Dale's job performance. If Dale is 99.9 percent accurate on the job, his boss will find the 0.1 percent flaw in it.

Dale became depressed. He learned that no matter what he did, the result was going to be negative. Dale had learned to be depressed through punishment and unfair treatment.

Extinction—or ignoring behavior—is another way in which depression can be learned. Think for a moment what it would be like if you received no recognition whatsoever. Whenever you said good morning to people, they simply pretended you were not there. Whenever you offered a handshake, people acted as if you didn't exist. Whenever you called friends to talk, they hung up. These are extreme examples of extinction, but they can occur on a much more subtle and pervasive level as well.

One of the most dramatic examples of learned depression through extinction or ignoring of behaviors is the example of Jill, a neglected child. Jill's depression became apparent at the age of 16, yet the roots of her depressive disorder were there since childhood.

Jill's father was a workaholic who had no time for his wife or daughter. Jill's mother, receiving little attention or affection from her husband, turned to her friends and to recreation to meet her basic needs. Consequently, she spent a great deal of time out of the house.

Jill was dumped off at day-care centers and baby-sitters, none of whom really cared much for her. No matter what Jill did, she felt ignored and neglected.

By the time Jill was 16, she had a clear understanding that she did not count to her parents and felt that she really never would matter to anybody.

As a result of never receiving healthy support from others, Jill had just about lost hope. She felt that no matter what she did or didn't do, she would never be noticed by other people. Jill suffers from another form of depression.

In contrast to ways in which depression can be learned, there are ways in which depression can be *unlearned* or *changed*.

One way in which *nondepressive* behavior can be learned is by arranging behaviors which have very pleasurable consequences.

Peter Lewinsohn and his colleagues at the University of Oregon have depressed patients engage in pleasant-events scheduling of naturally enjoyable activities which depressed people no longer do on their own.

Social-learning theory suggests that lack of enjoyable activities greatly contributes to continuing depression. The more depressed people feel, the less likely they are to do anything that makes them feel good. Dr. Lewinsohn and his colleagues, and other social-learning theorists, believe that people can affect depression at a behavioral level: by forcing themselves to do previously enjoyable activities, they can alter the way they feel. Typical examples of pleasant events are jogging, swimming, going to movies, reading entertaining books, being at social gatherings with others, and doing any activities which gave them a great deal of pleasure in the past. I know it sounds easy, but it's true.

It is important to do previously enjoyable activities whether you feel like them or not. Once you start engaging in these activities, enjoyable consequences are likely to modify the way you feel.

To overcome the effects of depression due to punishment or neglect, find situations in which your behavior is likely to be rewarded. If you find that you are continually doing everything you can to impress your spouse or your boss and never receiving any positive strokes, it's time to look to other sources for favorable feedback.

Cognitive therapy is another major tool in the treatment of depression. This concept assumes that you will tend to meet the expectations and prophecies that you have for yourself. Chief among these techniques is self-talk. Most depressed patients find themselves beset with damaging self-talk sentences, such as: "I am worthless and always will be," "I am no good," "Things will never get better," and "Life is not worth it."

Cognitive therapists teach depressed patients to substitute positive self-talk for the negative. They are encouraged to develop such philosophies as: "My mind is perfectly calm, crystal clear, and totally aware," "My life is full of things that keep me interested and enthused," "I am capable of overcoming any adversity," and "Things are definitely going to get better."

Recent evidence from behavior therapists indicates that simply engaging in large-muscle aerobic activity is highly effective in treating almost all forms of depressive disorders. Research in many laboratories throughout the world is showing that when you keep your heart rate between 60 and 80 percent of its maximum level for a period of 30 to 90 minutes, the effects of depression are greatly reduced or eliminated. This may be due to the release of enkephalons, natural opiatelike substances in your brain, which dramatically alter your mood and behavior.

There have been some major improvements in the treatment of depression with drugs. Psychiatrists and physicians have known for years that the drug lithium carbonate is often effective in controlling and managing manic-depressive disorders.

Recently, such tricyclic antidepressant medications as Elavil and Desyvel have shown a great deal of promise in altering the neurochemical pathways associated with depression.

One of the most recent wonder drugs is Prozac. Despite some bad press, Prozac has shown a great deal of promise in treating many forms of depression. These pharmacological treatments are often even more effective when combined with cognitive behavioral treatment strategies.

The family-systems approach to treating depression focuses on going back into the patient's early life and discovering the roots of feelings of worthlessness and depression. Patients are taught that the lessons they learned as a child are not necessarily valid, and that they *are* worthwhile as human beings. Such therapists as John Bradshaw have patients working in groups return to their childhood for "reparenting," in which their groups give them the support and strokes they never got as children. In workshops, Bradshaw and others have patients reexperience and relive their childhood hurts and traumas. Once such feelings are expressed and understood, people can learn new, more adaptive beliefs about themselves. In a supportive group context, patients are then reassured with self-esteem-building comments from other group members.

Finally, electroconvulsive therapy (ECT) is a last resort. Although considered barbaric by many psychologists and therapists, electroconvulsive (shock) therapy is often effective in the treatment of extremely severe depression. Recent developments in electroconvulsive therapy involve unilateral placement of electrodes and the use of medication to minimize damaging side effects.

Yes, depression is a very treatable disorder. With the recent progress in psychological, psychiatric, and family-systems therapies, many professionals believe that depression may be completely and totally eliminated by the early twenty-first century.

CHAPTER **7**

DO I HAVE AN EATING DISORDER?

SINCE THE MID–1970S MANY PEOPLE—PARTICULARLY WOMEN—HAVE BECOME VIRTU-ally addicted to self-criticism about their physical appearance. Some women have come to believe that what they see is all they really are. The mirror is the modern woman's most powerful adversary.

But why do weight and appearance matter so much? Intrinsic to human nature is the desire to judge, evaluate, and compare ourselves to others. Appearance—particularly body weight—has started to re-place self-worth as a measure of people's social values.

The ideal model for today's women is slim but physically fit. Women believe that the extent to which they can match their physi-cal ideal for beauty—especially weight—will gauge how successful they will be in life.

Women are barraged with commercials, magazine ads, movies, and television shows in which successful, happy, loved, self-assured women match an ideal of physical beauty based on a slender body. Although overweight TV characters and entertainers are often adored, the adulation seems to come from the person's ability to make fun of herself, particularly her weight.

But there is another compelling reason why some women often seem obsessed by achieving an "ideal weight and shape."

We live in a world of rapidly changing values and customs. What was normal and acceptable twenty years ago is now out of vogue. With the advent of the "self" psychologies of the 1970s, altruistic values began to be replaced by the idealization of the self. Paramount in this self-adulation is the concept of perfect body measurements. So, while values and beliefs continue to shift, many women like to hold on to one thing they feel they have some control over: their weight. In short, controlling their weight provides a convenient escape from the things over which women feel powerless.

Dr. Judith Rodin surveyed *Ladies Home Journal* issues from the 1960s and found an average of only one diet article every six months. But by the 1970s, it seemed that almost every woman in America was trying some kind of diet. Losing weight had become a national obsession. In 1987 a *Psychology Today* survey found that 55 percent of all of the women and 48 percent of the men polled were dissatisfied with their body weight.

People in general—and women in particular—learn early in life that there is something shameful and disgusting about being obese. In a culture where the slim ideal is strictly defined, deviations are obvious, and the obese are usually ridiculed or stigmatized.

However, obesity may not be as controllable as we once thought. Genes play a major role in setting our body metabolism as well as our shape and size. Our genetic structure influences how much fat we burn, where it is distributed in our bodies, and how easily we can store it.

Frame size is also important in determining our weight. Some people have large bone structures, while others have small ones.

People are usually not ridiculed because of their height. That, it is believed, is something over which they have no control. Weight, on the other hand, is something we have been led to believe is *completely* within our sphere of influence.

One final point to consider is the fact that, despite the advances made by the women's liberation movement, women are still often equated with how they look, while men are evaluated in terms of what they have accomplished.

With these considerations in mind, let's look at what happened to Jeannie, a typical teen-ager.

ANOREXIA

Jeannie was a rather shy, studious 16-year-old who tried hard to please everyone. Nevertheless, she was not popular with boys. One day her father jokingly remarked, "You'll never get a date if you don't lose ten pounds."

Jeannie began to diet relentlessly, never stopping or believing she was thin enough although she eventually looked like a famine victim.

Jeannie's menstrual periods stopped. As anorexia began to take hold, she became obsessed with food and developed strange eating rituals. Each day she would weigh all the food she would eat on a kitchen scale, cut the solids into tiny pieces, and measure liquids precisely in ounces. She would then put her daily ration in small containers, lining them up in neat little rows.

Jeannie began to exercise compulsively, doing 1–½ to 2 hours of aerobics daily, as well as swimming and jogging. Eventually, Jeannie weakened and began fainting. Despite the fact that Jeannie was now 20 pounds underweight, she continued her obsessive-compulsive rituals. Jeannie's mom, dad, teachers, and friends all tried to convince her that she was in danger, but to no avail.

Finally, Jeannie's doctor insisted that she be hospitalized for treatment. While in the hospital, although watched carefully, she continued her obsessive rituals, doing sit-ups in the bathroom, numerous knee-bends in the closet, and stashing her food in her cheeks and not swallowing it.

It took several hospitalizations and many hours of intense individual and family outpatient psychotherapy for Jeannie to realize the seriousness of her problem and to begin solving it.

But all anorexic outcomes are not as successful as Jeannie's. Singer-songwriter Karen Carpenter spiraled downward in the grips of anorexia until she died in 1983. In fact, different studies show that 6 to 18 percent of all women with anorexia will die.

Anorexia nervosa involves a severe weight loss—at least 15 percent below normal body weight. Anorexics literally starve themselves, even though they suffer terribly from hunger pains. For reasons not yet understood, they become terrified of the idea of gaining too much weight. When an anorexic looks in the mirror, her perception of herself is far different from what other people see. Although being emaciated, she is likely to actually perceive herself as hideously obese.

Food and weight become obsessions to her. She may collect recipes and prepare gourmet foods for others, yet impose odd eating rituals on herself. The anorexic may refuse to eat with other people and indulge in strenuous, obsessive exercise programs to keep off the offending weight.

One of the more frightening aspects of this disorder is that the anorexic continues to think she is overweight even when she is emaciated. A severely distorted self-perception leads the anorexic down the path of starvation and, in some cases, to death.

BULIMIA

Debra became bulimic at the age of 18. Her unhealthy eating behavior began when she started to diet. She dieted and exercised to lose weight; but, unlike Jeannie, she regularly ate huge amounts of food in one or two sittings and maintained her normal body weight by forcing herself to vomit.

In counseling, Debra said she often felt like an emotional powder keg. She was alternately angry, frightened, and depressed—all within minutes. She stole things on impulse. Sometimes she drank too much. She experimented with drugs, and often she could not stop eating for hours.

Unable to comprehend her own behavior, Debra thought no one else would understand either. She began to feel isolated and lonely. When things were not going well, Debra would be overcome with an uncontrollable desire for sweets. She once ate four 8-ounce boxes of candy and two chocolate cakes at one sitting, and often would not stop eating until her stomach was badly distended and she was in pain. Then, overwhelmed with shame, guilt, and disgust with herself, Debra would force herself to vomit.

Debra knew something was wrong. Her eating habits so embarrassed her that she kept them secret. Finally, depressed by her mounting problems and disgusted with herself, she attempted suicide. Fortunately, she did not succeed. While recuperating in the hospital, she was referred to an eating-disorders clinic where she became involved in group therapy. In the first session, Debra showed others the scars on the back of her hand that she got by forcing her fingers so far down her throat to make herself vomit that her teeth cut her hand.

In group therapy, Debra received the understanding and support she so desperately needed from others who shared her problem. Debra was no longer isolated, but on the way to recovery.

While Debra used forced vomiting to purge herself of excessive food, other bulimics resort to laxatives and diuretics. Some use a combination of all forms of purging. Eventually, half of those who are anorexic will also become bulimic.

Anorexics who go on eating binges are called "bulimic anorexics," in contrast to "restricting anorexics," who control weight solely by restricting food intake.

Many bulimics remain at a normal body weight. Their binges can range from once or twice a week to several times a day. Using this method of bingeing and purging, normal-weight bulimics are able to keep their eating disorders a secret for years. As with anorexia, bulimia usually begins during adolescence, but many bulimics, ashamed of their eating habits, do not seek help until they are in their thirties or forties.

Fortunately, because of increased public awareness regarding bulimia, many bulimics are now seeking help sooner. Just as with anorexia, the sooner treatment is begun for bulimia, the better the chance for recovery.

MEDICAL COMPLICATIONS

Eating disorders will kill up to 10 percent of those affected. Common causes of death include starvation, cardiac arrest, and suicide.

The medical complications of anorexia involve the symptoms of starvation. As the body tries to protect its vital organs—the heart and the brain—it goes into slower gear. Metabolism is greatly reduced.

Menstrual periods stop, breath rate decreases, pulse and blood pressure drop, and thyroid function slows. The nails and hair become brittle. The skin dries, yellows, and becomes covered with a soft hair called "lanugo." Water imbalance contributes to constipation, and reduced body fat leads to lowered body temperature and the inability to withstand cold.

Other symptoms of anorexia include mild anemia, swollen joints, reduced muscle mass, and light-headedness. If anorexia becomes severe, osteoporosis (thinning of bones), irregular heart rhythm, and heart failure can occur. The anorexic who turns to purging or bulimic episodes is in particular danger. The abuse of drugs to stimulate vomiting, bowel movements, and urination will increase the risk of heart failure.

Depression, weakness, and obsession with food may also accompany starvation. Personality changes can occur. Outbursts of hostility and anger or social withdrawal may surprise those who have become used to the typical compliancy of the anorexic.

The bulimic is also in danger from binge eating and purging. In rare instances, binge eating causes the stomach to rupture. Purging may result in heart failure due to the body's loss of such vital minerals as potassium. The acid in the bulimic's vomit wears down the teeth, and forcing the fingers down the back of the throats often leads to permanent scars on the backs of the hands. Furthermore, the bulimic's esophagus may become inflamed, and the glands near the cheek become swollen. The bulimic's menstrual cycles may become irregular, and interest in sex may decrease.

Classic bulimics often speak of being hooked on certain foods, usually carbohydrates. They describe needing to feed their habit, as drug addicts need to feed their addiction. This addictive tendency seems to carry over into other areas, including the abuse of drugs and alcohol. Bulimics may also engage in kleptomania (compulsive stealing). Many bulimic people suffer from serious depression which, combined with their impulsive tendencies, places them at increased risk for suicide.

CAUSES OF EATING DISORDERS

Psychologists and psychiatrists have spent years trying to understand the causes of eating disorders. Researchers have studied the personalities, family backgrounds, environments, and biochemistry of people who have become anorexic or bulimic. As more and more research is done, scientists are recognizing that eating disorders are an extremely complex set of diseases.

Biochemical abnormalities found in people with eating disorders may be a result of their eating behaviors, or an inherited vulnerability that places them at risk. At this point, most scientists agree that it's usually a combination of genetics, biochemistry, and environment which leads to eating disorders.

THE EATING-DISORDERED PERSONALITY

Anorexics and bulimics seem fundamentally different in personality. Bulimics are usually described by others as impulsive, and are more apt to abuse drugs or alcohol than are anorexics.

Anorexics are usually described by family and friends as having been "ideal people" or "too good to be true." As children, anorexics' parents indicate that they rarely disobeyed, kept their feelings to themselves, tended to be perfectionists, were good students, and excelled as athletes.

Bulimics and anorexics, however, share a lack of self-esteem. They both develop an obsessive fear of fat. In both these disorders, eating behavior serves the function of helping the person handle stress and anxiety. The bulimic consumes huge amounts of food—often empty-calorie or junk food—in search of comfort to ease the demands of living. Unfortunately, after the binge, the bulimic suffers severe guilt and depression. The relief of these feelings comes only with purging.

The anorexic tends to restrict food—particularly carbohydrates—to gain a sense of self-control in some area of her life. Having followed the wishes of others for most of her life compulsively, she has not learned how to cope with the typical problems of adolescence or young adulthood. Controlling her weight appears to offer two advantages: she can take control of her body and gain approval from others, and eventually other people will realize that she is out of control and will pay attention to her. She is crying out for help.

FAMILY BACKGROUNDS

Anorexia and bulimia tend to run in families. Female relatives are particularly vulnerable to these eating disorders. There is probably a strong genetic factor which may predispose some people to eating disorders. However, complicating the case for genetics is the possibility that the anorexic may be imitating the disturbed eating behavior of her mother or female relatives.

Social scientists have compared families of anorexic and bulimics to families of people who do not suffer from eating disorders and have found some interesting differences. Families of bulimics tend to be hostile or contentious, compared with those with no eating disorder. Families of anorexics, on the other hand, are often described as providing a warmer and more supportive environment for their children than families whose young women do not develop eating disorders.

Studies of the parents of anorexics suggest that there may be a high incidence of marital problems, and some mental-health specialists have theorized that the anorexic child serves as a kind of psychological lightning rod for adults who cannot face or resolve their marital problems.

Statistically, people with eating disorders almost always come from white middle- or upper-class families. Apparently, higher socioeconomic status is an important risk factor here. International studies offer further evidence to support these findings. During the past twenty years, eating disorders have increased dramatically in industrialized nations, while remaining virtually unheard-of in Third World countries. These facts raise clear questions about the cultural influences that place people at risk. In Third World countries, starvation is a clear threat to survival. Thinness is not admired among the poor, whose hunger is not a matter of choice.

The "thinning" of the ideal woman in industrialized countries, as represented in Western art, has been a gradual process over the past several hundred years. By today's standards, women in paintings portrayed as beautiful hundreds of years ago, would be considered morbidly obese. The artists depicting these women probably were following the cultural standards of their time regarding female beauty.

THE BIOCHEMISTRY OF EATING DISORDERS

One of the first signs of anorexia in women is loss of menstrual periods. This is a clear indication that a hormone imbalance is involved in the disorder. However, since loss of periods often occurs before apparent weight loss, it is not clear which comes first: the hormone imbalance or the eating disorder. Anorexic males also suffer an imbalance in male hormones, which may lead to impotence. The relationship between weight, eating habits, and hormone production is a complex one which is not understood fully.

Recently, behavioral scientists have began to focus on the neuroendocrine system, which consists of the central nervous system and hormonal systems interacting with one another. Feedback mechanisms of the neuroendocrine system regulate sexual function, physical growth and development, appetite and digestion, sleep, heart and kidney function, emotions, thinking, and memory. The neuroendocrine system is crucially involved in the regulation of the mind and body. Many of these mechanisms are seriously disrupted in people who have eating disorders.

At a different level, scientists have studied neurotransmitters, the chemical messengers that play a major role in regulating hormone production. Researchers have found that anorexics and bulimics tend to have abnormal levels of certain neurotransmitters. Low levels of the neurotransmitter serotonin are linked to bulimia, mood disorders, and impulsive behavior. Low serotonin levels could also contribute to the impulsiveness and depressive symptoms associated with bulimia, as well as the bulimic's binge eating of food high in carbohydrates.

Even though serotonin is strongly implicated in bulimia, the crucial question remains: Is the low serotonin a result of disturbed eating, or the cause of it?

Anorexics typically suffer lower levels of beta-endorphins, a natural brain opiate, and the neurotransmitter norepinephrine, a natural stimulant.

Some fascinating research on norepinephrine levels has found that they are low in anorexic patients who have gained weight, implying the possibility that the abnormally low levels of this neurotransmitter precedes weight loss and may, in fact, indicate an inherited predisposition to anorexia. On the other hand, the same low norepinephrine level could be caused by starvation, the low-carbohydrate/high-protein diet typical of anorexics, or be due to a coexisting depressive disorder.

The relationship between depression and eating disorders has been studied for many years. People with eating disorders also suffer from depression, and scientists have wondered whether depression triggers the eating disorder, or vice versa. Certainly there are similarities in neurochemical abnormalities in both these disorders. Low levels of serotonin and norepinephrine are also associated with depressive disorders, and antidepressant medication may help some people, especially bulimics.

Both anorexics and depressed people tend to have higher-than-normal levels of the hormone cortisol, which is released in response to stress. Scientists have traced cortisol levels and found that there is an excess of cortisol in both depressed and anorexic people in an area of the brain called the hypothalamus. The hypothalamus is involved in the neuroendocrine system and regulates such bodily functions as hormonal secretion, temperature, water balance, and sugar and fat metabolism.

Other scientists have noticed elevated hormone levels in people who are experiencing very stressful times in their lives.

Thus, genetic, environmental, hormonal, neurochemical, and anatomical factors have all been implicated in the development of eating disorders.

DANGER SIGNALS FOR EATING DISORDERS

Eating disorders may be prevented or treated easily if they are detected early. A person who has several of the following signs may be developing or already have an eating disorder:

Anorexia

The person—usually a woman—has:

- lost a great deal of weight in a relatively short period of time
- continued to diet although bone thin
- reached a diet goal and immediately set another goal for further weight loss
- remained dissatisfied with her appearance, claiming to feel fat, even after reaching her weight-loss goal
- preferred dieting in isolation to joining a diet group
- stopped menstruating
- developed an unusual interest in food, to the point of fixation
- developed strange eating rituals, like eating small units of food; cutting food into tiny pieces or measuring everything before eating extremely small quantities
- become a secret eater
- become obsessive about exercising
- appeared depressed much of the time
- begun to binge and purge

Bulimia

The person has:

- binged regularly (eaten large amounts of food over a short period of time)

- purged regularly (forced vomiting and/or used drugs to stimulate vomiting, bowel movements, and urination)
- dieted and exercised often, but maintained or regained weight
- become an secret eater
- eaten enormous amounts of food at one sitting, but does not gain weight
- disappeared into the bathroom for a long period of time (to induce vomiting)
- abused drugs or alcohol, or stolen regularly
- appeared depressed much of the time
- had swollen neck glands
- had scars on the back of their hands from forced vomiting

THE OTHER SIDE OF THE COIN

But there is another side to the eating-disorder coin. Anyone who is severely underweight or overweight is suffering from a kind of illness. By definition, an obese person weighs 30 percent or more over what he or she should. Obese individuals may suffer from one or more of the following:

- an overworked heart and poor circulation
- shortness of breath
- a tendency to high blood pressure
- a tendency to diabetes
- poor adjustment to hot weather and changes of temperature
- increased strain on joints and ligaments, often leading to chronic back and joint pain
- reduced capacity for physical exercise and sometimes reduced mental clarity
- increased susceptibility to infectious disease
- personality problems due to poor appearance

Being overweight actually shortens your life span. Actuarial statistics indicate that "the larger the waistline, the shorter the lifeline."

The mortality from circulatory disease is 44 percent higher in men who are 5 to 15 percent overweight than it is for men whose weight is within normal limits.

WHAT IS NORMAL WEIGHT?

Since one of the essential criteria for diagnosing anorexia is determining whether you weigh 85 percent or less of what you should, it is necessary to look at some statistics regarding what is normal for your height and body frame.

The following may be considered a general guide to determining your approximate normal weight.

Normal Weights for Men and Women*

Women

Height (with shoes on)		Small Frame	Medium Frame	Large Frame
Ft.	In.			
4	11	104–111	110–118	117–127
5	0	105–113	112–120	119–129
5	1	107–115	114–122	121–131
5	2	110–118	117–125	124–135
5	3	113–121	120–128	127–138
5	4	116–125	124–132	131–142
5	5	119–128	127–135	133–145
5	6	123–132	130–140	138–150
5	7	126–136	134–144	142–154
5	8	129–139	137–147	145–158
5	9	133–143	141–151	149–162

| 5 | 10 | 136–147 | 145–155 | 152–166 |
| 5 | 11 | 139–150 | 148–158 | 155–169 |

Men

Height (with shoes on)		Small Frame	Medium Frame	Large Frame
Ft.	In.			
5	2	116–125	124–133	131–142
5	3	119–128	127–136	133–144
5	4	122–132	130–140	137–149
5	5	126–136	134–144	141–153
5	6	129–139	137–147	145–157
5	7	133–143	141–151	149–162
5	8	136–147	145–160	153–166
5	9	140–151	149–160	157–170
5	10	144–155	153–164	161–175
5	11	148–164	157–168	165–180
6	0	152–164	161–173	169–185
6	1	157–169	166–178	174–190
6	2	163–175	171–184	179–196
6	3	168–180	176–189	184–202

*Adapted from "Overweight and Underweight," Metropolitan Life Insurance Company, 1978.

By looking at the table, you can get a quick and clear idea of the normal weight range for your height and body frame. Remember: your body frame is extremely important in determining your desirable weight. For example, a woman who is 5'5" with a petite frame would be squarely within normal limits at 123 pounds, while a woman the same height with a large frame would look good at 140 pounds.

A WORD ON OBESITY

The *DSM III-R* does not consider obesity as an eating disorder. Obesity can, however, be thought of as a psychological disorder affecting physical condition. Not to include morbid obesity as an eating disorder seems negligent. Isn't the 600-pound women who is so obese that she cannot get out of a chair at as high a risk of mortality as the emaciated anorexic who is being sustained on IV fluids?

Keep one important point in mind. In spite of all the statistics and research involving neurochemistry, genes, stress, environment, family background, and personality structure, the one most powerful principle that determines your body weight is this:

> Your weight is a result of the amount and kind of food you eat and the amount of energy you expend through your basal metabolic rate and physical activity level.

So find your target weight zone and stay in that zone by dieting and exercising.

ANOREXIA NERVOSA

The anorexic usually comes for professional help when her weight has dropped to 85 percent or less of her normal body weight. Use the above table to help you determine 85 percent of your normal body weight.

Perhaps the greatest problem with anorexia is that people with this disorder tend to deny or minimize the severity of their illness until they are in a desperate situation. Anorexia may also delay the psychosexual development of adolescents and have a strong diminishing effect on the sexual interest of adults. Since anorexia is a compulsive behavior, other compulsive behaviors, such as hand washing, may be present with this disorder.

FAST FACTS REGARDING ANOREXIA

- Anorexia usually begins in early to late adolescence, although some patients have developed this disorder in their early thirties.
- Anorexia is predominantly a woman's disease; 95 percent of all anorexics are female.
- The *DSM III-R* cites studies from different populations indicating that in Western cultures as many as 1 out of every 100 young women between the ages of 12 and 18 have anorexia.
- Most anorexic disorders consist of a single episode, with return to normal weight. However, in some women, anorexia may be chronic.
- In severe cases of anorexia, hospitalization is required to prevent death by starvation.
- Mortality rates indicate that between 5 and 18 percent of all people with anorexia will die.
- Anorexia is more common among sisters and the daughters of anorexics than in the general population.
- About 33 percent of the people who develop anorexia are mildly overweight before the onset of the disease.
- Many people who develop anorexia are described as having been perfectionistic, or model children.

Anorexia Questionnaire

Directions: Answer the following questions as honestly as possible. Do not deny or minimize your responses, but do not answer questions that do not apply to you.

Note: Remember that anorexia is a disease characterized by denial, so check your responses with the observations of people you love and trust.

1. Have you consistently maintained a body weight 15 percent below that which is expected for your height and body frame? (Use table to determine normal weight).
2. Even though your weight is within normal limits, or you are underweight, do you have an intense fear of gaining weight or becoming fat?
3. When you look in the mirror, do you perceive your body as fat or overweight, even though other people tell you that you are thin?
4. Has your obsession with becoming thin or losing weight had any life-damaging consequences, such as problems with your family, friends, job, or your physical health?
5. For women: have you missed at least three consecutive menstrual periods?

Scoring: If you answered yes to question 1 and yes to at least one other question, you are likely to have anorexia nervosa.

BULIMIA

Bulimia involves recurrent episodes of eating large amounts of food in a very short period of time, feeling a lack of control over your binge-eating behavior during these episodes, self-induced vomiting, use of laxatives or diuretics, overly harsh dieting or fasting, vigorous exercise in order to prevent weight gain, and a persistent concern with body shape and weight.

In order to be diagnosed as bulimic in the strict clinical sense, you must have had a minimum of at least two eating binges a week for at least three months.

But what exactly is an eating binge? During an eating binge, the food consumed often has high a caloric content, a sweet taste, and a texture that enables you to eat it rapidly. The binger usually eats food as secretly as possible. The food is typically gobbled down rapidly, with little chewing. Once an eating binge has begun, additional food may be sought to continue the binge.

A binge is usually stopped only by severe abdominal discomfort, sleep, interruption by others, or induced vomiting. Vomiting serves the twofold purpose of relieving abdominal discomfort and expiating the guilt and shame over the amount of food consumed.

The range of emotions during an eating binge range from euphoria during the actual eating, to shame, guilt, self-anger, and depression immediately after.

Unlike the anorexic, most bulimics' weight is within normal range, and some may even be slightly underweight.

FAST FACTS REGARDING BULIMIA

- Like anorexia, bulimia typically develops in adolescence or early adult life.
- Unlike many single-episode anorexics, bulimia is usually chronic and intermittent over a period of many years.
- Parents of bulimics are often obese.
- Although seldom incapacitating, bulimia may result in electrolyte imbalance, dehydration, cardiac irregularities and, occasionally, sudden death.
- Rare complications may include esophageal tears and gastric ruptures.
- A study cited by *DSM III-R* found that 4.5 percent of college freshwomen females and 0.4 percent of college freshmen had a history of bulimia.
- There is some evidence that obesity in adolescents predisposes people to bulimia in adulthood.

Bulimia Questionnaire

Directions: Answer the following questions as honestly as possible. Do not deny or minimize your responses, but do not answer yes to questions that do not apply to you.

1. Have you had recurrent episodes of rapidly eating large amounts of food in a relatively short period of time?
2. Do you feel a lack of control over your eating behavior during these eating binges?
3. After these eating binges, do you regularly engage in self-induced vomiting, use of laxatives, use of diuretics, strict dieting or fasting, or vigorous exercise in order to prevent weight gain?
4. Have you had an average of at least two eating binges a week for at least three months?
5. Do you have a persistent overconcern with your body shape and weight?
6. Have your eating binges led to life-damaging consequences, such as disturbance of family relations, social relations, occupation, or physical health?

Scoring: If you answered yes to questions 1 and 4, and yes to any one of the remaining four questions, you are likely to have bulimia.

TREATMENT APPROACHES

If you suspect that you have anorexia, first get a thorough physical examination to rule out any other illness that might cause your low weight. Weight loss is common for many physical diseases. If anorexia is diagnosed, get immediate treatment. Beginning and maintaining treatment is crucial for the treatment of anorexia.

While bulimics are more likely to seek help than anorexics, many have a low tolerance for frustration and are very impulsive. Bulimics are likely to leave treatment if their symptoms are not relieved immediately.

The longer that eating disorders persist, the more difficult it is to treat them. If treatment is not sought during their early phases, long-term care or hospitalization may be required. Hospitalization is usually required due to such medical complications as serious metabolic disturbance, severe depression or risk of suicide, or serious gastrointestinal problems.

Due to the complex nature of eating disorders, a multifaceted team approach usually works best. An ideal treatment team would include an internist, nutritionist, individual or group psychologist or psychiatrist, family counselor, and psychopharmacologist (a doctor specializing in psychoactive medication).

The internist would treat the medical complications, the nutritionist advise on diet and eating regimens, and the individual and family therapists focus on personality, emotional, and family issues which may contribute to the eating disturbance.

Anorexics at low weight—or even after their weight gain—require 30 to 50 percent more calories to maintain their proper weight than do bulimic patients. This is an important finding because consuming extra calories is exactly what the anorexic is most afraid of.

On the other hand, some normal-weight bulimics maintain a stable weight on just 75 percent of the calories needed by normal individuals of similar weight and age.

Group therapy has been extremely useful for anorexic and bulimic individuals; they are usually greatly relieved to find that they are not alone in their difficulty. Participation in a group allows them a chance to give and receive help from others who share their problems.

The role of the family therapist cannot be overemphasized. Family therapists not only deal with the family problems associated with the eating disorder, but may also provide crucial information and directions to family members in order to observe and even at times confront the eating-disordered patient's self-destructive behavior.

Psychologists specializing in cognitive and behavioral therapy use a mixture of reinforcing appropriate eating behaviors and modeling desired eating behaviors for the anorexic or bulimic. These psychologists focus on helping the patient change distorted and rigid thinking patterns associated with their eating disorder.

At a pharmacological level, some medications have proven ex-

tremely effective in cases where depressive symptoms are not prominent. Medications with promise for treating bulimia include
desipramine, imipramine, and phenelzine. Amitriptyline and the anti-
histamine cyproheptadine have shown some promise in treating certain anorexic patients.

Friends, teachers, relatives, and doctors may all play an important
role in helping the person with an eating disorder start and stay with
needed treatment.

Often it is not enough just to get the anorexic or bulimic into
treatment. Usually, many family members and friends will need to
give ongoing encouragement, caring, support, and will need to be
persistent to convince the eating-disordered person that it's time to
get help.

ADDITIONAL INFORMATION

For additional information on eating disorders check your local hospital or university medical center for an eating disorders clinic, or
contact any of the following:

> National Institute of Mental Health
> Eating Disorders Program
> Building 10, Rm 3S–231
> Bethesda, MD 20892
> (301) 496–1891
>
> National Association of Anorexia Nervosa and Associated
> Disorders
> P.O. Box 7
> Highland Park, IL 60035
> (312) 831–3438

American Anorexia/Bulimia Association, Inc.
133 Cedar Lane
Teaneck, NJ 07666
(201) 836–1800

Center for the Study of Anorexia and Bulimia
1 West 91st Street
New York, NY 10024
(212) 595–3449

National Anorexic Aids Society, Inc.
P.O. Box 29461
Columbus, OH 43229
(614) 436–1112

Overeaters Anonymous World Service Office
P.O. Box 92870
Los Angeles, CA 90009
(Ask for local chapter. Groups available for bulimics.)
(213) 657–6252

CHAPTER 8

DO I HAVE A SEXUAL DISORDER?

WHAT IS SEXUALLY NORMAL?

On Sunday, February 16, 1992, a Milwaukee jury found Jeffrey Dahmer guilty of one of the most gruesome, sexually motivated, mass-murder cases in American history.

Dahmer would typically pick up young men for sex, drug them, strangle them and, in some cases, drill a hole through their skulls in the bizarre hope of creating zombies who would serve as his sexual slaves. He admitted to boiling the skulls of his victims, eating body parts, and having sex with corpses.

Yet the Milwaukee jury found Dahmer not to be insane. To be insane, according to Wisconsin law, he must have had a mental disease that kept him from knowing right from wrong, or made him unable to stop himself from continuing to commit the crimes.

Although some would argue that Jeffrey Dahmer is obviously crazy, "insane" is a legal term used to determine responsibility for actions. Certainly, everyone agrees that Jeffrey Dahmer represents an extreme example of what is sexually abnormal. Specifically, his behavior was consistent with that of individuals suffering from sexual sadism and necrophilia (obtaining sexual gratification from having intercourse with corpses).

At the other end of the spectrum is Bob, a 34-year-old account executive who has noticed in the past couple of years that his sex drive has decreased considerably. Bob has been married for five years, and his desire for sexual intercourse has dropped from three or five times a week to once every two or three weeks. While Bob is mildly distressed, he doesn't see any major problems with his developing hyposexuality (unusually low sex drive).

Between these two extreme points on the spectrum of sexual disorders lie numerous sexual problems.

Two of the most controversial sexual issues in the past few years have involved date rape and sexual harassment.

While few people would disagree that rape is a violent crime requiring prosecution and incarceration, you might be shocked to know that, according to the *DSM III-R,* not all rapists suffer from psychosexual disorders. The *DSM III-R* states that studies of rapists indicate that fewer than 10 percent experience sexual sadism, a clinical disorder in which the physical suffering of the victim creates sexual excitation. In most cases, the rapist is not motivated by the prospect of inflicting suffering. He rapes to satisfy his sexual needs.

Assuming that a date rape occurs in the context of a man's wanting to have his sexual needs met without injuring the woman, according to the *DSM III-R,* such an act would not fall into the category of a psychosexual disorder. Of course, it would still be considered a crime.

The highly publicized trials of William Kennedy Smith and heavyweight boxing champion Mike Tyson highlighted a growing public tendency to prosecute for rape even if the victim has willingly placed herself in a situation that invites sexual abuse. For example, in the William Kennedy Smith case, the defense argued that the woman involved had been drinking. Furthermore, if she was not interested in a sexual liaison with Mr. Smith, she should not have gone at 2:00 A.M. to the estate where he was living. Similarly, the defense in the Tyson trial argued that the 18-year-old Miss Black America contestant should have known better then to go up to Mr. Tyson's room and, by implication, was agreeing to have sex.

These cases gave a clear and compelling message to all would-be date rapists that forcible sex with an unconsenting partner, no matter what the context or situation, is a prosecutable crime.

Another sexual issue in the late 1980s and 1990s is that of sexual harassment. Before 1980, sexual harassment was seldom heard of. With the nomination of Supreme Court Justice Clarence Thomas, attorney Anita Hill claimed that Mr. Thomas sexually harassed her while she served as his assistant. Highly publicized Senate confirmation proceedings brought this issue to the forefront of American public awareness.

Homosexuality, which in the middle part of the twentieth century was considered to be a psychosexual disorder, became a "lifestyle preference" in the 1970s and is no longer considered a disorder unless it is extremely distressing to the person's sense of identity.

Free love—or sexual promiscuity—which was common during the hippie era of the 1960s and early 1970s has declined gradually, in part because of the fear of AIDS. In 1992 one out of every one hundred men had the AIDS virus, and it was spreading at a rate of one new victim every 13 minutes.

We clearly live in a time of rapidly fluctuating sexual norms.

Although people could argue for years over what is and is not sexually normal, a specialized group of psychiatrists and psychologists in 1987 wrote the diagnostic criteria for sexual disorders in the *Diagnostic and Statistical Manual of Mental and Emotional Disorders (DSM III-R)*. In this classic text, sexual disorders were divided into three categories: paraphilias, sexual dysfunctions, and other sexual disorders.

PARAPHILIAS

In general, paraphilias involve sexual arousal by objects or situations that in some way interfere with the ability for mutual, reciprocal, affectionate sexual activity.

Common to all paraphilias are recurrent severe sexual urges and sexual fantasies usually involving either (1) nonhuman objects, (2) the actual physical or emotional suffering or humiliation of yourself or your partner, or (3) children or other people not capable of consenting to sexual acts. A diagnosis of a sexual paraphilia is made only if: (1) you have acted on these urges, or (2) you are extremely distressed or upset about the urges.

In short, paraphilias or sexual deviations point out that these particular problems lie in the object or person to which you are sexually attracted.

Some people with paraphilias require these fantasies to achieve sexual arousal, while others require these abnormal fantasies only under conditions of severe stress.

Just because you are sexually excited by a nonhuman object does not mean that you have a sexual paraphilia. For instance, many men are sexually aroused by seeing or touching female undergarments. As long as these arousing thoughts or acts are not distressing to the men or interfere with their ability for sexual relationships with their partners, they would not be considered to have the paraphilia known as fetishism (deriving sexual urges and sexual fantasies from nonliving objects).

The fantasies in a paraphilia—e.g., being degraded by one's partner or raping the partner—may be relatively harmless and even shared with a consenting partner. Often such sexual fantasies arouse one partner and are not communicated to the other who may feel estranged from the interaction. But recurrent sexual fantasies involving injury to oneself or others may lead to actual behaviors involving harm.

When sexual paraphilias involve a nonconsenting partner, they usually become the focus of the legal, rather than the mental-health system. Sadistic rape falls into this category. Often people with sexual paraphilias do not think of themselves as mentally ill, and come to the attention of the mental-health system only when their sexual behavior has gotten them into trouble with the law.

People seen in mental-health systems for paraphilias have an average of three to four different paraphilias. These sexual deviations may also be blended with other emotional and substance-abuse disorders.

The *DSM III-R* does not distinguish between people who *fantasize* about the sexual act and people who actually *act* on it. It does, however, require that the individual be genuinely distressed and upset over the recurring sexual urge or fantasy.

Three factors make it likely that a person will act on deviant sexual urges or fantasies:

(1) The presence of an antisocial personality disorder: individuals who tend to be impulsive, rebellious, and who have great difficulty controlling their urges.
(2) Severely stressful situations. People who are undergoing extreme emotional or physical stress are more likely to act on a deviant

sexual urge or fantasy than when they are not under extreme stress.
(3) People who use alcohol or drugs. Many drugs—especially alcohol—lower inhibitions and result in impulsive acts, which would normally be successfully restrained.

Another important distinction to make is between people who *consistently* act on deviant sexual urges and those who do so only *occasionally*. Sexually deviant behavior can be *chronic* or *episodic*.

Specific situations may be sought out by individuals suffering from one or more paraphilias. For example, a pedophile may seek out situations which brings him/her into contact with children; a fetishist may take a job selling women's shoes or undergarments; a sexual sadist may work as an ambulance attendant.

The object that sexually motivates the paraphiliac may be very specific, such as ten-year-old thin black males; or general, for instance, all female undergarments.

Sometimes individuals with paraphilias report extreme guilt, shame, and distress at having to use deviant sexual stimulus that is socially unacceptable to others or that they consider immoral, such as a sexual attraction to animals. Other times, individuals with paraphilias see nothing wrong with what excites them and see the problem only as what other people think of them; for example, enjoying cross-dressing (dressing as the opposite sex).

In any case, there is always a clear set of problems in the paraphiliac's ability to initiate and maintain mutually consensual and reciprocal sexual activity.

Interestingly, approximately half of the people with diagnosed sexual paraphilias are married. Often their desires significantly interfere with their marital relationship. Paraphiliacs and their spouses frequently seek marriage counseling.

Paraphilias are rarely diagnosed in mental-health settings. However, given the great demand for pornography and sexual paraphernalia, the prevalence of sexual paraphilias in the general public is believed to be far higher than clinical statistics suggest. Due to the chronic nature of sexual paraphilias, many innocent people have been and will continue to be victimized by people with these disorders.

According to mental-health statistics, other than sexual masochism, paraphilias are rarely seen in women.

Sexual paraphilias may also be examined in terms of the severity of the specific deviation. In mild sexual paraphilias, the person is noticeably upset about the recurrent sexual urges, but has never acted on them.

In a moderate sexual paraphilia, the person has occasionally or episodically acted on the sexually deviant urge.

The individual with a severe paraphilia acts repeatedly on the distressing or harmful sexual urge.

In short, sexual paraphilias (deviant sexual urges and behaviors) are an actual clinical problem if:

(1) they are harmful to yourself or others,
(2) the sexual urges, fantasies, or behaviors cause you emotional distress (shame, guilt, depression),
(3) the sexual behaviors interfere with your occupation, education, or ability to function in life, or
(4) the recurrent sexual urges or behaviors interfere with your developing and maintaining a mutually satisfying sexual relationship with another person.

SPECIFIC TYPES OF PARAPHILIAS

Fetishism

Fetishism is a psychosexual disorder involving chronic, intense sexual urges, fantasies, and behaviors over a period of at least six months involving the use of nonliving objects for sexual arousal and gratification. A fetishist has either acted on these urges and suffered some life-damaging consequences, or is extremely upset about these urges and fantasies.

Ray, a 19-year-old college sophomore is suffering from a fetish. Ray is sexually stimulated by women's underwear and frequently sneaks into female coed dorm rooms to steal undergarments. He is aroused only by the sight, feel, and smell of these articles, and has no other sexual relationship with women or men.

Since Ray's interest involves a nonliving object which is sufficient for his sexual gratification, it necessarily interferes with his ability for a sexual relationship with a consenting partner and is therefore a fetishism.

James, on the other hand, a 22-year-old college senior, is extremely turned on when his girlfriend wears thigh-high black leather boots. When he sees her in these boots, he has strong sexual urges. The touch and smell of the leather while he is having sex with her greatly enhances his arousal and performance. When he sees or handles leather boots when his girlfriend is not around, he has pleasant memories of these satisfying encounters.

Although James is sexually excited by the leather boots, they do not interfere with his life, cause him distress or shame, or interfere with his relationship with his girlfriend. In fact, the nonliving objects (boots) actually serve to enhance his sex life. James does not have a fetish.

Fetishism Questionnaire

Directions: Answer the following questions as honestly as possible. Do not deny or minimize your responses, but do not answer yes to questions that do not apply to you.

1. Over a period of at least six months, have you had strong, recurrent, intense sexual urges or fantasies involving nonliving objects?
2. Have you acted on these sexual urges or fantasies?
3. Are you markedly distressed by these sexual urges or fantasies?
4. Have these urges, fantasies, or behaviors interfered with your education, your occupation, or your social relations?
5. Have they prevented you from achieving and maintaining a satisfying sexual relationship with another person?
6. Have these sexual urges, fantasies, or behaviors ever gotten you into trouble with authorities?

Scoring: If you answered yes to question 1, yes to question 2 or 3, and yes to any of the questions 4–6, you may be suffering from a sexual fetishism.

Exhibitionism

Exhibitionism is a psychosexual disorder in which the individual experiences intense, chronic sexual urges, fantasies, or behaviors over a period of at least six months involving exposing their genitals to strangers or nonconsenting others. The exhibitionist has either acted on these sexual urges or fantasies, or is noticeably distressed and emotionally upset about them. Frequently the exhibitionist will masturbate while exposing himself, or masturbate while he fantasizes about exposing himself. Most exhibitionists expose themselves for one of two reasons: to shock or surprise the observer, or to sexually arouse the person that is observing them. In the strict clinical sense of the term, exhibitionism is extremely rare in women, and the target of the exhibitionistic display is almost always women or children.

Exhibitionistic tendencies usually begin before the age of 18. Despite occasional newspaper stories involving "dirty old men" who expose themselves, clinical statistics indicate that this condition becomes much less severe after the age of 40.

Christy is a 21-year-old model who, when she realized she could make a lot more money stripping, gave up her career and started dancing at a strip joint. Although Christy earned over $100,000 last year working 15 days a month, she performed because she found sexual excitement and satisfaction in exposing herself and arousing males in the audience. Her dances are seductively exciting and sexually attractive to both her audience and herself.

Since Christy's audience consist of patrons who want to see Christy expose herself, and since Christy's dancing seems to enhance rather than distract from her relationship with her boyfriend, she is not an exhibitionist.

George, on the other hand, is a 34-year-old transient who has been arrested on eight different occasions for exposing himself to unwilling women and children. George gets a great sense of sexual satisfaction out of his exhibitionism, and uses the memories of his victims' reactions as fantasy stimulation for masturbation. Due to George's numerous legal difficulties and his lack of desire for a mutually fulfilling sexual relationship, George is clearly an exhibitionist.

Exhibitionism Questionnaire

Directions: Answer the following questions as honestly as possible. Do not deny or minimize your responses, but do not answer yes to questions that do not apply to you.

1. During a period of at least six months, have you had strong, recurrent sexual urges or fantasies involving exposing your sex organs to unsuspecting or unwilling strangers?
2. Have you actually acted upon these sexual urges or fantasies to expose yourself to unwilling others?
3. Have you been clearly upset or distressed about recurrent urges or fantasies to expose yourself to unwilling others?
4. Have these urges to expose yourself ever interfered with your education, occupation, or social relations?
5. Have these exhibitionistic urges or acts prevented you from initiating and maintaining a satisfying sexual relationship with another person?
6. Have these behaviors ever gotten you into trouble with authorities?

Scoring: If you answered yes to question 1, yes to questions 2 or 3, and yes to any of the questions 4–6, you are likely to have exhibitionistic tendencies or to be an exhibitionist.

Frotteurism

Frotteurism is a psychosexual disorder in which the individual has long-term intense sexual urges and fantasies involving rubbing or touching his or her genitals against a nonconsenting person or sexually fondling a nonconsenting person.

People with this psychosexual disorder usually commit frottage in crowded, busy places like buses, subways, sidewalks, or at public events such as concerts. Committing frottage in a crowded public place offers two advantages to the disturbed person: it gives them an easy escape, and many victims of frottage believe that the sexual contact was accidental.

There are varying degrees of frottage, ranging from brushing your genitals against the buttocks of a woman as you pass by to manually fondling her genitals through tight jeans.

Frotteurs report that they often fantasize an exclusive, caring relationship with the person they are victimizing.

Frotteurism usually begins by adolescence, and most acts occur between ages of 15 and 25. After this time, there is a gradual decrease in its frequency.

Jerry, a 42-year-old construction supervisor, still gets sexually turned on when he brushes his genitals against his wife's hips and fondles her breasts through her blouse. Jerry's wife is thrilled that he still finds her desirable after twenty years of marriage, and his behavior excites them both. Clearly, Jerry is not suffering from frotteurism.

Keith, on the other hand, is a 21-year-old packaging worker who gets his sexual thrills by reaching up women's skirts and stroking them just before the bus doors open and he makes his escape. Even though Keith has a relatively good relationship with his girlfriend, his behavior has caused him trouble with other women. He was once punched by a woman's husband before he could make it out the door of the bus.

Keith is suffering from frotteurism.

Frotteurism Questionnaire

Directions: Answer the following questions as honestly as possible. Do not deny or minimize your responses, but do not answer yes to questions that do not apply to you.

1. During a period of at least six months, have you had strong recurrent sexual urges or fantasies involving touching or rubbing against a nonconsenting person?
2. Have you acted on these sexual urges to touch or rub against a nonconsenting person?
3. Have you been emotionally distressed or upset over these urges or fantasies?
4. Have these urges to sexually touch or rub against a nonconsenting person ever interfered with your education, occupation, or social relationships?
5. Have these urges or acts ever prevented you from initiating and maintaining a satisfying sexual relationship with another person?
6. Have you ever gotten into trouble with authorities for sexually touching or rubbing against a nonconsenting person?

Scoring: If you answered yes to question 1, yes to questions 2 or 3, and yes to any of the questions 4–6, you are likely to have a problem with frotteurism.

One final point to make about frotteurism: It is the actual physical touching or rubbing—not the coercive nature of the act—that is sexually stimulating.

Pedophilia

To the general public, pedophilia is probably one of the most reprehensible of all the psychosexual disorders. Pedophilia involves intense urges or fantasies for sexual activity with a prepubescent child, typically age 13 or under.

Borrowing from child-molestation statutes in various states, the *DSM III-R* states that the earliest age at which one can be accused of pedophilia is 16, and the individual must be at least five years older than the child victimized.

Pedophiles typically report an attraction to children in a specific age range. Those attracted to girls usually prefer them in the 8- to 10-year-old age group; those attracted to boys usually prefer them in the 10- to 12-year-old age group. Pedophilic attraction to girls is about twice as common as it is to boys. Some pedophiles, however, are attracted to both.

A common misconception about pedophiles is that they are sexually attracted only to children. While this is true of the "exclusive" pedophile, many people with this affliction are also sexually attracted to adults.

The pedophile's sexual exploitation of children may take many forms. It can vary from dressing and undressing the child, to peeping on the child when he or she is naked, to masturbating in the presence of the child, to genital touching or fondling of the child, to actual intercourse.

Pedophiles often justify their deviant behavior with excuses such as they are "teaching the child about sex," or that "the child was deriving sexual pleasure from the act." Pedophiles often see children as "sexually provocative" and feel that the child actually wants sexual relations with them.

Pedophilia may also occur in an incestuous relationship with the pedophile's own children, grandchildren, or other relatives. Often pedophiles will threaten the child with severe harm if he or she discloses the sexual abuse. Other pedophiles will engage in complicated long-term strategies to arrange for situations in which they will have the opportunity to victimize children sexually. A pedophile may marry a woman simply to have the opportunity for sexual exploitation of her young daughter. Vladimir Nabokov used this strategy as the plot for *Lolita*.

While the vast majority of people who enjoy working with children are honorable, pedophiles often slip into professions or volunteer positions in which they can exploit children sexually. Every year newspaper articles point out child sexual abuse from such generally trusted figures as scout leaders, priests, volunteer coaches, and trusted family friends.

Except in cases involving forcible rape, pedophiles may be very loving, caring, and generous to the child's needs in all areas but the sexual one.

Pedophilia, like most other paraphilias, usually begins in adolescence, although a number of men report becoming pedophiles in middle age.

Behavior involving young boys is usually chronic and often varies with the amount of stress the pedophile is under. The relapse rate for pedophilias is about twice as high among those who prefer the same sex as opposed to those who prefer the opposite sex. Statistics show that about 40 to 50 percent of individuals diagnosed as pedophiliacs were themselves victims of childhood sexual abuse.

Mike is an 18-year-old high-school senior who was sentenced to thirty days in the county jail for a sexual relationship he had with his 15-year-old girlfriend. Charges were filed against Mike when the girl's father caught them in the act in her bedroom and chose to press charges on her behalf. Despite her protest that she was willing and desirous of the sexual relationship, the court found Mike guilty of a sexual relationship with a minor under the age of 18. Since the girl was postpubescent and over the age of 14, as well as consenting, Mike fell in the unusual category of not having a psychosexual disorder (pedophilia), but being guilty of an illegal sexual act with a minor.

Mike's case points up the distinctions which often arise between the mental-health and legal systems.

Joe, a 26-year-old state unemployment-eligibility worker, has a different kind of problem. A muscular, attractive young man, Joe recently married a 39-year-old woman with two daughters aged 10 and 12. After winning his wife's trust during the courtship, Joe began laying plans for how he would create a sexual relationship with Lisa, the 12-year-old daughter. After the wedding, Joe began to casually expose himself to Lisa and convinced Lisa that it was okay for her to be nude in his presence. Before long, Joe and Lisa were showering together, began fondling each other, and soon had sex.

The sexual relationship went on for a year before Lisa's mother discovered it, at which point she contacted authorities and filed charges.

Joe was arrested for lewd and lascivious acts with a child under the age of 14 and sentenced to two years in jail and mandatory psychotherapy for one year. During Joe's therapy, he admitted that although he had sexual relationships with his wife, these sexual acts with her were spurred only by sexual fantasies involving her daughter.

Joe is clearly a pedophile.

Pedophilia Questionnaire

Directions: Answer the following questions as honestly as possible. Do not deny or minimize your responses, but do not answer yes to questions that do not apply to you.

1. During a period of at least six months, have you had strong recurrent sexual urges or fantasies involving sexual relationships with prepubescent children or a child under the age of 14?
2. Have you acted on these sexual urges or fantasies involving children?
3. Have you been clearly distressed or emotionally upset about these desires involving children?
4. Have these sexual urges, fantasies, or behaviors ever interfered with your education, occupation, or social relationships?
5. Has this behavior prevented you from initiating and maintaining a satisfying sexual relationship with a consenting adult?
6. Have these sexual urges, fantasies, or behaviors with children ever gotten you into trouble with authorities?

Scoring: If you answered yes to question 1, yes to questions 2 or 3, or yes to any of the questions 4–6, you are likely to be diagnosed as having either exclusive or nonexclusive pedophilia and should seek help immediately.

SEXUAL MASOCHISM

Sexual masochism involves a recurrent sexual urge or fantasy of being physically abused, beaten, bound, humiliated, or made to suffer. The masochist has acted on these sexual urges or is noticeably emotionally distressed by the thought of them.

Masochists often have recurrent sexual fantasies involving being raped, bound, or held in a position from which there is no escape. These sexual fantasies typically occur while the individual is either masturbating or during sexual intercourse. Some masochists act on their fantasies by inflicting pain on themselves, such as electrically shocking themselves, cutting themselves, or having their partner whip them or bind them. Other typical masochistic fantasies include being forced to crawl and bark like a dog, being subjected to verbal degradation, or being urinated or defecated upon.

Masochistic sexual fantasies usually begin sometime during childhood; actual activities usually occur by adolescence or early adulthood.

Some people engage in ritualistic compulsive masochistic acts, such as whipping and bondage, while others increase the severity of masochistic acts over time creating greater risk of injury and potential death.

Although such fantasies may be distressing to most people, the diagnosis of sexual masochism is made only if the person having the fantasies is emotionally distressed by such fantasies, or has acted on them with life-damaging consequences.

Leah is an attractive 24-year-old nurse who enjoys playing sexual games with her husband that involve fantasies of being tied up and raped. Leah and her husband have bought handcuffs at an adult bookstore, masks, gloves, and other sexual paraphernalia to act out these fantasies. Leah reports that her husband will sometimes sneak away from work, slip into the house dressed up like someone else, and *simulate* raping her. On other occasions he will handcuff her to the headboard of the bed and force sex upon her despite her insincere pleading that he stop. The couple had decided in advance to act out these fantasies and her simulated resistance was required. Rape is a violent and disgusting crime, but Leah's *simulated* masochistic fantasies have never lead to life-damaging consequences for her or her husband. They serve as a tool for mutual sexual excitement. Despite having some masochistic leanings and acting on them, Leah is not distressed by them, and is therefore not a sexual masochist.

Art, a 42-year-old CEO, is an extremely domineering man. He exercises nearly complete control over all aspects of his business, interpersonal, and family life. Yet Art has a deep-seated need to be dominated by women, a need which is met only through his encounters with Helga, a 34-year-old prostitute. In Art's encounters with Helga, it is prearranged that he will be completely subservient and obey all of her demands. Art has the money to afford his weekly sessions with Helga, and the sessions do not interfere with his work. Art and Helga have a mutual understanding as to how far she will go, and Art never experiences any serious physical or psychological damage.

After several years of this secretive behavior, Art's wife becomes suspicious and follows him. Art is caught, and his seemingly harmless fantasy causes serious marital problems. Because Art's masochistic fantasies with a prostitute interfered with his marriage, Art would meet the criteria for the diagnosis of sexual masochism.

Sexual Masochism Questionnaire

Directions: Answer the following questions as honestly as possible. Do not deny or minimize your responses, but do not answer yes to questions that do not apply to you.

1. During a period of at least six months, have you had strong, recurrent sexual urges or fantasies involving the actual act (not simulated) of being physically abused, bound, humiliated, or otherwise made to suffer?
2. Have you acted on these urges or fantasies to be physically abused or degraded?
3. Have you been emotionally distressed or upset by these urges or fantasies?
4. Have these masochistic sexual urges or behaviors ever interfered with your education, occupation, social relationships, or family life?
5. Have these masochistic urges or acts prevented you from initiat-

ing and maintaining a mutually satisfying sexual relationship with another person?

6. Have these masochistic urges, fantasies, or acts gotten you into trouble with authorities?

Scoring: If you answered yes to question 1, yes to questions 2 or 3, and yes to any of the questions 4–6, you may be a sexual masochist.

SEXUAL SADISM

Sexual sadism is a psychosexual disorder in which the individual has recurrent, strong sexual urges and fantasies involving the actual commission of acts (not simulated) in which his or her victim is forced to endure physical or emotional suffering, including humiliation or degradation. For the sexual sadist, the victim's suffering is sexually exciting. The sadist may have acted on these urges, or may be emotionally distressed about them. Just like sexual masochism, some people may have sadistic fantasies while they engage in sexual activities with a consenting partner, but otherwise not act upon these fantasies. Usually the fantasies of a sexual sadist involve total control over a victim who is terrified by anticipation of the impending sadistic sexual act. Other people with sadistic sexual urges may find a consenting partner (usually a sexual masochist) who willingly suffers pain and humiliation.

Perhaps the most dangerous of all the sexual sadists are those who act on their sadistic urges with nonconsenting victims.

Sadistic fantasies typically originate in childhood; yet, like masochism, sadistic activities generally begin only in late adolescence or early adulthood.

When sexually sadistic behavior is practiced with a nonconsenting partner or a victim, the activity is likely to be repeated until the sadist is apprehended by authorities.

Some people with sadistic fantasies may engage in sadistic acts for years without inflicting serious physical damage on their partner. However, unlike masochism, the severity of sadistic acts tends to increase over time. When sexual sadism is found in the context of an antisocial personality disorder, sadists may seriously injure or kill their victim due to poor impulse control and bad judgment.

Just because a person commits rape or another form of sexual assault does not mean that he or she are sadistic. The true sadist takes great pleasure in inflicting physical and psychological suffering on the victim far in excess of what is necessary to obtain sexual compliance. The visible pain of the suffering victim is what is arousing to the true sadist. *DSM III-R* cites a study of rapists showing that fewer than 10 percent have sadistic thoughts or fantasies, and a significant number actually found the physical suffering of the victim during rape interfering with their sexual arousal.

Sadistic behavior also occurs outside of a sexual context; for example, torture used to interrogate prisoners, torture used in cult rituals, and professions in which people enjoy inflicting pain on others, like a dentist who enjoys the pain of his patients.

An example of a sadistic fantasy without actual sexual sadism is the previously discussed case of Leah. Leah's husband, Ed, found the simulated acts of bondage and rape sexually exciting. There were no life-damaging consequences of this behavior to Ed or Leah. These behaviors did not interfere with Ed's occupation, interpersonal relations, or any other area of his life. He never got in trouble for this behavior, and not only did it not interfere with his relationship with Leah, it actually stimulated mutual sexual excitement between them. While having sadistic sexual fantasies, Ed does not meet the criteria for sexual sadism.

But sexual sadism can lead to bizarre and grotesque atrocities.

On May 19, 1977, a 24-year-old lumber-mill worker named Cameron Hooker and his wife kidnapped Colleen Stan, a 20-year-old college student. She was blindfolded, handcuffed, and put in a "head box." She was taken to the Hookers' small home in Red Bluff, California, and kept in bondage in their basement for more than seven years.

Besides Hooker's blindfolding, handcuffing, stripping, whipping, raping, and sodomizing Colleen on numerous occasions, Hooker devised even more grotesque techniques for the physical and psychological torment of his victim. In addition to the suffocating head box, which prevented sights and sounds from reaching her, Hooker would leave her naked, strapped to a large wood table, for hours or even days at a time. On numerous occasions he hung her from the basement ceiling beam by leather wrist cuffs and whipped her mercilessly with a leather strap. The suffering of Hooker's victim excited him sexually. On the first night of Colleen's captivity, he had intercourse with his wife as Colleen lay next to them strapped to a table, blindfolded.

Despite her initial terror, Colleen Stan, for unknown reasons, did not escape when the opportunity arose. Hooker was finally apprehended when his wife became jealous of his relationship with Colleen and reported him to authorities.

Cameron Hooker's case represents one of the most bizarre forms of sexual sadism. For his crimes, Hooker was sentenced to 60–104 years in state prison. The life-damaging consequences to Hooker's victim are incomprehensible to most of us.

Sadism Questionnaire

Directions: Answer the following questions as honestly as possible. Do not deny or minimize your responses, but do not answer yes to questions that do not apply to you.

1. During a period of at least six months, have you had recurrent strong sexual urges and fantasies involving actually inflicting psychological or physical suffering on a victim, and found this sexually exciting?
2. Have you acted on these sexual urges or fantasies?
3. Have you been emotionally distressed or upset about these recurrent desires?
4. Have these sadistic sexual urges, fantasies, or behaviors ever interfered with your education, occupation, or social relations?
5. Have these urges or acts prevented you from initiating and maintaining a mutually satisfying sexual relationship with another person?

6. Have these sadistic sexual fantasies or behaviors ever gotten you into trouble with the authorities?

Scoring: If you answered yes to question 1, yes to questions 2 or 3, and yes to any of the questions 4–6, you may be suffering from sexual sadism.

Again, it is very important to notice the distinction between sexual fantasies and urges, and the actual commission of damaging acts. By definition, if you inflict harm on another person to achieve your own sexual gratification, you are sexually sadistic and should seek help immediately. At the milder end of the continuum, if you are recurrently distressed or bothered by sexual fantasies involving inflicting pain or suffering on others, yet never feel the need to commit these acts, it is still best to seek psychotherapeutic assistance. Recurrent sexual fantasies often lead to the actual commission of these acts.

TRANSVESTISM

Transvestism involves a long-term, intense, recurrent sexual urge or fantasy involving cross-dressing. The transvestite either engages in actual cross-dressing, or is very upset about his fantasies and urges. The transvestite usually keeps a collection of women's clothes that he often uses to cross-dress when alone. Typically, the cross-dressed transvestite will masturbate and imagine that other males are attracted to him as a woman in his female clothing. Transvestism has been described only in heterosexual males.

It is important to distinguish between transvestism and transsexualism. Transsexualism is the compelling desire to actually change sexes through surgery and hormone-replacement therapy.

Transvestism can range from wearing one or more female garments occasionally to extensive involvement in a club or subculture.

Transvestism usually begins with cross-dressing during childhood or early adolescence. In most cases, the cross-dressing is not done in public until adulthood. Individuals may covertly cross-dress—e.g., wearing female hosiery or underwear under their normal masculine attire. Transvestism may also be considered a form of fetishism because the female clothing is sexually exciting in and of itself and may be the stimulus for masturbation and, later, intercourse.

Only a small number of transvestites develop a desire to become women and request surgical or hormonal transformation. When this occurs, the disorder shifts from transvestism to transsexualism.

Bart, a 31-year-old account executive, first dressed up like a woman while masquerading at Mardi Gras. He found the behavior sexually exciting and reported that he had been considering cross-dressing for a long time. Cross-dressing has never been particularly distressing to Bart, but he does admit that since he is sexually satisfied by masturbating when he cross-dresses, he has not been motivated to find a sexual partner.

Bart could be described as a transvestite since his cross-dressing serves as a substitute for a mutually consensual and satisfying sexual relationship.

Transvestism Questionnaire

Directions: Answer the following questions as honestly as possible. Do not deny or minimize your responses, but do not answer yes to questions that do not apply to you.

1. During a period of at least six months, have you had a recurrent intense sexual urge or fantasy involving cross-dressing?
2. Have you acted on these cross-dressing sexual urges?
3. Have you been emotionally distressed or upset about the cross-dressing urges, fantasies, or behaviors?
4. Has this need to cross-dress ever interfered with your education, occupation, or social relationships?
5. Have these cross-dressing urges, acts, or fantasies prevented you from initiating and maintaining a mutually satisfying sexual relationship with another person?

6. Have you ever gotten into trouble with authorities because of your cross-dressing?

Scoring: If you answered yes to question 1, yes to questions 2 or 3, and yes to any one of the questions 4–6, you are likely to be a transvestite.

VOYEURISM

Voyeurism is a psychosexual disorder characterized by intense recurrent sexual urges or behaviors involving observing unsuspecting people—usually strangers—who are either engaging in sexual activity, or are nude.

The classic case of the "peeping tom" is a stereotype of voyeurism. The peeping is done for the purpose of achieving sexual excitement; no sexual interaction other than watching the person is sought. Usually, voyeurs masturbate either during or after their voyeuristic activity and achieve their orgasm based on these observations or memories. Frequently, voyeurs enjoy the fantasy of having a sexual relationship with the person observed, but in reality this rarely occurs. In its purest form, voyeurism constitutes the exclusive use of secretly observing others in sexual behavior or in the nude.

Voyeurism typically begins at or before the age of 15 and tends to be a chronic problem.

Norman, a 38-year-old bartender, gets his sexual thrills after work when he sneaks around the back of apartment complexes and catches glimpses of women through the curtains either engaging in sex or disrobing. Norman was once caught peeping, and charges were filed. Norman's life has been damaged, and he may be described as a voyeur.

On the other hand, Matt, a 24-year-old body builder, frequently enjoys watching adult pornographic films and live strip shows. Matt finds these materials sexually exciting, and he uses the memories and fantasies about the people he observes to enhance his own sex life with his girlfriend.

Since the actors and actresses Matt observes know that they are being seen, Matt is not a voyeur.

Voyeurism Questionnaire

Directions: Answer the following questions as honestly as possible. Do not deny or minimize your responses, but do not answer yes to questions that do not apply to you.

1. During a period of at least six months, have you had strong recurrent sexual urges or fantasies about observing an unsuspecting person who is either naked or engaging in sexual activity?
2. Have you acted on these urges to observe unsuspecting people?
3. Have you been emotionally distressed or upset about the mere thought, urge, or fantasy of observing people's nudity or sexual behavior without their consent?
4. Have these sexual "peeping" urges or behaviors ever interfered with your education, occupation, or social relationships?
5. Have these urges to secretly watch others prevented you from initiating and maintaining a mutually satisfying sexual relationship with another person?
6. Have these activities ever gotten you into trouble with the authorities?

Scoring: If you answered yes to question 1, yes to questions 2 or 3, and yes to any of the questions 4–6, you are likely to be a voyeur.

OTHER PARAPHILIAS

Although much less common, the following sexual disorders are also classified as paraphilias:

telephone scatologia: receiving sexual excitement and gratification through sexually explicit or lewd telephone conversation

necrophilia: receiving sexual stimulation and gratification from sexual interaction with corpses

partialism: sexual excitement or gratification by exclusive focus on one part of the body (e.g., the feet)

zoophilia: sexual excitement or gratification through sexual activity with animals

coprophilia: sexual excitement or gratification through interaction with feces

klismaphilia: sexual excitement or gratification through receiving enemas

urophilia: sexual excitement or gratification through urinating on others or being urinated on

SEXUAL DYSFUNCTIONS

In contrast to the sexual paraphilias, in which the problem lies in the object which creates sexual excitement and gratification, sexual dysfunctions involve some type of disturbance in the sexual-response cycle. A diagnosis of sexual dysfunction is not made if the sexual problem is due to physical disorder or illness.

Researchers have found that the human sexual response cycle can be divided into four phases:

(1) Appetitive—This phase consists of fantasies about sexual activity and the desire to have sexual relations.

(2) Excitement—This phase consists of the subjective sense of sexual pleasure and accompanying physiological changes. In the male, these consist mainly of penile erection; in the female, the excitement

phase consists of vasocongestion in the pelvis, vaginal lubrication, and swelling of the external genitalia.

(3) Orgasm—This phase consists of a peaking of sexual pleasure involving the release of sexual tension in rhythmic contractions of the reproductive organs. In the male, there is ejaculation of semen; in the female, there are involuntary contractions in the outer third of the vagina. (4) Resolution—This phase consists of a general sense of relaxation, well-being, and complacency. During the resolution phase, men are typically unable to regain erectile potence, while women are capable of responding immediately to additional sexual stimulation.

Almost invariably, inhibitions in the sexual-response cycle occur during the appetitive, excitement, or orgasmic phase. Sexual dysfunctions involving the typical sexual-response cycle may be purely psychological, partly biological, acquired over time, specific (limited only to certain partners or situations), or generalized to all sexual activity.

Usually related to sexual dysfunctions are such emotional symptoms as depression, guilt, shame, frustration, and sometimes monitoring oneself with extreme sensitivity to the ability to please the sexual partner. This oversensitivity involving performance leads to impaired sexual functioning.

Most sexual-dysfunction problems have their onset in early adulthood, although premature ejaculation commonly begins with the first few sexual encounters. The most common age for presentation of sexual dysfunctions are in the late twenties and early thirties, and the dysfunctions usually become noticeable after the individual has established and sustained a sexual relationship with someone.

Sexual dysfunctions are rarely associated with educational or occupational status, but major complications often occur as a result of disrupted marital or other sexual relationships.

Studies in Europe and the United States indicate that in the young adult population, approximately 8 percent of the men have had a male erectile disorder and approximately 20 percent of the total population have a hyposexual disorder (lack of normal sexual desire). Thirty percent of the men have had premature-ejaculation problems at some point, and approximately 30 percent of the women have inhibited female orgasms.

Women are more prone to sexual dysfunctions involving hyposexual disorder and inhibited orgasm, while men suffer more from premature ejaculation.

TYPES OF SEXUAL DYSFUNCTIONS

Hypoactive Sexual Desire Disorder

This disorder consists of a consistent deficiency or absence of sexual fantasies and urges for sexual activity. When determining what is normal or abnormal in terms of sexual desire, such factors as age and physical health must be taken into account. When diagnosing hyposexual desire disorder, the possibility of depression must be ruled out, as it almost invariably leads to a significant reduction in sexual drive.

Sexual-Aversion Disorder

Sexual-aversion disorders involve aversion to virtually all genital sexual contact with your sexual partner.

Brad, a 61-year-old retired engineer, has not had sexual relations with his 59-year-old wife in twenty-two years. Brad stated that when he turned 39 his already-fading sexual desire for his wife disappeared completely. Brad is still sexually turned on by attractive females and masturbates to sexually stimulating movies and magazines, but is unable to generalize these fantasies and urges to his wife.

The result of Brad's sexual negligence towards his wife has been devastating to the couple. Wisely, they are finally planning to divorce.

Female Sexual-Arousal Disorder

A female sexual-arousal disorder consists of a partial or complete failure to achieve or maintain the sexual-excitement phase. It may also involve a consistent and recurrent lack of enjoyment or excitement during sexual activity.

Male Erectile Disorder

A male erectile disorder involves a consistent partial or complete failure to achieve and maintain an erection until orgasm.

Inhibited Female Orgasm

Inhibited female orgasm involves a recurrent delay or absence of orgasm following a normal sexual-excitement phase. Although times vary considerably, the necessary amount of foreplay to stimulate women to orgasm may involve anywhere from twenty to thirty minutes. Frequently women are able to achieve orgasm during clitoral stimulation, but are unable to experience it during sexual intercourse without manual stimulation of the clitoris. Just because a woman requires manual clitoral stimulation during intercourse does not justify the diagnosis of inhibited female orgasm.

The range of sexual stimuli necessary to excite a woman to orgasm ranges from pure sexual imagery, with no physical contact, to prolonged stimulation with a vibrator. Typical male-female coitus lies somewhere in the middle, with oral stimulation and manual stimulation reportedly more effective in helping females achieve orgasm.

Inhibited Male Orgasm

Inhibited male orgasm consists of delay or absence of orgasm following a normal phase of sexual excitement in sexual activity. Usually, inhibited male orgasm involves the inability to achieve an orgasm while the penis is within the vagina.

Premature Ejaculation

Premature ejaculation involves ejaculating with very minimal sexual stimulation, ejaculate either before or shortly after penetration. Usually premature ejaculation occurs despite the man's attempts to stop it, and this disorder is much more common with a new partner, or when the man is young or sexually inexperienced.

Dyspareunia

Dyspareunia is a recurrent or consistent genital pain in either men or women before, during, or after sexual intercourse.

Vaginismus

Vaginismus is the involuntary spasm of the muscles of the outer third of the vagina, which interferes with sexual intercourse. It is not uncommon in women attempting sexual intercourse for the first time.

Other Types of Sexual Disorders

There are a myriad of possible sexual disorders which are not included in this chapter. Typically, feelings of inadequacy may develop as a result of distress over body size and shape, size and shape of sex organs, sexual performance, or other characteristics related to self-imposed standards of ideal masculinity or femininity. When appearance or performance doesn't measure up to these standards, considerable distress results, and this affects sexual performance.

There may also be distress—particularly guilt—about a pattern of sexual conquests in which sexual partners are viewed as objects only to be used.

Some budding homosexuals experience homosexual panic. They realize that they have a homosexual orientation, and this orientation comes into direct conflict with their conscience, or ideal of what they think they should be.

HOPE FOR THE FUTURE

A small, but growing number of clinics for the treatment of sexual dysfunctions and sexual compulsivity (paraphilias) have begun to appear throughout the United States. At the end of this chapter a resource list of such treatment centers is provided by geographical location.

Perhaps the most well established, and certainly the most widely known of all the sexual treatment centers is the Masters and Johnson Institute in St. Louis, Missouri. Centers such as this focus on a wide range of sexual disorders, including: impotence, inability to ejaculate, premature ejaculation, inability to experience orgasm, pain with intercourse (dyspareunia), and vaginal contractions which interfere with intercourse (vaginismus).

Pioneering research by Drs. Masters and Johnson established the value of both sexual partners which comprise the couple participating in the therapy process. It's easy to realize that when one partner has a sexual problem he/she both influences, and is influenced by the other partner. Cooperation between both partners is considered essential to the resolution of most sexual problems. In the Masters and Johnson program, privacy is respected, and sexual relations between the couples are not observed.

The therapy team usually includes a wide variety of professional disciplines including: physicians, psychologists, social workers, and other specialists who have received postgraduate training in the treatment of sexual disorders.

Clinics specializing in the treatment of sexual compulsions or paraphilias are usually more difficult to find.

One such state-of-the-art facility is the River Oaks Sexual Compulsion Program in New Orleans, Louisiana. Research on hundreds of patients with sexual compulsions has revealed that these patients were frequently the target of physical or sexual traumas in their own childhood. In short, these victimizers were often victimized themselves as children.

Similar to other addictive disorders, compulsive sexual behavior can fill a void in the sufferer's life, and become a means of escape from stress and the difficulties of life. Four common features of sexual compulsion include:

- A sense of powerlessness and passive rage.
- An inability to form close loving relationships with other adults.
- Frequent use of denial, rationalization, and/or minimization to hide both the problem and the underlying shame.
- Sexual acting out (e.g., voyeurism, rape, pedophilia, fetishism), despite serious consequences and repeated attempts at control.

The treatment process at River Oaks includes an eclectic orientation involving: behavioral, psychodynamic, cognitive, and 12-step approaches to develop and maintain control of self-destructive behavior patterns. Specifically, this eclectic approach is used to:

- Help the patient remember and acknowledge sexual compulsivity.
- Accept responsibility for the past.
- Reduce deviant arousal patterns and damaging sexual impulses.
- Maintain abstinence from sexually compulsive behavior.
- Resolve family or early trauma issues.

- Develop empathy and awareness of the impact of their behavior on others.
- Develop the life skills to cope with a new sense of power and effectiveness.
- Deal with guilt and shame resulting from a clear perception of the past.
- Develop healthy, intimate adult sexual relationships.

Expressive therapy is often considered essential in the treatment of sexual compulsivity. Therapeutic modalities such as: art therapy, psychodrama, and music can sometimes release buried feelings that traditional talk therapy cannot.

Didactic groups focus on helping patients develop self-esteem, and deal with topics such as: assertiveness, family roles, sex education, personal boundaries, and communication skills. Collateral issues such as substance abuse, eating disorders, and codependency are addressed when appropriate.

The River Oaks program, and others like it, recommend that after a two-to-four-week inpatient program, patients commit to outpatient therapy for a minimum of two years.

SUMMARY

Sexual disorders may be divided into paraphilias and sexual dysfunctions.

Paraphilias involve a deviation in the object, which creates sexual excitement and gratification. Usually, the object of the paraphilia creates the problem because it has some form of life-damaging consequences.

Certainly, a good sexual fantasy life will involve variations of typical sexual themes. The problem occurs only when recurrent sexual fantasies or urges lead to the likelihood of commission of sexual acts which may have life-damaging consequences.

Sexual dysfunctions represent a different type of sexual disorder.

They occur in the human sexual-response cycle and involve the appetitive, excitement, or orgasmic phases of this cycle.

There is much room for discussion of what is normal in the area of human sexual behavior. There are moral or ethical questions such as: Is homosexuality sexually acceptable? Should pornography be legalized? and Is it ever acceptable to have a sexual affair when you are married? These are all questions that must be dealt with in the context of your own conscience and society's mores.

RESOURCES

CALIFORNIA

University of California School of Medicine
924 Westwood Blvd., Suite 335
Los Angeles, CA 90024
(310) 825-0243
Codirectors: Joshua S. Golden, M.D.
            Anna Heinrich, Ph.D.
            Susan Price, Ph.D.
Patients Treated: Couples, Singles
Special Aspects: Treatment of dysfunctions secondary to physical illness or disability
Physician Training: yes

Center for Marital and Sexual Studies
5251 Los Altos Plaza
Long Beach, CA 90815
(310) 597-4425
Codirectors: William E. Hartman, Ph.D.
            Marilyn A. Fithian, B.A.
Patients Treated: Couples, Singles
Special Aspects: Two-week, ten-day or day treatment programs tailored to patients needs and financial means, preorgasmic woman's group
Physician Training: yes

The Institute for the Advanced Study of Human Sexuality
1523 Franklin St.
San Francisco, CA 94109
(415) 928-1133

Codirectors: Wardell B. Pomeroy, Ph.D.
            Maggi Rubanstein, R.N.
Patients Treated: Couples, Singles
Special Aspects: Treatment of homosexual and transsexual
            disorders; surrogates used when appropriate;
            weekend courses offered in human sexuality
Physician Training: yes

CONNECTICUT

Hartford Hospital
SEX THERAPY PROGRAM
Hartford, CT 06115
(203) 524-2396
Codirectors: Alan J. Wabrek, M.D.
            Carolyn P. Wabrek, M.Ed.
Patients Treated: Couples, Singles
Special Aspects: Medical evaluation for impotence
Physician Training: no

Yale-New Haven Hospital
DANA PSYCHIATRIC CLINIC
20 York St.
New Haven, CT 06504
(203) 785-4242
Director: M.T. Dreyfus, M.S.W.
Patients Treated: Couples, Singles
Special Aspects: Sex therapy in a psychotherapy modality
Physician Training: yes

DISTRICT OF COLUMBIA

Howard University Hospital
DEPARTMENT OF OB/GYN

2041 Georgia Ave., N.W.
Washington, DC 20059
(202) 865-6100
Director: William Brown, M.D.
Patients Treated: Couples, adolescents
Special Aspects: Problem pregnancies; surgical procedures re-
                lated to male and female reproductive sys-
                tems
Physician Training: yes

ILLINOIS

University of Chicago Hospital
SEXUAL DYSFUNCTION CLINIC
5841 S. Maryland Ave., Box 411
Chicago, IL 60637
(312) 702-1000

Cook County Hospital
SOCIAL EVALUATION CLINIC
1825 West Harrison
Chicago, IL 60612
(312) 633-6676
Patients Treated: Couples, singles
Special Aspects: Short-term treatment with one year follow-
                up; arthritic and other handicapped patients;
                hormonal tests, team approach to sex therapy
Physician Training: yes

American Association of Sex Education Counselors and Therapists
435 North Michigan, Suite 1717
Chicago, IL 60611
Special Aspects: Send $2.00 and a self-addressed stamped en-
                velope, AASECT will send to you a list of
                qualified professionals in your area.

Loyola University of Chicago
SEXUAL DYSFUNCTION CLINIC
2160 South First Ave.
Building 54, Room 205
Maywood, IL 60153
(708) 216-9000
Director: Domeena C. Renshaw, M.D.
Patients Treated: Married Couples only; singles in modified
program
Special Aspects: Sexological examinations given
Physician Training: yes

LOUISIANA

River Oaks Psychiatric Hospital
1525 River Oaks Road, West
New Orleans, LA 70123
(504) 734-1740
(800) 733-3242
Director: Dr. Mark Schwartz

MARYLAND

The Johns Hopkins University School of Medicine
SEXUAL BEHAVIORS CONSULTATION UNIT
600 N. Wolfe St.
Baltimore, MD 21205
(410) 955-3618
Director: Jon K. Meyer, M.D.
Patients Treated: Couples, singles, children, adolescents, el-
derly
Special Aspects: Treatment of intersex conditions, gender

identity disorders; postoperative and traumatic sexual dysfunctions
Physician Training: yes

MASSACHUSETTS

Beth Israel Hospital-Harvard Medical School
SEXUAL DYSFUNCTION UNIT
330 Brookline Ave.
Boston, MA 02215
(617) 735-2168
Codirectors: Norman S. Fartel, M.D.
            Ester G. Feuer, R.N.
Patients Treated: Couples, singles
Special Aspects: Sex and marital therapy for orthodox Jewish
                couples and singles, and for people with
                physical disabilities

MISSOURI

University of Missouri-Columbia School of Medicine
HUMAN SEXUALITY CLINIC
Clinic 6, Outpatient
Columbia, MO 65212
(314) 882-2511
Director: Joseph Lambert, M.D.
Patients Treated: Couples, singles
Special Aspects: Hypnosis, biofeedback
Physician Training: no

The Masters and Johnson Institute
4910 Forest Park Blvd.
St. Louis, MO 63108
(314) 361-2377

CoDirectors: William H. Masters, M.D.
            Virginia F. Johnson, D.Sc. (Hon)
Patients Treated: Couples only
Special Aspects: Treatment of homosexual dysfunction and
            dissatisfaction; infertility problems
Physician Training: yes

NEW YORK

Long Island Jewish-Hillside Medical Center
HUMAN SEXUALITY CENTER
7559 63rd Street
Glenoaks, NY 10014
(718) 470-7000
Director: Robert Marantz, M.D.
Patients Treated: Couples, singles
Physician Training: yes

Mt. Sinai School of Medicine
HUMAN SEXUALITY PROGRAM
Department of Psychiatry
1 Gustave L. Leavey Place
Box 1084
New York, NY 10029-6574
(212) 241-6634
Director: Raul C. Schlavl, M.D.
Patients Treated: Couples, singles
Special Aspects: Assessment of sexual problems associated
            with medical illnesses; nocturnal penile tu-
            mescence monitoring
Physician Training: yes

Cornell University College of Medicine
PAYNE WHITNEY CLINIC
New York Hospital
525 East 68th St.
New York, NY 10021

(212) 746-5454
Director: Helen Singer Kaplan, M.D.
Patients Treated: Couples, singles
Special Aspects: Short-term treatment model
Physician Training: yes

State University Hospital Downstate Medical Center
CENTER FOR HUMAN SEXUALITY
Department of Psychiatry
450 Clarkson, Box 1203
Brooklyn, NY 11203
(718) 270-1000
Director: Robert Dickes, M.D.
Patient Treated: Couple, singles
Physician Training: yes

NORTH CAROLINA

The John Reckless Clinic P.A.
Crossdalle Office Park
1816 Front St., Suite 310
Durham, NC 27705
(919) 383-1502
Director: John Reckless, M.D.
Patients Treated: Couples, singles
Physician Training: no

PENNSYLVANIA

University of Pennsylvania School of Medicine
MARRIAGE COUNCIL OF PHILADELPHIA
Division of Family Study
4025 Chestnut St.

Philadelphia, PA 19104
(215) 382-6680
Director: Harold I. Lief, M.D.
Patients Treated: Couples, singles
Special Aspects: Treatment of dysfunctional homosexual couples
Physician Training: yes

Temple University Medical School
MOSS REHABILITATION HOSPITAL
1200 West Tabor Rd.
Philadelphia, PA 19141
(215) 456-9900
Director: Dorothea Glass, M.D.
Patients Treated: Couples, singles, all ages
Physician Training: no

Hahnemann Medical College and Hospital
CENTER FOR FAMILIES IN TRANSITION
Outpatient Psychiatry
1427 Vine St., 8th Floor, Mail Stop 950
Philadelphia, PA 19102
(215) 762-7000
Director: Ilda V. Ficher, Ph.D.
Patient Treated: Couples, singles
Physician: yes

TENNESSEE

University of Tennessee Medical School
SEXUAL THERAPY CLINIC
Department of Psychiatry
66 N. Pauline, Suite 663
Memphis, TN 38105
(901) 577-4570
Director: Peter Hoon, Ph.D.

Patients Treated: Couples
Special Aspects: Main orientation toward women with sexual
                        problems; physiologic assessment via com-
                        puter, biofeedback
Physician Training: no

University of Tennessee Medical School
SPECIAL PROBLEMS UNIT
Department of Psychiatry
66 N. Pauline, Suite 663
Memphis, TN 38105
(901) 528-5489
Special Aspects: Sex offenders

VIRGINIA

The Johns Hopkins Medical Institutions / Fairfax Hospital
DEPARTMENT OF PSYCHIATRY
3300 Gallows Rd.
Falls Church, VA 22046
(703) 698-1110
Director: Thomas N. Wise, M.D.
Patients Treated: Couples, singles
Special Aspects: By referral only
Physician Training: no

WISCONSIN

Medical College of Wisconsin
DEPARTMENT OF PSYCHIATRY
9191 Watertown Plank Rd.
Milwaukee, WI 53226

Director: David B. Marcotte, M.D.
Patient Treated: Couples, singles
Special Aspects: Treatment of gender dysphoria
Physician Training: no

CHAPTER 9

AM I SCHIZOPHRENIC?

In 1911 the Swiss psychiatrist Eugen Bleuler first coined the term: "the group of schizophrenias." Since that time, despite disagreement among various scientists as to exactly what the condition refers to, the term has been commonly used in the fields of psychology and psychiatry.

Prior to that time, schizophrenia was thought of as "madness," "insanity," or "craziness." Now "schizophrenia" is a term used to describe an extremely complex condition which is the most disabling of all the major mental illnesses.

Because schizophrenia represents such a wide spectrum of disorders, it is difficult to make any generalizations about one particular type of schizophrenia. One useful distinction is the categorization of acute schizophrenia, which refers to the onset of severe psychotic symptoms. "Psychotic" refers to an individual's being out of touch with reality and being unable to separate the real from the unreal. Rarely do people have only one schizophrenic episode. Most have numerous episodes during a lifetime, yet lead relatively normal lives between the episodes.

The term "chronic schizophrenia" refers to individuals who never return fully to normal functioning. They typically require long-term treatment, including psychotropic medication to control their symptoms.

Approximately 1 million people in the United States will develop schizophrenia at some point during their lifetimes. This disorder affects women and men with equal frequency. Usually, the first symptoms of schizophrenia develop in the late teens and early twenties in men, and in the twenties or early thirties in women. Often preceding more severe symptoms are less obvious problems, such as social isolation, withdrawal, unusual speech, distorted thinking, and odd or eccentric behavior.

A DIFFERENT REALITY

Just as you and I view our worlds from our own perspectives, so schizophrenic people, too, have their own particular perceptions of reality. Unfortunately, the view of the schizophrenic is strikingly different from the reality shared by most people around them. A schizophrenic's world can appear distorted, changeable, and lacking in reliable landmarks that most of us use to anchor our reality. For example, to a schizophrenic, a solid wall may appear liquid, or a carpet may seem to be growing. When schizophrenics notice things changing that other people don't, they quickly become anxious and confused. To normal people, they often seem detached, distant, or preoccupied. A schizophrenic may sit for hours at a time, not moving or uttering a sound, or may move about incessantly, seem hypervigilant, alert, and paranoid.

HALLUCINATIONS

Perhaps the most frightening part of the schizophrenic's world is the phenomenon called "hallucination." When hallucinating, a person actually senses things that do not exist. Auditory hallucinations—hearing voices without knowing where they are coming from—are the most common. Usually, the voices that schizophrenics hear seem to be coming from outside of their heads. The voices are often described as carrying on a conversation, warning of impending dangers, or telling the schizophrenics what to do. But occasionally, visual hallucinations, in which the schizophrenic sees people or objects that other people don't see; or tactile hallucinations, in which the schizophrenic feels sensations that have no exterior source, are also experienced.

DELUSIONS

Delusions are faulty beliefs which are not subject to reason or evidence. Delusions are common symptoms of schizophrenia and can involve themes of persecution, in which the schizophrenic feels that other people are out to get him; or delusions of grandeur, in which the schizophrenic feels that he is extremely different or special from everyone else in some unrealistic way—for example, believing that he has the power to create an earthquake.

Veronica, a 32-year-old brunette, was trying to make sense of the voices she was hearing, and developed delusions (a set of faulty beliefs) that aliens were trying to communicate with her from an astral plane. She reasoned that since no one else was having these experiences, she must be a special person who was chosen by these aliens for some special purpose.

Perhaps more common are delusions of persecution, which are usually seen in paranoid schizophrenia. These are beliefs in which the schizophrenic wrongly believes that he is being harassed, cheated, spied on, poisoned, or conspired against.

DISORDERED THINKING

If the schizophrenic senses things that other people don't sense and believes things that are often ludicrous or absurd, it is only logical that his thinking will also be affected by this disorder. Schizophrenics often complain of not being able to think clearly. Thoughts may come and go so rapidly that they are not able to hold them or make sense of them. Schizophrenics are usually unable to concentrate for very long and are distracted easily.

Schizophrenics are unable to sort out what is relevant and not relevant to any particular situation. They may not be capable of connecting thoughts into logical sequences, and their thinking may become disorganized and fragmented. When schizophrenics try to articulate what is happening, their speech skips from topic to topic in a way that is confusing to others.

Other forms of distorted thinking common in schizophrenia include *thought broadcasting,* in which the schizophrenic believes that his own thoughts are broadcast outside his head into the external world so that other people can hear them; *thought insertion,* in which the schizophrenic feels that someone is forcing thoughts into his mind; *thought withdrawal,* in which the schizophrenic feels that his thoughts are being stolen; and *delusions of being controlled,* in which the schizophrenic feels his thoughts or actions are not his own, but are imposed on him by some outside force.

Other, less common forms of distorted thinking include *somatic delusions,* in which the schizophrenic feels his body is rotting or being eaten away; *religious delusions,* in which the schizophrenic feels that he is some remarkable religious figure; and *nihilistic delusions,* in which the schizophrenic feels that all is for nothing and that life is worthless and empty.

In addition to the thought-*content* problems just mentioned, the *form* of thought is also affected in schizophrenia. Often there is what is known as *loosening of associations,* in which the schizophrenic's ideas shift rapidly from one subject to a completely unrelated subject without his realizing that the two topics are unconnected. For instance, "I've got to get some milk for breakfast, the war in Vietnam is over now, and you could probably get that job yourself." Other thought-form problems, such as *neologisms,* in which the schizophrenic makes up his own words, or *perseveration,* in which he repeats the same word or phrase again and again may also occur.

The term *affect* refers to the expression of emotions. Typically, the schizophrenic will exhibit a blunting, flattening, or inappropriateness of affect. *Blunted affect* refers to a severe reduction in the intensity of the emotional expression, like the weary news anchorman droning on about events of the day. *Flat affect* indicates virtually no sign of emotional expression. Usually the voice is monotonous and the face has no expression, with an overall appearance that indicates nothing really matters. *Inappropriate affect* refers to exhibiting emotions which are clearly inconsistent with what the schizophrenic is talking about and feeling—for instance, laughing while discussing the death of a loved one. *Labile affect,* in which sudden and unpredictable changes in emotional expression—for example, from laughing to screaming to crying, is also seen.

SELF-CONCEPT

A schizophrenic often has trouble recognizing his own individuality and personality. Since a schizophrenic is often reacting to and desperately trying to cope with bizarre hallucinations, it is quite understandable that his sense of identity would be severely compromised.

DISTURBED VOLITION

In schizophrenia there is frequently a disruption of self-initiated behavior, which results in severe impairment in work and social relations. This usually takes the form of an utter inability to set goals and follow through on achieving them.

DISTURBED INTERPERSONAL RELATIONSHIPS

An inability to initiate and maintain close personal relationships is invariably seen in schizophrenia. This usually takes the form of withdrawal from family and friends and emotional detachment. The schizophrenic is often preoccupied with such sensory experiences as voices and visions which no one else can hear or see, and delusions, in which he tries to make sense of these phenomena.

At the opposite extreme, some schizophrenics may exhibit an overwhelming dependency on other people, intrude upon strangers, and fail to recognize the demands they make upon other people. One way or another, the schizophrenic's behavior usually makes other people feel uncomfortable and leads to their eventual withdrawal from the schizophrenic, which results in even more isolation.

BEHAVIOR

During the acute stage of schizophrenia, odd behavior is apparent. Schizophrenics may be seen talking to individuals who are not present, swat at things that are not there, or exhibit marked increases or decreases in reactions to an ordinary environment. One of the most severe forms of schizophrenic behavior is *catatonic posturing,* in which the schizophrenic maintains a mannequinlike rigidity for hours at a time.

SCHIZOPHRENICS CAN LOOK NORMAL

Just as normal people sometimes may feel or act in ways that resemble schizophrenia, so, too, can schizophrenics think and act in a normal fashion for extended periods of time. Being psychotic, or out of touch with reality, does not mean that the schizophrenic is living in a completely different world. However, there are areas of the schizophrenic's world that are not shared by others and have no basis in reality. For example, hearing a voice out of the air warning you that someone is spying on you is an experience clearly not shared by most people, yet it is only a distortion of one area of reality. The schizophrenic may, in fact, be aware of such facts as time, date, and world and personal events which are occurring around him.

CAUSES OF SCHIZOPHRENIA

Scientists have found no specific cause for schizophrenia. It appears that genetic factors produce a predisposition or vulnerability to schizophrenia, with environmental factors playing a triggering role. Thus far, no gene or biochemical defect has been isolated as responsible for schizophrenia. And no specific or stressful event in your environment can predict a schizophrenic episode.

It has been known for a long time that schizophrenia tends to run in families. Close relatives of schizophrenics are much more likely to develop schizophrenia than nonrelatives. Researchers have found that a child who has one schizophrenic parent has about a 10 percent chance of developing schizophrenia, while a child who has no schizophrenic parent has only a 1 percent chance.

Researchers determine the genetic versus environmental factors which determine disorders like schizophrenia by studying identical and fraternal twins. Twin studies involving schizophrenics have found that there is a 40 to 60 percent probability of an identical twin's developing schizophrenia if the other twin has it, while the fraternal twin of a schizophrenic has only about a 10 percent chance. These studies indicate that even with the identical genetic structure, only about half of the people with this disorder may be explained through genetic influences.

In Denmark, an exhaustive study was made of the mental health of children who were adopted from schizophrenic parents. These children were compared with adopted children whose biological parents have no history of mental illness. The comparison was also made of the rates of mental disorder among the biological relatives of the two groups of adoptees—one known to be schizophrenic and the other without a history of mental illness. The findings of the adoption studies have shown that being biologically related to a schizophrenic person increases the risk for schizophrenia, even when the related individuals have had little or no contact with each other.

Scientists agree that what is inherited is a *potential* to develop schizophrenia. Given a certain set of genetic factors interacting with environmental stressors, schizophrenia is more likely to occur. But, at this time, we do not know what genetic or enzyme defect is specifically responsible for this predisposition.

ARE THE PARENTS TO BE BLAMED?

Virtually all schizophrenia researchers in the 1990s agree that parents do not cause schizophrenia in their children. In the middle part of the twentieth century, there was a tendency for mental-health workers to blame parents for their children's disorders. In the early 1990s, this attitude is generally recognized as not only inaccurate, but actually counterproductive. Professionals are now trying to enlist family members to help the schizophrenic manage through a difficult and often unpredictable life.

RECENT RESEARCH ON SCHIZOPHRENIA

All of our experience and behavior occurs through a series of neurochemical reactions within the brain. Knowledge of brain chemistry is expanding rapidly in the search to find a cure for schizophrenia.

Neurotransmitters—substances that allow for communication between nerve cells—are likely to be involved in the onset of schizophrenia. It is probable that schizophrenia is associated with some imbalance in the neurochemical pathways within the brain. In fact, the effectiveness of such major tranquilizers as Haldol has been traced to how the drug affects these neurochemical pathways.

In the 1970s, research was assisted by computerized axial tomography (CAT scan), an X-ray technique for visualizing the living brain. Some studies using CAT scans have found that schizophrenic patients are more likely to have such abnormal brain structures as enlargement of the cavities in the interior of the brain compared to people who are normal. However, these abnormalities are not characteristic of all schizophrenic patients, nor do they occur only in schizophrenics.

Positron emission tomography (PET scan) is a technique which produces brain images by measuring metabolic activity of specific areas of the brain. While research is continuing in this field, PET scan results indicate that metabolic rates in certain areas of the schizophrenic's brain are different from those of the normal brain.

Magnetic resonance imaging (MRI) is a technique involving the precise measurement of brain structures based on the effects of the magnetic field on substances in the brain. RCBF (regional cerebral blood flow) involves inhaling a radioactive gas and monitoring its rate of disappearance from different areas of the brain to give information about the relative activity of the brain regions during various mental activities. Computerized electroencephalographs (EEGs) are brain wave tests that map electrical responses of the brain as it reacts to different types of information. While all of these imaging techniques are being used for research, none has been developed into a form of treatment.

TYPES OF SCHIZOPHRENIA

Schizophrenia is diagnosed along a scale from acute (short-term) to chronic (long-term). There are five basic types of schizophrenia.

Catatonic Schizophrenia

The hallmark of catatonic schizophrenia is severe impairment in behavior and functioning, which may involve such symptoms as a stuporous appearance, rigidity, uncontrollable excited behavior, and unusual posturing. The catatonic may go for hours, days, or even weeks at a time not uttering a sound. Such vegetative behavior may be interrupted suddenly by a frenetic episode of hyperactivity in which the patient runs about, talks incessantly, and appears incoherent.

Disorganized Type

The disorganized type of schizophrenia used to be known as hebephrenic schizophrenia. Its key features are a loosening of associations, severely disjointed behavior, incoherence, and bizarre or inappropriate emotional expression. Because of the severity of disorganization in thinking, this person does not have the mental wherewithal to even organize a system of delusions. The delusions of the disorganized type are often fragmentary and change from moment to moment. While the catatonic appears to be both physically and psychologically frozen, the disorganized type appears to ramble about purposelessly.

Paranoid Type

The hallmark of this paranoid schizophrenia is a preoccupation with one or more highly organized sets of delusions, with frequent auditory hallucinations related to a particular theme. Paranoid schizophrenics are able to organize their delusions, which are often attempts to make sense of their hallucinations. One schizophrenic told me during an evaluation that he felt pressure pushing in from the outside of his head, and made sense of this by developing the idea (delusion) that his mind was holding up a large dam at a hydroelectric power plant.

Excessive and unfocused anger, anxiety, argumentativeness, and violence are also commonly seen in paranoid schizophrenia. In an attempt to compensate for these strong feelings, paranoid schizophrenics often become extremely intense in trying to control themselves during interactions with other people. They look as if they are desperately trying to keep themselves and their worlds together.

Schizophrenia, Undifferentiated Type

The undifferentiated schizophrenic is a catch-all term used to describe schizophrenic disorders which do not meet the criteria for disorganized, catatonic, or paranoid types. Still, the hallmark features of schizophrenia, such as hallucinations, delusions, and disorganized behaviors, are apparent.

Residual Type

The residual type of schizophrenia represents a milder form of the disorder. There is an absence of prominent delusions, hallucinations, and grossly disorganized behavior. However, social withdrawal, inappropriate responses, eccentric behavior, illogical thinking, and a mild loosening of associations are likely.

PARANOID (DELUSIONAL DISORDERS)

Often confused with the schizophrenic disorders are a group of problems called *paranoid disorders*. The hallmark of paranoid disorders is the presence of a delusional system which is not quite bizarre, and which usually does not have hallucinations.

Auditory and visual hallucinations, if present at all, are not usually noticeable. A person with a paranoid disorder who does not have schizophrenia is likely to have a coherent and tightly organized system of beliefs which are not quite in sync with reality. There are five basic types of paranoid disorders:

Erotomanic Type

A central faulty belief of the erotomanic type is the delusion that he or she is loved by another person. The delusion usually concerns some idealized romantic love and some kind of spiritual union with a person whom the paranoid individual has little or no relationship with. The erotomanic individual may persistently telephone, write letters, send gifts, make unexpected visits, and even spy on the beloved. Usually the erotomanic keeps the delusions a secret.

Sometimes, people with this disorder run into trouble with the law due to their incessant efforts, which may be manifested as harassment of public figures. John Hinckley, Jr. showed signs of this disorder in his obsessive preoccupation with actress Jodie Foster.

Grandiose Type

The grandiose individual usually has a specific set of beliefs that he has some special secret, talent, or discovery which he may take to various governmental agencies. Another common theme in the grandiose type is believing that he or she are the unrecognized son or daughter of a famous person. Grandiose delusions may have a religious content, and in some cases can lead to disaster. The Reverend Jim Jones, leader of the People's Temple cult, was an example of how religious grandiosity can lead to tragedy. In November 1978 he forced 911 followers in Jonestown, Guyana to commit suicide by drinking cyanide-laced Kool-Aid.

Jealous Type

Probably one of the most common types of paranoia is the jealous type. People with this disorder are convinced that their spouses or lovers are being unfaithful even though they have little or no evidence to support this belief. The perceived or imagined infidelity becomes the main source of emotional investment in the jealous person's life. He or she may spy on the lover or spouse, hire a private detective to follow them around, or make farfetched or illogical connections of a perceived relationship with someone else. Recently, a patient who has paranoid jealousy informed me that he was sure his wife and his best friend were having an affair because while his wife had gone to a birthday party, his best friend was not at home. Therefore, they must have been together. Often these individuals make desperate attempts to restrict the movement of the spouse or lover and insist that he or she never leave without supervision of some kind. Jealous types can be extremely dangerous and have been known to physically attack the spouse, lover, or perceived object of affection.

Somatic Type

Somatic delusions refer to distorted beliefs about one's body. Usually the somatic paranoid individual is convinced that he has a strange physical problem such as infestation of insects on or in the skin, internal parasites, parts of the body that are rotting away, parts of the body that are ugly or misshapen, or parts of the body that are not working at all.

Persecutory Type

The persecutory type of paranoia is the most common. The persecutory-type paranoid feels that he is being cheated, spied upon, followed, poisoned, drugged, harassed, or talked about behind his back. Social slights, such as forgetting to say hello or return a phone call, may be incorporated into this individual's delusional system, and you may become his enemy. Such people are characterized by anger and resentment, and eventually they may resort to violence against those whom they believe have hurt them.

Typically, paranoid disorders, if not of the schizophrenic type, begin much later in life and usually occur between the ages of 40 and 55.

Impairment of daily functioning, such as job and personal care, is usually slight. Such individuals often live out their lives without their friends or coworkers realizing the true nature of their illness. It is only when their delusional system is tripped by some unwitting act and the paranoid individual engages in bizarre behavior that atten tion is called to the disorder.

True paranoid disorders are extremely rare. The prevalence in the population is estimated to be somewhere around 0.03 percent.

Schizophrenia Questionnaire

Since schizophrenia represents such a broad spectrum of disorders, the questionnaire for schizophrenia is much longer than any of the other diagnostic entities in this book.

Obviously, the most apparent problem with diagnosing yourself as schizophrenic is the probability that if you have this disorder, you may be unable to read and comprehend the test. On the other hand, if not exhibiting an acute phase of the disorder, you may look back over the course of your life and find that some of these questions apply to you.

This questionnaire is more likely to be useful in helping determine whether friends, loved ones, or family members may be suffering from this serious disorder so that you can get them the professional help that they need.

Directions: Answer the following questions as honestly as possible. Try not to deny or minimize problems that apply to you, but do not exaggerate or answer yes to questions that do not apply to you, or how you really feel. Also, make sure that any positive responses to these questions are not the result of either using or withdrawing from drugs or alcohol.

Key Questions

1. Have you ever heard voices without knowing where they're coming from or seen things, people, or animals around you no one else can see?
2. Have you ever felt that your body or mind was being secretly controlled against your will?
3. Have you ever felt that others wanted to hurt you because you have some special secrets or powers?
4. Have you ever had odd, peculiar, or strange things happen in which you felt your mind was playing tricks on you?

If you answered no to questions 1–4, stop here. You are not likely to be schizophrenic.

5. If you answered yes to any of the above questions, did these events happen even though you were not drinking or taking drugs, or withdrawing from these substances?
6. Did these unusual experiences happen on and off for at least several days at a time?

If you answered no to questions 5 or 6, stop here. The odds are your problems are drug or alcohol related, or a temporary psychotic episode.

Interpersonal Significance

7. Did these unusual experiences (questions 1–4) cause you significant discomfort or distress in your life?
8. Did these experiences interfere with your education, your occupation, or your work around your home?
9. Did these problems cause your family to worry about you or cause you conflict with your family?
10. Did these problems interfere with your friendships or social life?

11. Did these experiences (hallucinations, beliefs of being controlled, or feelings that other people were out to get you) ever get you in trouble with the authorities?
12. Did you ever receive any type of treatment or medication for these problems?
13. Were you ever placed in a psychiatric hospital because of these problems?

Adjunctive Questions

Group I

Did you ever:
14. Feel that someone was using secret devices to control your body or your mind?
15. Hear voices which appear to come out of the air that no one else around you could hear?
16. See people or animals around you that no one else could see?
17. Feel that someone was trying to force thoughts into your mind through strange or unusual methods?
18. Feel that a person or group of people were plotting against you because you had some special powers?
19. Feel that your thoughts were somehow being taken away from you against your will?
20. Feel that you had been chosen to do something extraordinary or secret by some special force or power?
21. Believe that something strange or terrible was happening to your body or your mind (for instance, your intestines were rotting away, your brain was disintegrating, or you were infested with parasites)?
22. Feel that other people thought you were homosexual even though you were not?
23. Believe that you were receiving messages from outer space, an astral plane, the TV, the radio, or from someone else through ESP?
24. Believe that you actually have the power to perform miracles?
25. Feel that thoughts were somehow being inserted or forced into your mind against your will?
26. Notice that unusual signs had special meaning for you (for in-

stance, the weather report had some special significance only you recognized)?

27. Notice that other people could read your mind?
28. Notice that the world and people seem to be strange, unreal, or dreamlike?
29. Notice that the thoughts inside your head were so loud that people could actually hear them, even though you were not talking?
30. Notice that you had stopped being real, and felt as if you were turning into something else?
31. Notice that something seemed to be blocking or stopping your thoughts against your will?
32. Feel bothered by your mind suddenly going blank and resisting further thoughts?
33. Notice that a voice inside your head kept repeating your thoughts like an echo?
34. Hear voices inside your head that seemed to talk with each other and seemed to have a life of their own?
35. Hear voices inside your head that talked about what you're doing or thinking and seemed to have a life of their own?
36. Hear voices inside of your head that tried to tell you what to do, which seemed to have a life of their own? (This voice inside your head does not refer to the self-talk phenomenon, in which you say things to yourself like, "I have to go to the bathroom," "I wonder what's for dinner tonight," or "I think I'll go play golf." It is an ego-alien voice which does not come from your intention.)
37. Feel as if parts of your body were missing?
38. Have other people frequently tell you that the way you talked was crazy and that they could make no sense of it?
39. Did you ever notice that other people seemed bothered or upset by the way you talked?

Group II

Did you ever:
40. Feel worried because other people were talking about you behind your back or laughing at you?

41. Feel afraid that someone or something was secretly out to kill you or hurt you?
42. Feel that other people were trying to take unfair advantage of you?
43. Feel that someone was out to get you?
44. Feel that someone was spying on you?
45. Feel as if someone was trying to poison you?
46. Feel that you could have been much more successful in life if other people hadn't had it in for you?
47. Feel that some group or organization was out to secretly take over the country?

Group III

48. Did any of the previously mentioned problems (1–47) start before you were 45 years old?
49. Have you always been single?
50. Before these problems (1–47) started, would you describe yourself as a shy and withdrawn person who had difficulty making friends?
51. Before these symptoms (1–47) started happening to you, did you have trouble keeping up with your schoolwork or holding down jobs which you were qualified to do?
52. Have any of your close relatives—mother, father, or siblings—ever been diagnosed as having a schizophrenic disorder?
53. During the year before you started having these symptoms (1–47), were you drinking heavily or taking drugs?
54. Have you noticed that your life has gone pretty much straight downhill since you started having these problems?
55. Have these problems bothered you off and on for six months or more at at a time?
56. Have you ever taken medication to stop these problems from happening?

Chronological Questions

57. How old were you when you first noticed any of the problems mentioned in Questions 1–47?

58. How old were you when you last noticed any of these prob-
    lems?
59. Have you noticed any of these problems in the past month?
60. Have you noticed any of these problems in the last two years?

Scoring: In order to meet the scoring criteria for a schizophrenic
disorder, the following is necessary:
1. At least one question answered true in questions 1–4.
2. No to questions 5 and 6.
3. At least one item answered yes in Group I or II.
4. At least two items marked yes in Group III.
5. Item 55 must be marked yes.

   The chronology questions 57–60 give a time frame for the disorder. If you once had these problems but have not experienced them
for the past two years, your schizophrenia is probably in remission
(not active), or you may have had some other disorder which has
been resolved.
   If you or your loved ones meet the criteria for a schizophrenic
disorder, it is very important to seek qualified professional help as
soon as possible. But remember that a number of nonpsychotic
problems can cause schizophrenic-like behavior. Heavy dosages of
alcohol, amphetamines, hallucinogens, or even marijuana can produce schizophrenic-like symptoms. Undergoing a period of extreme
stress or pressure can lead to unusual behavior without indicating the
presence of an underlying schizophrenic disorder. Even excessive
sleeplessness or very high doses of caffeine can produce hallucinations and delusions.

CASE HISTORIES

Jack was a 42-year-old transient who was referred to me by a college
counselor after informing the counselor while scheduling some

classes at the community college that he was having strong urges to rape college coeds.

In my first interview with Jack, I found that he was a man who had been a drifter all of his life. At first his thinking seemed clear, but as he talked, I began to have trouble following what he said. Then it became apparent that Jack was engrossed in a delusion system of sadistic sexual fantasies. He told me that he believed a number of young women from colleges around the United States were being kidnapped and taken to South America. They then had holes cut in their throats, and their captors would put a straw in and suck out all their blood.

Jack's mother had been diagnosed as having a schizophrenic disorder, paranoid type. She would routinely neglect and abuse Jack while he was a child. On one occasion, one of her boyfriends apparently tried to kill Jack by firing three shots at him as he was running away. Although Jack had a lot of anger towards his mother, he reported that he frequently heard her voice calling his name and telling him to rape or murder certain women. Jack realized that this was wrong and thought that the real people he should be killing were the ones in South America who were drinking the blood of the young women.

In short, Jack felt that his behavior was being controlled by a dead person (his mother), and had a tightly organized delusional system involving people in South America kidnapping and killing American women. Jack's delusional system turned out to represent a projection of his own feelings of hostility and rage towards women.

On an emotional level, Jack's affect was initially quite stilted. He smiled a lot, and there was excessive tension on his face. He appeared to be so brittle in his bodily movements that it looked as if he might break. He laughed with a weird tenseness when describing the ritualistic killings he believed were occurring in South America. Then, suddenly, his demeanor became one of excessive anger, and he announced that certain people deserved to be killed.

Obviously Jack had been unable to hold down any job for very long. He had been unable to attend college after his first semester and had drifted from job to job around the country. He had no close relationships or friendships, and had written off his family as not only uncaring, but potentially murderous.

Jack went on to tell me that his first hospitalization occurred at the age of 18, when he thought that other students and teachers were constantly talking about him and plotting how to get rid of him.

Jack has a classic schizophrenic disorder, paranoid type.

Surprisingly, I was able to establish rapport with Jack despite his delusions. The turning point in Jack's therapy was his allowing me to refer him to a psychiatrist for treatment with Haldol, a neuroleptic medication which is often very effective in controlling hallucinations and delusions.

Within one week, Jack's thought processes were clear and coherent. He realized his previous beliefs about the kidnapping of American women were bizarre. He reported no longer hearing the voice of his dead mother telling him to rape and murder women.

After four additional months of medication and therapy, Jack established a cordial relationship with a woman whom he began to date.

But Jack and I both knew that the possibility of relapse, even on medication, was 50 percent. As is standard in the treatment of most schizophrenic patients, I educated him about the early warning signs of an acute schizophrenic episode, and he agreed to call me or his psychiatrist at the first sign of such an episode. Under this plan, Jack functioned well for two years, completed his BA degree, and moved back east.

Anita is a 26-year-old amphetamine addict. I was asked to evaluate Anita by the medical director of a drug-rehab unit to determine whether she was simply drug addicted or schizophrenic.

When I began talking with Anita, she told me that her mind had been playing bizarre tricks on her. She said that last night, while she was looking out a window of her hospital room, she suddenly saw the face of a gypsy superimposed on her reflection. This startled her, and she said that the face did not go away no matter how hard she tried to make it disappear. Later that night, when she was trying to sleep, she reported hearing someone calling her name very clearly. She began looking about her room, but soon realized that no one was there. Anita became frightened and confused and thought that she may be tormented by a dead spirit. At this point, a delusional system began to set in to try to explain Anita's hallucinations.

The next morning, when Anita woke up, she saw, heard, and felt a swarm of bees around her bed. She began swatting at them with noticeable intensity and actually felt herself hitting some. The nursing staff was called and calmed her down with a shot of a major tranquilizer.

During my history taking with Anita, she told me that she had been strung out on amphetamines since the age of 13. She had never gone more than two days without using crank. She was now on her third day of detox and was suffering from acute amphetamine withdrawal and amphetamine-induced hallucinations.

With extensive reassurance from the nursing staff and daily counseling, Anita was able to withstand the frightening symptoms she experienced while she withdrew from amphetamines.

Despite hallucinations, delusions, and bizarre behavior, Anita was not schizophrenic. She was suffering from a drug-induced, temporary psychotic episode.

After two weeks, with no medication and a lot of reassurance, Anita's behavior had returned to normal.

Many times the schizophrenic patient can be his or her own worst enemy by not complying with treatment recommendations.

Veronica, the 32-year-old diagnosed paranoid schizophrenic discussed earlier, was referred to me for a court-ordered custody evaluation to determine whether she was competent to take care of her 12- and 4-year-old children. Veronica had been given custody of her children with the stipulation that she would see a psychiatrist on a biweekly basis and take her neuroleptic medication to control her symptoms.

Veronica told me that her problems began when she was about 16 years old and started hearing voices without knowing where they came from. She reported that the voices were not like the voice you hear inside of your head that tells you what to make for breakfast or what time to go to school, but voices that came out of the air, as if someone else was actually in the room. Veronica said that the voices were telling her that she had been put on earth for a very special purpose—to teach people to love each other—and she was the only one who could accomplish this goal. She told me that people on some astral plane had instructed her to tell other people about them so they would know that there are higher forces in the universe.

Veronica's behavior never became outrageous. She knew that when she talked to the people on the astral plane other people would think she was crazy, so she had these conversations in private.

Most notable was a blunted and eventually flattened quality to Veronica's appearance. She had a waxy, expressionless quality to her

face, and her movements appeared to be in slow motion and somewhat mechanical.

When I evaluated Veronica, she had been off her medication for
about one week and reported that she was feeling better. After seeing her the second week, I agreed with her. Her behavior appeared
to be getting more and more normal.

I recommended close monitoring of Veronica's visitation with her
children over a trial period of three months to see whether her
schizophrenia was actually in check. Unfortunately, after two
months, Veronica had an acute episode in which she was found
standing in the middle of a busy intersection preaching what people
on the astral plane had commanded her to do.

Obviously, such behavior is not consistent with competent parenting. But miraculously, Veronica's story did have a happy ending. All
the psychologists, psychiatrists, and social workers who had observed Veronica for the past three years noticed that when she was
on her neuroleptic medication, she never exhibited schizophrenic
behavior, nor did she ever abuse or neglect her children. In fact,
Veronica was thought of as a warm, responsible, caring mother. With
my recommendation, the court decided to give Veronica a trial custody period provided she come in for biweekly Prolixin shots.
Prolixin is a long-lasting neuroleptic, which typically keeps schizophrenic symptoms in check for at least two weeks at a time. If Veronica failed to show up for her appointment, a social worker would
remove the children from her custody immediately.

I kept track of Veronica for two-and-one-half years and had numerous opportunities to talk with both of her children. The plan
worked extremely well. Like Jack, Veronica was informed about the
warning signs of an acute episode of schizophrenia, which could
occur even if she was taking Prolixin. Only once during that two-
and-one-half-year period did Veronica experience the warning signs
of a developing schizophrenic episode. And, as agreed to by the
courts, during this time her parents took custody of the children for a
few days while Veronica went into a short-term psychiatric hospital
to get stabilized.

I recently saw Veronica's daughter, who told me that things had
worked out fairly well with her, her mom, and her younger brother.
She related that her mother had had her ups and downs, but basically
provided a good upbringing for her and her brother. She reported

that she is married, still visits her mother every week, and that her little brother would soon be graduating from high school.

Richard is a 25-year-old, single unemployed male who only recently moved out of his parents' house into his own apartment. Richard has been collecting disability insurance ever since he had a nervous breakdown while at college. Richard told me that he felt other people were talking about him incessantly, and thought he was homosexual even though he was not. Richard had developed a sensitivity to nonverbal behavior and frequently thought that people were mocking him or making sexual advances towards him. When Richard checked this out with some of his friends, they did not notice the behavior and started thinking that Richard was kind of strange. Before long, he had alienated all of his friends with his disquieting beliefs, and was considered by most people to be peculiar. This social ostracism magnified Richard's suspiciousness, sensitivity, and paranoia, and his condition got much worse.

Richard denied ever hearing voices without knowing where they came from or seeing people or animals around him that other people couldn't see. He did, however, report some perceptual distortions in which he saw wavy outlines around tree branches and a wavy outline around a baseboard in his room. Richard told me that the perceptual distortion or outlines did not bother him much, but other people talking about him and mocking him really did. In one of our sessions, I went for a walk with Richard and confirmed his delusions. Sure enough, Richard felt that everyone that drove by us was making lewd sexual comments about him and about us being a homosexual couple.

At an emotional level, Richard's presentation appeared to be more or less normal. He would get angry and irritated rather easily, but most of the time presented a normal emotional facade. On one occasion he was sad because his aunt had died, and on another occasion he was happy because he got a new car.

Richard was able to meet his basic needs of daily living such as providing a home for himself, managing his money, maintaining his personal hygiene, and preparing meals for himself. Richard's disorder most strongly affected the social and occupational areas of his life. He had absolutely no friends, felt too threatened to go to college, and was too paranoid even to go to a group for paranoid patients which I recommended to him.

On one occasion, I must have tripped Richard's delusional system inadvertently because he quit coming into therapy for over a month and half. After repeated phone calls, I was able to coax Richard back into therapy, and his behavior has again begun to stabilize.

While not having a schizophrenic disorder, Richard has a paranoid disorder, persecutory type.

HOPE FOR THE FUTURE

Since schizophrenia is not a single condition and its causes are not clearly known, current treatment methods focus on reducing the symptoms of schizophrenia and lessening their severity.

Neuroleptics—antipsychotic medications—are the biggest breakthrough in the treatment of schizophrenia. Prior to the mid–1950s, schizophrenics were looked at as hopelessly insane. But now neuroleptic medications reduce the severity and duration of hallucinations and delusions and allow the patient to function much more effectively and appropriately. While antipsychotic drugs such as Haldol, Melaril, stelazine, Prolixin, and thorazine are the best treatments currently available, they do not cure the schizophrenic disorder or ensure that there will be no further psychotic episodes.

Antipsychotic medications are particularly effective in treating auditory, visual, and tactile hallucinations and delusions. A large majority of schizophrenic patients show immediate improvement upon taking these neuroleptics.

During my internship at a large inner-city hospital, I had the opportunity to observe an acutely schizophrenic man who was in a three-point restraint, talking to people who were not there and picking what he thought to be imaginary bugs out of the air and eating them. The man was confused, disoriented, and did not know what city he was in or even what year it was. Through a process called rapid tranquilization (intravenous injections of Haldol every thirty minutes), within two hours the patient was oriented to where he was and what was going around him, completely free of hallucinations, and out of restraints.

Sometimes patients and families become worried about the addic-

tive potential of antipsychotic medications used to treat schizophrenia. Researchers have found that antipsychotic or neuroleptic medications did not produce a high or euphoric feeling or a strong
physical dependence as some other drugs do. Therefore, their addiction potential is quite low. Furthermore, the present trend in psychiatry favors using the lowest dosage possible to allow the schizophrenic person to function independently.

Another misconception about antipsychotic drugs is that they represent a type of mind control in which the patient loses the ability to
think for himself. Quite the opposite, antipsychotic drugs do not
control a person's thoughts, but instead help him differentiate between the psychotic symptoms and the real world so that he can
control his own thoughts.

Antipsychotic drugs also reduce the risk of future psychotic episodes in recovering patients. With continued treatment, about 40 percent of recovering schizophrenics will suffer relapses within two
years of discharge from the hospital. Yet this is far better than the 80
percent or more who suffer a relapse when medication is discontinued. In short, in most cases, antipsychotic medication does not prevent relapses, but it does reduce their frequency.

One of the biggest problems in helping schizophrenic patients
maintain normal functioning is getting them to take their antipsychotic medication. This often requires close supervision, and many
schizophrenic patients will actually stash their medication in their
cheeks or hide it under their tongue and feign swallowing it. For
patients who are especially resistant to taking their antipsychotic
medication, a long-acting injectable antipsychotic medication, such
as Prolixin, may be used on a biweekly basis.

Another major concern about antipsychotic drugs is their side effects. In the early stages of antipsychotic drug treatment, the schizophrenic patient may be troubled by restlessness, drowsiness, muscle
spasms, tremor, blurring of vision, and dry mouth. Usually these side
effects can be corrected by lowering the dosage of the medication or
offering patients other medications, such as cogentin, to control the
side effects.

Perhaps the most serious long-term side effect of antipsychotic
medication is tardive dyskinesia (TD), a disorder characterized by
involuntary movements usually affecting the mouth, lips, tongue,
and occasionally the trunk and other parts of the body. Often smack-
ing of the lips or rolling of the mouth indicates the likelihood that

tardive dyskinesia has begun. Tardive dyskinesia typically occurs in about 15 to 20 percent of the patients who have been receiving antipsychotic drugs for many years, but TD can also occur in patients who have been taking these drugs for shorter periods of time.

For patients who develop TD, the use of psychotropic medications must be reevaluated. It basically comes down to a cost-benefit analysis: is the "cost" of TD worth the elimination of hallucinations and delusions and other bizarre behavior. Recent research suggests that TD, which was once considered irreversible, often improves when patients continue to receive antipsychotic medications.

PSYCHOSOCIAL TREATMENTS

While antipsychotic drugs have proven to be very effective in reducing hallucinations, delusions, and bizarre behavior, they do not relieve all of the symptoms of schizophrenia, especially those in the psychosocial area of the schizophrenic's life. Even when schizophrenic patients are free of symptoms, they may still have a difficult time establishing and maintaining relationships with others. Because schizophrenic patients frequently become ill during the critical career-forming years of life (ages 18 to 35), they are less likely to have a career or means of personal support.

While psychosocial treatments are of limited value for people with acute schizophrenic episodes, psychosocial-therapy approaches are very important for individuals who have been stabilized on medication. These approaches work on improving the patient's functioning as a social being, whether in the hospital, the community, at home, or on the job.

One aspect of this approach is rehabilitation: the wide array of nonmedical interventions for people with schizophrenia. Rehabilitation programs emphasize social and vocational training and typically include counseling, on-the-job training, cognitive or thinking strategies, problem solving, money-management skills, how to use public transportation, social-skills instruction, and training in independent living.

Individual psychotherapy is another aspect of psychosocial treatment. By sharing his experiences with a trained, empathetic professional and by talking about his world with someone who is outside of it, the schizophrenic patient may gradually come to understand more about himself and his problems. The therapist can also help the patient sort out real from unreal and distorted versions of reality.

The National Institute for Mental Health reports that recent studies indicate that supportive, reality-oriented therapy is generally of much more benefit to schizophrenic outpatients than more probing, psychoanalytic, or insight-oriented therapy.

Family therapy is also a crucial part of the multifaceted approach to treating the schizophrenic. It is essential to teach the schizophrenic's family what to expect from the patient. If the family members have a clear understanding of what schizophrenia is and what may happen, they can easily be prepared to deal with it. They can also support the schizophrenic, while gently challenging and confronting him on his interpretation of reality which is not consistent with their own.

Group therapy is another method used to treat schizophrenics. Typically, anywhere from six to twelve patients and one or two trained therapists conduct these groups. They focus on learning from the experiences of others and testing the patient's perceptions against those of others. Correcting distorted thinking and maladaptive behavior by means of feedback from other members of the group often goes a long way towards helping the schizophrenic learn behaviors that are appropriate.

Self-help groups are another way in which schizophrenics attempt to help themselves. Although not led by professional therapists, self-help groups for schizophrenics are therapeutic because members—usually ex-patients or family members of schizophrenics—provide continuing mutual support as well as the comfort that comes from knowing they are not alone in the problems they face. Reassurance from someone who has been through the problem of schizophrenia and recovered from it successfully is sometimes more therapeutic than work with a trained professional.

Family- and peer-support and advocacy groups are now very active and provide useful information and assistance for patients and their families.

Sometimes, even with the most thorough multifaceted treatment approach and psychotropic medications, relapses occur, and the patient requires residential care. Prolonged hospitalization is now much less common than it was twenty or thirty years ago. In the 1960s, approximately 300,000 schizophrenic patients were residents in state and county mental institutions. Many of these patients were committed to these institutions for most of their lives.

The new trend in residental care is towards brief, short-term, goal-directed relief from acute schizophrenic episodes. Short-term residental care in a well-staffed facility can give patients the few days to several weeks they may need to recover from stressful situations and reorganize themselves so that they can be released back into the community. Newer programs for schizophrenics, such as partial hospitalization (day care or night care) or halfway houses, are keeping hundreds of thousands of schizophrenics out of mental hospitals and allowing them to function adequately within the community.

Despite being the most frightening of all psychiatric disorders, schizophrenia is manageable, and hundreds of thousands of patients who in the 1950s would have been committed to a lifetime in a mental institution, are now living reasonably productive lives within their communities and with their families.

For further information on schizophrenia and other severe mental illnesses, contact the following advocacy groups:

The National Alliance for the Mentally Ill
1901 North Fort Myer Drive, Suite 500
Arlington, VA 22209
(703) 524–7600

National Mental Health Association
1021 Prince Street
Alexandria, VA 22314–2971
(703) 684–7722

The National Mental Health Consumers Association
311 South Juniper Street
Room 902
Philadelphia, PA 19107
(215) 735–2465

CHAPTER 10

IS IT ALZHEIMER'S DISEASE?

Samuel is a 75-year-old retired middle-management executive. He has two daughters, ages 25 and 30, who have become concerned about his apparent failing memory. Louise, Samuel's older daughter, recently noticed that her dad went to the post office on Sunday morning, thinking it was Monday. About two weeks earlier, Sandy, Samuel's younger daughter, overheard him telling his wife that when he went to go play golf with one of his friends, he forgot to bring his clubs along.

Armed with recent articles and literature about Alzheimer's disease, Sandy and Louise feel quite certain that their dad is suffering from the illness. They immediately call their mom and set up a lunch appointment to discuss their dad's future.

Confused and upset by her daughters' distressing comments, Sam's wife, Betty, begins to think about the problems Sam has been having with his memory. As she looks back, Betty can remember that Sam's once-sharp mind is not nearly as clear as it used to be. She remembers that he used to be able to recall names of every one of the sales representatives in his company and all of his major accounts. In the past few years, Betty told her daughters, Sam sometimes has trouble remembering the names of people he has known all of his life.

Samuel's daughters know enough about Alzheimer's disease to really upset themselves and their mother. They point out that Alzheimer's is a chronic, irreversible brain disease that usually leads to death within seven to ten years of the initial diagnosis. The disease develops as a slow, insidious decline in general intellectual functioning, beginning initially with memory impairment. Betty fearfully recounts the sequence of events that led up to the nursing-home stay and eventual death of her friend's mother, whose autopsy revealed the presence of neuritic tangles and neurofibrillary plaques characteristic of Alzheimer's disease.

Based on their information, the three women decide that their husband and father is clearly suffering from Alzheimer's disease and before long will need to be placed in a nursing home.

When I interviewed Samuel, he found the whole sequence of events quite amusing. "Sure, I'm not quite as sharp as I was when I was twenty-five or thirty, but there's nothing wrong with my mind that's not going on with anyone else my age."

After a careful mental-status examination, I tested Sam's coordination and found it to be age-appropriate and normal. I then administered a series of intellectual and memory tests to determine his level of cognitive functioning compared to his age mates. Sam's overall IQ tested at 115, which is in the bright-normal range, and his memory quotient turned out to be 112, which is also clearly above average. A review of Sam's history indicated that he had always been an above-average student and worker, and his present level of intellectual and memory functioning was consistent with the history he, his daughters, and his wife gave me.

No, Sam wasn't suffering from Alzheimer's disease. He had become an unwitting target of an often-hysterical overreaction to recent highly publicized accounts of that ailment.

Let's face it. As we get older, we are not quite as mentally quick as we were in our prime. But, the gradual decline in intellectual power is far less than most people realize.

To understand this concept, let's look at one of the best-known of all the tests of intelligence, the Wechsler Adult Intelligence Scale-Revised. This test, known as the WAIS-R, has been standardized on hundreds of thousands of people and administered to millions. The WAIS-R provides an accurate overall estimate of the level of intellectual functioning. It is divided into two major categories which measure verbal and performance intelligence. The verbal subscales consist of a series of six tests measuring such intellectual abilities as long-term memory and general fund of information, short-term memory and concentration capacity, word knowledge, arithmetic reasoning ability, degree of socialization and social judgment, and concept-formation ability. The performance scales measure the ability to visually differentiate essential from nonessential details, the ability to understand and arrange pictures into a meaningful sequence, the ability to analyze and synthesize a series of geometric blocks into a meaningful design, perceptual and organizational ability, and speed of mental operation through hand-eye coordination.

Each subtest has a raw score, which is converted into a scaled score. The scale scores are then combined, to yield the sum of scaled scores in both the verbal and performance dimensions of intelligence. The sum of these scaled scores for verbal and performance is then divided by the patient's age and yields three scores: verbal IQ, performance IQ, and full-scale IQ.

To get an idea of the change of intellectual functioning over time, let's look at how a person with an average IQ score of 100 would do relative to himself taking this same test over the course of a lifetime.

At the age of 17, our hypothetical person would have a sum of scaled scores equaling 98, which converts to an IQ score of 100. At the age of 19, he would need a sum of scaled scores equaling 101 to achieve the same full-scale IQ score of 100.

At the age of 24, our average person would need to significantly increase his sum of scaled scores to 111 to achieve the same average IQ score of 100.

At the age of 34, he would need a sum of scaled scored equaling 114 to have an IQ score of 100.

Practically speaking, the actual performance on the WAIS-R intelligence test has shown that overall intellectual power seems to increase between the ages of 17 and 34. Then a shift occurs. At the age of 44, our average person needs a sum of scaled scores of 108 to achieve a full-scale IQ score of 100. This is six points lower than that needed by our 34-year-old.

At the age of 54, he would need a sum of scaled scores equaling 103, which is about the same as his IQ sum of scaled scores he achieved when he was 19 years old, but somewhat less than his peak performance on the test, which hypothetically occurred when he was around 34.

By the time our hypothetical person is 64 years old, he needs sum of scaled scores equaling only 96 to have an IQ score of 100. This is only 4 points below the sum of scaled scores required by our 19-year-old to have an IQ score of 100, and falls within such a small variation that it is known as the standard error of measurement for this test. The standard error of measurement is a statistical term defined as the number of points above or below the test score that the score indicates. A standard error of measurement of 4 points means that the score could be 4 points higher or lower than indicated.

By the age of 69, the sum of scaled scores required for an IQ score of 100 has dropped to 90. This sum of scaled scores is still within the normal range for a 19-year-old, although near the bottom of that range.

By the age of 74, our hypothetical person needs a sum of scaled scores equaling only 81 to achieve a full-scale IQ score of 100. This is obviously considerably lower than any of the previous sum of scaled scores, and would in fact be considered in the below-average range if the person taking this test was 34 years old. But are we really getting more ignorant as we get older?

One of the ways to understand the decrease in apparent measured intelligence is to realize that as people get older they do not move as fast, which clearly affects the mechanics of test taking and, therefore, the score on the performance scales of the IQ test. For example, our average person should have a peak performance IQ score at or around the age of 34. The sum of scaled scores: 52, which equals a performance I.Q. score of 100 at 24, drops 21 points to 31, to achieve a performance I.Q. score of 100 at the age of 74. In short, a 75 year old can score 21 points lower than a 24 year old and have the same performance I.Q. score.

The verbal IQ score, on the other hand, is much more consistent over time. The hypothetical peak of measured verbal subscales for a verbal IQ of 100 is 64 and, according to WAIS-R age tables, occurs at or near the age of 34. But at the age of 64 our average person needs only a sum of verbal scaled scores equaling 57 to achieve a verbal IQ score of 100. This is only 7 points from the score in his verbal intellectual prime at the age of 34, and is, for most intents and purposes, not really noticeable.

In short, statistical data from the best-established of all adult intelligent scales shows us that while many aspects of motor performance in intellectual functioning may decline substantially with age, the verbal aspect of intelligence remains largely intact, even into very old age.

When assessing intelligence, experience is often overlooked. Although older people may not be as intellectually "quick" as younger ones, they have a vastly superior fund of information. The recognition of the need for life experience as well as knowledge or information may account for the required minimum age of 35 for the U.S. presidency. Nearly all the presidents were over 50, and many were in their 60s or 70s. We all know elderly people who remain intellectually and physically active well into their 70s, 80s, or even 90s. Margaret Mead, Arturo Toscanini, Duke Ellington, Pablo Picasso, and Bertrand Russell were intellectually and artistically productive after age 75, with Picasso and Russell remaining mentally active well into their 90s.

Given the greater knowledge and experience base in older people, some psychologists have suggested constructing a separate IQ test for older adults and calling it the WISE (Wechsler Intelligence Scale for the Elderly).

DEMENTIA

Dementia is a medical term used for a group of symptoms. It describes a general decline in intellectual ability severe enough to interfere with a person's ability to function. This decline means loss of several kinds of mental processes that may include short- and/or long-term memory, arithmetic reasoning, word knowledge, abstract thinking, judgment, concept-formation ability, speaking, and coordination. Just because you don't feel quite as sharp at the age of 70 as you did when you were 22 does not mean that you're developing dementia.

Other terms that are often synonymous with dementia include organic brain syndrome, senility, hardening of the arteries, or chronic brain syndrome.

In our present discussion, we will define dementia specifically as a loss or impairment of mental powers.

There are two major conditions that result in the symptoms of memory loss, confusion, disorientation, and intellectual impairment. The first is known as delirium. Delirium comprises a group of symptoms in which the person is less alert than normal. The delirious person is often drowsy, but may fluctuate between drowsiness and restlessness. Like the demented individual, the delirious person is also confused, disoriented, and forgetful. Delirious individuals have often been referred to as having "acute brain syndromes" or "reversible brain syndromes." Delirium often results from illnesses such as pneumonia or kidney infections, malnutrition, reactions to medications, or withdrawal from drugs or alcohol. Usually delirium is treatable and reversible.

What sets dementia apart from delirium is the fact that demented people have obviously impaired intellectual functioning while they are clearly awake and alert, while delirious people are obviously groggy, incoherent, and lapse in and out of sleep.

Thyroid disease or acute alcohol withdrawal are often associated with reversible delirium, while Alzheimer's disease appears to be the most frequent cause of irreversible dementia in adults.

SYMPTOMS OF DEMENTIA

Perhaps the most common symptoms of individuals suffering from dementia are memory problems. People with dementia tend to forget things very quickly. For the person suffering from dementia, life is like constantly coming into the middle of a movie, with no idea what has happened just before or what is happening right now. In the early phases of dementia, recent and short-term memory impairment is more obvious, while long-term memory is less affected. In the more advanced stages of dementia, both long- and short-term memory are affected.

Another characteristic of dementia is emotional overreactions in people who had no previous history of such outbursts of feelings.

Jacob, a previously stoic 65-year-old Alzheimer's patient was observed by his son bursting into tears over his inability to tie his own shoelaces.

Other hallmarks of dementia are problems with speech and communication. The demented individual may have difficulty in making himself understood. Frequently, he will have difficulty finding words to express his thoughts. Other times, he may ramble on quite fluently and seem as if he has no trouble talking, but when you think back upon what he has said, it makes very little sense.

Memory-impaired people also have difficulty understanding others. They may forget what you told them just a few moments before. One way to deal with this problem is to have the demented person recite back to you what he has just heard every few minutes.

Another hallmark of a generally developing dementia is loss of coordination. This may take its initial form in *apraxia,* noticeable change in handwriting. As the loss of coordination continues, the person has trouble balancing and walking. He may walk much more slowly, with an unsteady or shuffling gait.

The loss of coordination of dementia should not be confused with its loss in such common illnesses as rheumatoid or ostcoarthritis, or Parkinson's disease, which commonly affect the coordination and movements of older people.

Finally, one of the most obvious signs of developing dementia is a loss of sense of time. Normal people have an uncanny ability to judge the passage of time in both the long and the short term. The impaired person may ask you repeatedly what time it is, or feel that you have left him for hours when you have been gone only for a few minutes. He may want to leave a restaurant after two or three minutes, insisting that he's been there for several hours.

CAUSES OF DEMENTIA

Many conditions and diseases can cause dementia. Some of these are reversible, some irreversible.

Metabolic disorders are quite capable of causing temporary dementia. Problems involving thyroid or parathyroid dysfunction, or adrenal-gland dysfunction are commonly associated with dementia. Liver or kidney dysfunction may also lead to dementia as may certain vitamin deficiencies, such as low levels of vitamin B-12.

Structural problems of the brain have long been known to create dementia. Abnormal pressure (hydrocephalus), abnormal flow of spinal fluid, brain tumors, or traumatic injuries to the brain are capable of lowering intelligence. Subdural hematoma (bleeding between the brain and skull), can create pressure, which affects brain function.

Various infections are also known to cause dementia. Tuberculosis and syphilis, as well as other fungal, bacterial, and viral infections of the brain may cause dementia, as may such diseases as meningitis and encephalitis.

Toxins or poisons like carbon monoxide, lead, drugs, or alcohol may also cause dementia.

Fairly recently, such autoimmune diseases as temporal arthritis and lupus erythematosus have been discovered to cause dementia.

Psychiatric diseases such as depression and schizophrenia often mimic dementia. The slowed intellectual processes often seen in vegetative depression look very similar to dementia, but are clearly treatable and are usually reversible.

Transient ischemic attacks (TIAs), result in a temporary impairment due to an insufficient supply of blood to part of the brain. When TIA occurs, the person may be unable to speak or have slurred speech. They may become weak, paralyzed on one side, dizzy, or nauseated. These TIA attacks usually last for only a few minutes. TIAs should be regarded as a warning sign of possible stroke and should be reported to your doctor immediately.

In the past, dementia associated with old age was thought to be caused by a hardening of the arteries in the brain. Research has now proved otherwise. In multi-infarct dementia, repeated strokes within the brain, destroy small areas, and the cumulative affect of the damage leads to dementia. Multi-infarct dementia affects such intellectual functions as memory, coordination, and speech. The function affected is determined by the area of the brain that was damaged.

Multi-infarct dementia typically progresses in a steplike fashion, with the results of each "mini-stroke" becoming obvious quickly; e.g., sudden, slurred speech. You may be able to look back and recall that the ill person was worse after a specific time and then gets much better, as opposed to one with Alzheimer's disease, who experiences a gradual decline.

A major stroke, on the other hand, causes such obvious symptoms as a sudden paralysis on one side of the body, drooping of one side of the face, or speech problems. Strokes are often caused by blood clotting in the vessels of the brain, or by a blood vessel bursting and causing bleeding within the brain. Often the brain cells are injured or impaired by swelling but can recover when the swelling subsides.

Fortunately, the brain has a unique capacity called *neuroplasticity:* different areas of the brain can gradually learn to do the jobs of damaged sections. Through rehabilitation training, people are often able to regain most if not all the function they lost due to a stroke, even though part of their brain may have been destroyed.

ALZHEIMER'S DISEASE

In 1907 the German physician Alois Alzheimer described a disease occurring in a woman in her fifties which he called "presenile dementia." Physicians and neurologists now agree that the dementia which occurs in the elderly is the same as that which occurs in the presenile condition, and have grouped these two disorders together under one label: Alzheimer's disease.

The course of Alzheimer's disease is insidious, at first hardly perceptible, yet at the same time inevitable. Early in the disease, only memory may be impaired noticeably. A person may be a bit more forgetful than usual and have difficulty learning new tasks which require abstract reasoning and thinking. He may begin to have difficulty on the job and not enjoy reading or watching TV as much as he used to. He may become depressed as a result of this general decline.

As Alzheimer's disease progresses, impairment in both language and motor abilities are seen. Initially, the person with Alzheimer's disease may be unable to find the right word for things or will use the wrong word. Gradually, he will become unable to express himself. At this stage, he may have difficulty performing tasks which were once easy. His handwriting may change, and he may begin to walk with a stoop or shuffle and become clumsy. The Alzheimer's patient may get lost easily, misunderstand what is happening, show poor judgment, and show such personality changes as having paranoid moods or outbursts of anger.

Late-stage Alzheimer's disease is characterized by severe impairment in most areas of intellectual functioning, incontinence, and difficulty walking. Severe late-stage Alzheimer's patients may be unable to say more than a few words at a time, and may recognize only one or two people. Late-stage Alzheimer's patients are usually in need of nursing-home or custodial care by professionals.

Research from Johns Hopkins University in the early 1980s found that Alzheimer's disease usually leads to death in about 7 to 10 years, but sometimes it progresses more quickly (3 to 4 years) and other times more slowly, with survival rates reaching up to 15 years.

UNDER THE MICROSCOPE

It is difficult to differentiate Alzheimer's disease from other forms of organic brain dysfunction. The only true definitive test for Alzheimer's disease is a brain biopsy, in which a small part of the skull is pierced and a tiny piece of brain material is removed and analyzed under a microscope. The removal of the tiny bit of brain material itself does not reduce intellectual functioning to any extent.

Specifically, Alzheimer's disease is characterized by two abnormal structures in the brain tissue: neuritic plaques and neurofibrillary tangles.

Brain biopsies are not routinely performed at the present time because a cure for the disease has not yet been developed. The management of Alzheimer's disease is another story, and significant advances have been made in this area.

FAST FACTS ABOUT ALZHEIMER'S DISEASE

• Statistical data cited by Mace and Rabins in their classic, *The 36-Hour Day,* indicate that only 5 percent of the aged will suffer from severe intellectual impairment, and an additional 5 percent from some milder form of intellectual impairment.

- Alzheimer's disease alone accounts for 40 percent of the dementias, while an additional 40 percent are accounted for by a combination of Alzheimer's disease and stroke. The remaining 10 to 20 percent of dementias are accounted for by such other problems as toxins, infections, or structural damage to the brain.
- Despite senility's seemingly common appearance, 80 percent of the individuals who live to be over 80 years old will never suffer significant memory loss or dementia.
- However, 2 to 4 million Americans will suffer from some form of intellectual impairment during their lifetimes.
- According to several neurologists and neuropsychologists, virtually all patients with Down's Syndrome who live to be over 65 develop Alzheimer's disease. (However, most Down's Syndrome patients do not live past the age of 50.)
- Alzheimer's disease is much more common after the age of 65 than before. Rarely does Alzheimer's disease develop before the age of 49.
- It is estimated that between 2 and 4 percent of the population over the age of 65 suffers from Alzheimer's disease. The frequency increases with age, especially after 75. Most people over 75 do not develop Alzheimer's disease.
- Alzheimer's disease is slightly more common in women than in men.
- Multi-infarct dementia is differentiated from Alzheimer's disease by its patchy distribution: multi-infarct dementia affects some functions and not others.
- Delirium and withdrawal delirium, which are often confused with Alzheimer's disease, are seen frequently in alcohol and sedative withdrawal, amphetamine use or withdrawal, cocaine use or withdrawal, and PCP use or withdrawal.
- Alzheimer's kills over 100,000 people per year; it is the fourth leading cause of death among adults.

Dementia (Organic brain syndrome) Questionnaire

Note: Obviously, if the person is suffering from moderate to severe Alzheimer's disease or some other form of dementia, he will not be capable of understanding the test as it is meant to be interpreted. This test is therefore used more appropriately to help you screen and determine if the person you are concerned about has dementia or Alzheimer's disease. If he seems to, contact a professional immediately for a thorough evaluation.

1. I am going to say three words and I would like you to try to remember them. The words are *pen, boat,* and *hat.* Please repeat them. A little later I will ask you to recall and repeat these words. They are again: *pen, boat,* and *hat.*
2. What is your date of birth?
3. What day of the week is it today?
4. What month are we in right now?
5. What is today's date?
6. What year are we in?
7. Where are you right now?
8. What city or town are you in right now?
9. What are the names of our two most recent presidents of the United States?
10. Repeat the sentence just exactly as I say it:
    (A) Tomorrow I am going fishing with my friend.
    (B) Yesterday I went shopping with my daughter.
    (Both sentences must be repeated exactly as stated.)
11. Now tell me those three words I asked you to remember. (Recalling two of the three words is a correct response.)
12. Has your memory caused you any significant problems in the past few weeks?
13. Has your memory interfered with your ability to take care of your chores around the house or interfered with your job?
14. Have family members said that you were getting much more forgetful than you used to be, or that your memory was much worse?
15. Have friends or acquaintances told you that your memory is slipping?
16. If you have six apples and give two apples to Bob and two apples to Sue, how many apples are left?

17. Please count by serial sevens to 100. For example: 7, 14, . . .
18. A) How are cat and a mouse alike?
    B) How are an apple and an orange alike?
19. What did you have for your most recent meal? (Either breakfast, lunch, or dinner.)
20. Please copy the following design without lifting your pencil:

Scoring: If the person screened missed five or more questions, it is a good idea to consult your physician and have a more thorough workup done to test for possible dementia. Remember, use the previous questions only when the person you are trying to assess is clear, alert, and aware. Do not use this test on people who are sleepy, on drugs, on alcohol, or going through extremely stressful times.

Correct Responses:

1. The person repeats accurately the words pen, boat, and hat.
2. Exact date of birth must be given.
3. Exact day of the week must be given.
4. Correct month must be given.
5. The date must be given within one day of the correct date.
6. The exact year must be given.
7. The person must demonstrate he is clearly aware of where he is: e.g., his home, apartment, or school.
8. The city or town must be stated accurately.
9. Prior to the November 1992 election, the correct response is Bush and Reagan. After the 1992 election, the correct response would be Clinton and Bush.
10. The person must exactly repeat the sentences:
    (A) Tomorrow I am going fishing with my friend.
    (B) Yesterday I went shopping with my daughter.
11. The person must recall at least two of the three words presented in question 1 (pen, boat, and hat).
12. No.

13. No.
14. No.
15. No.
16. Two apples.
17. 7, 14, 21, 28, 35, 42, 49, 56, 63, 70, 77, 84, 91, and 98. Response must be given within 45 seconds.
18. (A) Both animals.
    (B) Both fruits.
19. Person must verbalize what they had for their most recent meal.
20. Sample of correct reproduction:

Incorrect reproductions:

CASE HISTORIES

You will recall that Alzheimer's disease represents one form of a general category of organic brain damage called dementia. Let's look at four of the major causes of dementia to help sort out what differentiates one from the other.

William, a 56-year-old civil engineer, was walking down the sidewalk toward a parking lot when he was struck by a vehicle driven by a drunken driver. For two weeks William lay in a hospital bed unconscious, and his fate was uncertain. He then gradually began to show signs of recovery. Within a week he was aware of his surroundings, although he had no memory of the accident. At first William did not recognize his wife or two children, but within two weeks, the faces of important people started to come back to him. During the first month of his hospital stay, William had to be reminded constantly where he was, the day of the week, and the situation which brought him into the hospital.

When William's physical injuries healed, I was asked to evaluate him to determine the extent to which he had suffered intellectual and memory impairment.

Before talking to him, I talked with his wife and daughters. They reported that William had a great deal of difficulty remembering recent events. What was more troubling to them was the fact that occasionally he would intermittently blurt out obscene and foul language, something that he had never done before. After the tirade of obscenities, he would quickly calm down and revert to his normal pleasant self.

Although William knew his wife, daughters, and doctors, he easily lost track of when he last saw these people. My evaluation with William took two days, and when I came to see him the second day, he said he remembered my face, but thought that he hadn't seen me for a few months.

Results of the intelligence testing indicated that, despite his recent traumatic head injury, he still had a full-scale I.Q. score of 110. This placed his present level of intellectual functioning in the above average range. William's memory quotient however, as measured by a test called Wechsler Memory Scale, indicated that he had a memory quotient of 96. This score, while still roughly within normal limits, is far below what we would expect from a man of above-average intelligence. In short, the testing confirmed that William had suffered significant short-term memory and concentration damage.

With continuing outpatient cognitive, occupational, and recreational therapy, William began to do things that used to make him feel good. He learned how to keep a notebook of important events, and how to schedule his day-to-day life. Within six months, William's memory quotient had improved to 109, which is consistent with what we would expect from his intelligence.

Based on my testing and reports from William's other doctors, within six months of his injury he was allowed to return back to limited work.

William performed relatively well, and his coworkers noticed only a slight difference in how he was doing his job. He was purposely given things that required him to do some thinking.

William continued to complain that he felt his mind just wasn't as sharp as it used to be. He told me that he could still get things done, but it took a lot more conscious effort, and it wasn't as easy as it used to be. He spoke with a hesitating and overly determined quality, and seemed to have to second-guess every sentence before he said it.

With encouragement from William's family, friends, and coworkers, he began to develop confidence in his skills. Nonetheless, his perception of his loss of memory and intellectual ability did lead to a moderate depression. He was placed on a low-dose antidepressant medication, which gave him a little more energy and helped him sleep better. But William told me that the major turning point in his therapy was being given the green light by his doctors to return to work.

I have continued to follow William for the past two years, and his progress has been steady. In fact, recently William's measured memory quotient had improved to 120, which is in the superior range. He no longer has trouble with names and faces. He no longer has to keep a memory workbook to help him keep appointments, and he is enjoying many of the activities he used to do, like fishing, and golf.

William still feels that something isn't quite right with his mind and that he is not as good as he used to be. But William's story is one of remarkable success. After his initial injury, William's physicians predicted that he would never return to work and considered placing him on permanent disability. But, through patience, hard work, a multidisciplinary team of professionals, and tremendous family support, William overcame his obstacles and has returned to being the well-adjusted, well-liked, civil engineer and family man he once was.

William had suffered from an acute brain trauma which proved to be very treatable and largely reversible.

Elizabeth, a 68-year-old retired schoolteacher, had been in the chemical-dependency unit for two days when I first saw her. Her problem was that she had been drinking at least a pint of vodka a day for the past four years.

My mental-status examination revealed that Elizabeth was not very clear. Her thoughts flowed in a slow and hesitating fashion. Elizabeth told me that the day she stopped drinking, she felt bugs crawling on her skin that weren't really there, and thought her deceased husband had come to visit her. She also reported seeing dots and floating clouds which her roommate couldn't see. Elizabeth was only marginally oriented. She knew she was in a hospital, but really wasn't sure why. She realized what city she was in, but had no idea of the day of the week or month of the year. She thought we were in 1972 when we were actually in 1992. At times during our interview, Elizabeth seemed to lapse into delirium. She became lethargic, tired, and her head would droop down to the table as she nodded off. With some coaxing I was able to awaken her, yet this pattern continued over the two hours of testing.

During her clearer moments, Elizabeth told me that she had received her master's degree with honors and had been an outstanding teacher. A social drinker, she never let alcohol create any problems for her until the death of her husband when she was 64. Then, in order to cope with the pain and the loneliness, Elizabeth began drinking heavily.

I gave Elizabeth a full scale IQ test, and found her measured IQ score to be 78. This score is in the borderline retarded range, and clearly not indicative of someone with a master's degree. However, Elizabeth's performance on the vocabulary subtest, which usually estimates her previous level of intellectual functioning, showed that she was still in the bright-normal range. Elizabeth's memory quotient also tested far below average, and there were obvious problems with her short-term memory and capacity for sustained attention. In fact, during the first two nights, the night staff noticed that Elizabeth roamed about the halls, asking people where she was.

Within a week, Elizabeth's symptoms began to recede gradually, and within two weeks she was nearly back to her normal self. However, without the alcohol, Elizabeth had to dwell on her sadness and loneliness since the death of her husband. She became actively involved in individual and group-counseling sessions and in several support groups, which helped her get her life back on track.

Two weeks after my initial assessment, Elizabeth complained to me about my bill, insisting that she had never before met me. I gently reminded her of details of her history, which few if any people knew about. She then realized that she had seen me, but had no memory whatsoever of our session.

While not suffering from the permanent memory loss due to heavy alcohol abuse called Korsakoff's syndrome, Elizabeth had been suffering from acute alcohol intoxication and withdrawal with delirium and dementia.

Carl, a 67-year-old retired middle-management executive, had not had too much difficulty giving up the six to eight beers a day he had been drinking before a stroke forced his early retirement at the age of

57. Carl did not have the disorientation, confusion, slowed thought processes, or delirium which Elizabeth experienced.

During my history taking, Carl told me that in 1982 he felt a sudden chill come over the right side of his body. He reported that his right leg wobbled and he fell down. He then found that he could not move his right arm or right leg and noticed that when he tried to talk, the right side of his mouth wouldn't move. His right eye, cheek, and jaw seemed to droop or sag, and he felt as if the right side of his body had completely gone to sleep. He was barely able to feel his right arm when it was touched, and feared the same sensation might spread to the left side of his body.

Carl had suffered a major stroke caused by a blood vessel's rupturing on the left side of his brain. Carl had a great deal of difficulty talking and could rarely find the words to express himself. He knew what things were, but couldn't find a name for them.

Through a process of rehabilitation training, the right side of Carl's brain began to take over most of the functions which had previously been handled by the damaged left side.

Carl's intelligence tests revealed that his performance IQ score was average at 107. His verbal IQ score however, which involved the left side of his brain, was measured at 86 (below average). Such a large discrepancy, coupled with the documentation of Carl's stroke, indicated that there was permanent damage to his brain. But his brain had reorganized and learned things in new ways.

For two or three years, Edna had known that her memory was slipping. At first she had trouble remembering the names of her friends, and one year forgot her husband's birthday. Edna compensated by trying to write down important things. She reasoned to herself that she was getting older, and at 65 she knew her mind would not be as sharp as it was when she was 20. Nonetheless, Edna frequently found herself groping for words which she had always known and used regularly. Edna had several friends who had become senile, but thought that by keeping her mind active with events, activities, and reading, she could ward off encroaching senility.

More recently, when Edna was talking with some friends and family members, she realized that she had forgotten more than just the name of her best friend's husband; she had entirely lost the thread of the conversation about her daughter's recent trip to Hawaii. Edna fought her memory lapses as best she could; she compensated for her inappropriate responses by saying that she was distracted by all of the volunteer work she had to do for the women's auxiliary and the upcoming election.

Despite her excuses and compensations, Edna knew that something was wrong with her mind. Her oldest daughter recognized this, too, and was afraid that her mother was slipping into senility. But there was no one Edna could express her feelings to for fear that she would be placed in a nursing home. Besides, what good would it do for Edna to worry about getting old and senile when there was nothing anyone can do about it anyway. She was still clearly able to enjoy life, manage on her own, and even have fun. In the fall of the following year, Edna became quite ill. One afternoon her daughter found her laying in bed semiconscious, feverish, and mumbling incoherently.

During her first three days in the hospital, Edna had only a vague notion of what was happening. The doctors informed her family that she had bacterial pneumonia and that her kidneys and liver were having problems. Edna was placed on a regimen of strong antibiotics to fight the infection.

Despite being reassured several times a day by nurses, family, and friends as to where she was and what was going on around her, Edna continuously forgot what had just happened. She lapsed into a delirium caused by her acute illness and aggravated by her confusion.

During her delirium, Edna was sure that her mother had come by to see her twice, yet was told by her daughter that her mom had been dead for over twenty years. Although living in northern California, Edna was convinced that she was in Arizona, where she had not lived for forty years.

Over the course of two-and-one-half weeks, Edna improved. Her infection cleared and she became able to speak and walk. Only during the acute phase of her infection did Edna imagine seeing and hearing things; but even after the fever and infection passed, Edna remained somewhat confused and forgetful.

While Edna had been able to function around her home with a severely impaired memory, she clearly was not capable of recalling recent events, and even had trouble recognizing where the bathroom was, although it was only four feet from her hospital bed.

Despite her problems, Edna's daughter and her son-in-law agreed to take her into their home. This was a house that Edna had been familiar with for over ten years. She would routinely go there at Christmas and Thanksgiving, and greatly enjoyed playing with her grandchildren and teaching them songs.

Shortly after arriving at her daughter's home, Edna became preoccupied with a retired neighbor's woodworking projects. Edna saw several rectangular shapes in the garage and became convinced that this man was building coffins and would eventually try to kill she and her grandchildren. At her daughter's insistence, Edna was taken over to chat with the man who described the bookshelves and end tables he was making, and even showed her a few of his finished products. Nonetheless, this was not enough proof for Edna, and she continued to be obsessed with the delusion that this man was building coffins.

On several occasions, Edna dialed 911 and told the police that her grandchildren had been kidnapped. Reacting to this serious report, the police quickly dispatched a number of patrol cars and even a search helicopter.

Edna also began to roam away from the house, and after she was picked up for the third time at 2:30 A.M. while walking aimlessly alongside a highway, Edna's daughter finally realized that they could no longer take care of her.

Edna was placed in a skilled nursing facility and lived in what amounted to a small studio apartment with around-the-clock care. Edna's meals were provided, and she was taken on supervised outings. Around-the-clock surveillance assured that Edna would not get lost, and initially she had daily visits with her family. Every weekend, one of Edna's children or her husband would bring her home for various family outings. Edna particularly enjoyed singing with the family, and continued to teach her two grandchildren new songs.

Despite a gradual decline in her memory, the quality of Edna's life remained acceptable to her and her family over the next nine years. Then, one evening, apparently in her sleep, Edna died of congenital heart failure.

After her death, a brain biopsy revealed neurofibrillary tangles, neuritic plaques, and granulovacuolar degeneration. The physiological evidence concluded what everyone close to Edna already knew: she had suffered from Alzheimer's disease.

HOPE FOR THE FUTURE

As is the case with most crippling diseases, the greatest hope for the management and cure of Alzheimer's disease comes from pharmacology. Six classes of drugs have shown considerable promise in controlling Alzheimer's symptoms:

- cerebral vasodilators and cerebral metabolic enhancers
- procaine solution
- psychostimulants
- nootropics
- neuropeptides
- neurotransmitter precursors or agonists

Cerebral Vasodilators and Cerebral Metabolic Enhancers

As their name implies, cerebral vasodilators dilate the blood vessels of the brain. It is thought that when the blood vessels are dilated, more blood can flow to the brain, thereby delivering more oxygen for enhanced performance. In 1981 Dr. Barry Reisberg cited evidence indicating that patients with Alzheimer's disease respond to a vasodilatory stimulus such as carbon dioxide. The vessels expand, and there is an increase in blood flow. Some cerebral vasodilators appear to help Alzheimer's patients, at least in the short run. However, they are of little or no benefit in cases of multi-infarct dementia, probably because the blood vessels are so clogged up that the vasodilators cannot open them.

The vasodilator which has been most widely used and studied most intensively is known technically as dihydroergotoxine, and is commonly listed under the trade name Hydergine.

Over 100 clinical studies of the efficacy of dihydroergotoxine have found that this drug significantly improves symptoms of Alzheimer's disease, including alertness, concentration, orientation, confusion, poor recent memory, depression, anxiety, lack of motivation, agitation, dizziness, and difficulty in movement.

European researcher Jay Kugler and his associates conducted a 15-month study of Hydergine and found that by giving patients a slightly higher dosage (4.5 milligrams), their overall cognitive performance was enhanced. Furthermore, results show that patients treated with Hydergine showed a slight increase in overall intelligence and an increase in cerebral blood flow. In contrast, patients receiving a placebo showed an overall decrease in intelligence and slightly decreased blood circulation within the brain.

Furthermore, studies of electrical activity in the cortex of the brain have indicated an increase in patients treated with Hydergine.

Reisberg cited studies showing that the exact mode of action of Hydergine may be vasodilation of blood vessels or the enhancement of metabolic activity within the neurons themselves.

Romanian Procaine

Romanian procaine, or Gerovital-H3 is another drug which has enjoyed considerable popularity in the treatment of Alzheimer's disease. Developed by Dr. Ana Aslan, a Romanian physician, the drug has been utilized in Romania for 25 years.

Gerovital-H3 decreases or inhibits the action of an enzyme known as monoamine oxidase, or MAO, an enzyme that breaks down certain kinds of neurotransmitter substances. Theoretically, if there is less MAO in the synapse between cells, there is more neurotransmitter substance to stimulate the firing of the cells. Therefore, the MAO inhibitory property of Gerovital-H3 appears to have an antidepressant effect: it reduces the activity of MAO, which tends to increase with aging.

Nootropics

Another promising class of drug which may prove valuable in treatment of Alzheimer's disease is piracetam, Nootropil.

Nootropil increases the electrical activity in that portion of the brain which carries information between the two cerebral hemispheres. Therefore, Nootropil may decrease the time which it would take for information to go from one part of the brain to another.

Despite their clear efficacy in enhancing the functioning of the brain, Nootropil or piracetam have no apparent side effects. They do not have any addiction potential and are not sleep producing or sedating. Even cerebral blood flow has not been found to change with treatment of piracetam.

Piracetam is believed to enhance the quantity of energy stored by the brain or to increase the efficacy of neural-cell metabolism.

Research studies have found that in unimpaired older adults and adults with mild to moderate age-related dementia, piracetam improves thinking and behavior. It is therefore hoped that piracetam (Nootropil) will be of considerable value in treating mild to moderate cases of dementia or Alzheimer's disease.

Neuropeptides

Neuropeptides are simple compounds composed of amino acids, the building blocks from which proteins are made. Certain kinds of neuropeptides have been discovered to act as hormones as well as transmitters in the nervous system and in other cell interphases throughout the body.

One of the most interesting of these neuropeptides is a substance called adrenocorticotropic hormone (ACTH), a pituitary hormone which stimulates the adrenal glands. Research has demonstrated that even with the adrenal glands removed, ACTH has a pronounced affect on learning ability.

Preliminary human experiments conducted with vasopressin, another peptide, indicate that when this nasal spray is given to people with memory disturbances, it appears to promote the return to normal memory. Other more carefully controlled studies have found that adult subjects taking vasopressin showed improved attention, concentration, and recall.

Research on enkephalins, the recently discovered natural opiates which play a crucial role in controlling pain, indicate that these substances may affect memory in much the same way as vasopressin. Enkephalins may act on specific neurotransmitters which teach specific cells to remember information. More research is needed to determine the exact benefits of enkephalins, vasopressin, and ACTH.

Neurotransmitters, Precursors, or Agonists

The neurotransmitter acetylcholine can also be crucial in the modification of Alzheimer's disease. Direct administration of the choline salts, which are precursors (building blocks) of acetylcholine, yield results that are disappointing. However, when some patients received lecithin, a natural source of acetylcholine, their thinking processes improved. Reisberg cites one study in which significant improvement in cognitive functioning was found in three of seven Alzheimer's patients treated with lecithin.

Finally, a substance known as physostigmine, a chemical which inhibits the enzyme which destroys acetylcholine in the synapse, has shown promise in the treatment of Alzheimer's disease. Theoretically, this chemical allows more acetylcholine to stay in the synapse and thereby promotes prolonged firing of the cells, allowing a longer duration of cell activity.

Research in pharmacology indicates that many different classes of chemicals appear to improve and reverse cognitive and intellectual deficits. It is probably only a matter of time before Alzheimer's disease can be arrested or reversed with appropriate drug treatment.

MULTIDISCIPLINARY TREATMENT APPROACHES

In order to enhance the quality of the life of the Alzheimer's patient, a comprehensive treatment program needs to be followed. It must include proper nutrition, regular exercise, personal hygiene, dental care, and prompt attention to any physical problems. A physician sympathetic to Alzheimer's patients should be found and should monitor the patient's condition since any health problem may exacerbate the patient's symptoms.

Alzheimer's patients are also likely to suffer from such emotional disorders as depression and anxiety in reaction to their intellectual decline. To control these feelings, the physician may discuss available medications or recommend appropriate counseling.

Psychologists can assist the Alzheimer's patient's family by teaching the patient self-care techniques and educating the family to reduce wandering and other inappropriate behaviors. Simple techniques such as labeling the contents of kitchen drawers can go a long way towards helping Alzheimer's patients daily lives.

FAMILY SUPPORT

About 3 of the 4 million Alzheimer's patients in the United States are cared for in the home by family members. Frequently, the patient is kept at home anywhere from 3 to 10 years after the initial diagnosis is made. While the early stage of Alzheimer's disease requires little supervision, as the disease progresses more and more supervision is required. The primary caregiver should not try to sustain the demanding responsibility of providing constant care to the patient. Other family members, if available, should be asked to provide mutual support. Care provided by another family member on a daily or weekly basis can give the primary caregiver a few hours or days to recharge his or her batteries and pursue his or her own interests.

Family counseling for the Alzheimer's patient's family may focus on discussing financial concerns and resolving feelings of anger, frustration, fear, hopelessness, and despair. Additionally, stress-coping strategies can be taught not only to the Alzheimer's patient, but also to family members.

COMMUNITY SERVICES/GROUP SUPPORT

Community services are often available to help the primary caregiver take care of the Alzheimer's patient. Such services as Meals on Wheels, respite care, visiting nurses, occupational or physical therapy, day treatment programs, or daycare programs are often available. You may need to contact several agencies to find out what services are available in your area and their costs.

Self-help groups for Alzheimer's families have grown in recent years and provide an extremely valuable support network. These groups are composed of Alzheimer's family members whose loved ones have been diagnosed as having the disease for two or more years. Such groups discuss the personality and mental changes, how to know what expectations are realistic, the proper ways to manage behavioral problems, and how to maintain as high a quality of life for the whole family as possible.

Finally, pets like dogs or cats often provide an invaluable companion to Alzheimer's patients. The devotion of the pet will give them a sense of love and being needed in their most lonely and emotionally destitute times. While the care and maintenance of the pet's health is up to other family members, the emotional support provided by the pet to the patient is well documented.

Alzheimer's Disease Societies

Gerontological Society
1835 K Street, N.W.
Washington, DC 20006

Yeshiva University
Alzheimer Project
Bronx, NY

National Alzheimer Foundation
4950 Olde Coventry Rd. West
Columbus, OH 43227
Attn: Ms. Nancy Schlegal, R.N.

Alzheimer's Disease Society
560 Sylvan Avenue
Englewood Cliffs, NJ 07632

R.E.A.C.H.
c/o Mental Health Association of Minnesota
4510 West 77th Street
Minneapolis, MN 55435

Alzheimer's Disease Society
32 Broadway
New York, NY 10004
Attn: Mr. Lonnie E. Wollin, Sec. Treas.

Pennsylvania School of Medicine
Alzheimer Project
Philadelphia, PA

Family Survival Project
Mental Health Foundation of San Francisco
1745 Van Ness Avenue
San Francisco, CA 94109

A.S.I.S.T.
(Alzheimer's Support Information and Services Team)
c/o Department of Psychiatry and Behavioral Sciences
RP-10
University of Washington
Seattle, WA 98195

Société Alzheimer Society
2 Surrey Place
Toronto, Ontario M5S 2C2
CANADA

CHAPTER 11

IS IT JUST AN ADJUSTMENT DISORDER?

AN ADJUSTMENT DISORDER IS THE COMMON COLD OF MENTAL HEALTH. THESE DISORders are very common, yet no definitive statistics have been kept on exactly how many people suffer from them.

Essential to the development of an adjustment disorder is a clear, identifiable psychosocial stressor or stressors which would provoke noticeable distress in even the most mentally healthy person. You already know from the chapter on psychosocial stressors that they range along a continuum from mild to catastrophic. People respond to a psychosocial stressor with a disturbed psychological reaction that shows up in either your feelings (moods) or your behaviors (conduct).

Let's face it: it's perfectly normal to be sad or even depressed when you are going through a divorce, upset or angry when you are laid off, or fearful and anxious when you learn that you have a chronic physical illness. But the key question to ask yourself when trying to determine whether you have an adjustment disorder is: "Do I or other people feel that I am having much more trouble handling this problem than most people would?"

Typically, adjustment disorders show up as disturbances in completing your work or school activities, engaging in your usual social activities, participating in typical family activities, or engaging in your usual recreations and pastimes.

An adjustment disorder is not just one instance of overreacting to a stress, but a continuing disruptive series of feelings and behaviors which interfere with your life.

One of the underlying assumptions of adjustment disorders is that when the stressor ceases to exist, the adjustment disorder will disappear. Another assumption is that if the stressor persists over six months, either a clearly identifiable emotional disorder will develop, or you will adjust and reach a new level of emotional functioning. With continuing psychosocial or other stressors, you will either gradually wear down and develop an actual clinical syndrome (disorder), or use your own psychological and emotional resources to learn to cope with the stressor and improve your functioning.

The stressors which trigger an adjustment disorder may be a single event, such as divorce or death of a loved one, or moving to a new city and the necessary adjustments; or multiple, recurrent stressors such as marital conflict, physical illness, seasonal business crises, or a prolonged illness. The stressor which triggers an adjustment disorder may occur in the context of family, job, social relations, community, or even religious- or cultural-group affiliation.

Often stressors may develop after passage into a new stage in life, such as going away to college, getting married, taking your first job, becoming a parent, or retiring from work.

Human beings vary considerably in their ability to adjust and adapt to psychosocial stressors. People who are psychologically vulnerable or fragile may have a very low tolerance for pressure and may react with an adjustment disorder to even a mild stressor. Psychologically resilient and emotionally strong people may have little or no reaction to even the most severe psychosocial stressors.

The death of one's spouse represents one of the most catastrophic stressors anyone can face, and this stressor deserves special attention. Rather than being called an adjustment disorder, the typical sadness, social withdrawal, and despair which usually accompany the death of a spouse is referred to as "uncomplicated bereavement." This is not to say that someone who loses a spouse cannot develop an adjustment disorder, but simply to point out the fact that severe emotional and behavioral reactions are typical when a wife or husband dies.

DURATION AND COURSE

Adjustment disorders are, by definition, time limited. An adjustment disorder must occur within three months of the stressor and not last longer than six months after it begins. If the disturbing reaction continues longer than six months, it is likely that another clinical syndrome has developed. Fortunately, in most cases, the stressor itself either disappears, or the person facing the stressor adjusts, adapts, and improves his or her psychological functioning.

TYPES OF ADJUSTMENT DISORDERS

Just as the range of psychosocial stressors can vary from anything as mild as making a C when you felt you deserved a B to being kidnapped and tortured, so your reaction to stressors can take many different directions.

When differentiating between an adjustment disorder and other emotional disorders such as anxiety disorders or depression, the key questions to keep in mind are: "Is my emotional reaction a response to a stressor which would provoke distress in virtually anyone?" and "Is my reaction to the stressor outside of the range of that of most people?"

Adjustment Disorder with Anxious Mood

Adjustment disorders with anxious mood consist of reacting to a stressor with feelings involving nervousness, irritability, and anxiety. If the stressor which occurs puts you on edge yet does not interfere with your job, family, friends, and hobbies, then you are probably not suffering from an adjustment disorder with anxious mood.

On the other hand, if your reactions to a clear and identifiable stressor make you so nervous that your lifestyle is affected, then it is likely that you are suffering from an adjustment disorder with anxious mood.

Anna, a 38-year-old editor at a paperback publishing house in southern California, has just learned that her position will be eliminated next month due to deteriorating economic conditions. Anna has spent 16 years with the same company and has been a devoted and competent employee. But Anna's diligence, competence, and devotion have not paid off in job security.

In response to the news of her impending layoff, Anna becomes irritable and edgy. Her friends report that she is not the same person; she tends to snap at people for no apparent reason. Anna's husband reports that she yells frequently at her two children and takes offense at her husband's most supportive comments. Anna's sleep becomes disturbed, and she finds it necessary to take two stiff drinks in order to get to sleep, only to find herself wide awake at 3:00 A.M., wondering what she is going to do with her life. Anna begins to notice other classic signs of anxiety, like cold hands and feet, unusual perspiration, occasional heart palpitations, frequent shortness of breath, and a feeling of impending doom. While nothing is actually threatening Anna's life, something certainly is threatening her financial future.

After a brief course of counseling (two sessions), Anna begins to contact publishing houses in the Los Angeles and San Francisco Bay areas. Within two weeks, she is called in for her first job interview, and within a month she has landed another position in the publishing industry.

Anna was suffering from an adjustment disorder with anxious mood, which resolved itself when she found a new job.

Adjustment Disorder with Depressed Mood

Steve, a 26-year-old account executive, was delighted with his recent promotion. He had worked long and hard over the past two years to achieve his new position and had to put in a lot of extra time at the office at the expense of ignoring his wife. While Steve was climbing his way up the corporate ladder, his wife's feelings of neglect became more and more upsetting. Feeling that she was unattractive and worthless set her up for the sexual advances of a man with whom she was working. A casual affair soon escalated and, two months later, she told Steve that she didn't love him anymore and was involved with another man.

Steve was emotionally shellshocked. Within two days, Steve moved out and found a partially furnished studio apartment in a section of town in which he thought he would never live. Steve's appetite began to dwindle, and within a month he had lost 10 pounds. His sleep patterns became erratic, and when he did go to sleep, he would usually wake up within two to three hours. Steve stopped doing the things he usually did to take care of himself, like jogging, playing tennis, and working out at the gym. He pulled away from his friends and refused weekly lunch meetings he often had with associates. In one of our first sessions, Steve confided, "I feel like my life is ruined. There's really nothing to live for. I spent all of my energy working my way up to a new level of income and prestige, and what did I get for it? I feel hopeless, worthless, and no good. Life just isn't fair."

Since Steve and his wife had no children, divorce proceedings went along rather smoothly and quickly. After an equitable property settlement was reached, Steve had little, if any, contact with his ex-wife.

Although his ex-wife was not around, Steve found himself obsessing about her and trying to find ways to get her back. But she was emotionally and physically gone, and Steve was left to try to fill up a large hole in the center of his life.

Despite the devastating effects of the sudden marital separation and divorce, within three months Steve's depression had improved markedly. Within four months he began going out with friends, and in the fifth month had his first date since the separation.

After five-and-one-half months of counseling, Steve was still angry and hurt about the divorce, but told me:

> "I really do feel the worst part is over now. For a while there I really thought I was doomed and there was nothing to live for. It was such a struggle just to get out of bed in the morning. I remember hanging out at the office as long as possible, doing extra work, to avoid coming home to that dingy apartment in that crummy neighborhood. Although I'm still afraid to trust women, I feel that at least I'm starting to accept the support and encouragement of my

friends. Getting back into tennis, working out, and jogging have really helped a lot. It seems like just pumping the weights or going for a long run has a sedating effect on my mood no matter how upset I am. I can honestly say I really see light at the end of the tunnel.

Soon Steve's appetite returned to normal, and he began sleeping better. He gradually resumed a normal level of social activity.

Steve was suffering from an adjustment disorder with depressed mood, in reaction to his marital separation and impending divorce. While Steve was going through one of the most difficult stressors that anyone can experience, he and his friends and family all knew that Steve was taking his divorce much harder than most men who have been through similar circumstances.

Adjustment Disorder with Disturbance of Behavior

Adjustment disorders with disturbance of behavior are distinctly different from adjustment disorders involving your feelings or emotions. As the name implies, adjustment disorders with disturbance of behavior or conduct are action responses to situational stressors. It's not simply a question of feeling anxious, depressed, or angry, it's a question of letting your emotions show through in your behaviors, and actually acting on your impulses. For this reason, many people suffering from the disorder run into trouble with other people or authority figures.

A case in point is Joe, a 34-year-old phone-company employee with 12 years of seniority. Joe's career has been checkered, and on several occasions he has been reprimanded for not getting along with fellow employees. About once a year Joe's boss has to sit him down and talk to him about how to relate to other people and how not to create trouble on the job.

Joe had a difficult childhood. His father left his mother when Joe was 6 years old, and he and his younger brother had to spend much of their time fending for themselves. Joe was raised in a rough neighborhood and learned to fight to take care of himself and his younger brother. Although his childhood and early adolescence were characterized by numerous brushes with authority figures, suspensions from school, and fistfights, at about the age of 17 Joe began to get his act together. By the age of 20 he had received his A.A. degree from a local community college, and shortly thereafter married a kind woman who was four years his senior.

One day Joe's employer told him that due to company cutbacks, his low seniority, and his spotted history, he would be laid off within two months.

Joe responded with extreme anger. He began yelling and shouting at his boss about how unfairly the company had treated him, and how he planned to get a lawyer and sue the company for every penny he could get. After a five-minute shouting and shoving match, Joe was escorted from the office and instructed not to return.

Joe took his anger directly to the neighborhood bar. He quickly downed three stiff drinks and, after ventilating his frustration on the bartender, began to look for trouble. Within half an hour, Joe was able to find another bar patron who looked at him the wrong way, and soon punches were being thrown. Although not arrested, Joe arrived home with bruised knuckles and a black eye, more angry than ever.

Within a day, Joe displaced his anger onto his wife, and even when he was not drinking, he slapped and pushed her around. Becoming frightened of Joe's behavior, his wife told him that if he didn't get immediate psychological help, she was going to leave. Joe agreed reluctantly, and the first time I saw him, I found a 5'9" 210-pound man who looked as if he was doing all he could to keep himself from exploding.

As Joe began to ventilate his anger regarding the unfairness of his layoff, his behavior started to get out of control. He began to pace around the office, pick things up, and even threaten to throw a candlestick. Although Joe's anger was not directed towards me, I let him know that I could not work with him if I was afraid of him and would not allow him to damage himself, me, or my office. Since Joe seemed incapable of sitting down and talking about his problems, I suggested we go for a long, brisk walk, which he agreed to.

Brisk walking appeared to give Joe a way of working off some of his frustration, and he admitted feeling a bit better when we came back an hour later.

We reached an agreement that when Joe felt the urge to abuse his wife physically, he would immediately leave the house and walk as long as he needed to until the urge abated. Joe was also educated on the effects of alcohol and how it tends to lower inhibitions and increase impulsiveness, thereby making inappropriate behavior and conduct more likely.

In our next session, Joe told me that he had spent much of the past week walking around his neighborhood. He asked if there was anything else he could do to work off his bound-up feelings, and we decided that he would join the local YMCA. During the initial days of his layoff, Joe reported spending four or five hours per day at the YMCA, lifting weights, running, playing basketball, or swimming. When Joe got home from these marathon physical activities, he reported feeling calm, sedate, and at peace. Joe's wife confirmed this, and said that on the days Joe worked out, she felt he was much calmer and was no physical threat to her.

Theoretically, Joe's adjustment disorder with disturbance of behavior was rechanneled from abusive behavior to vigorous physical exercise. The appropriateness of physical exercise as an anger-abatement technique is unquestioned, and Joe felt that working out gave him a great way of working off his stress and frustration.

Although the vigorous physical exercise did calm Joe down and prevent him from getting in further trouble, it did not solve the problem of a new job. For this, Joe spent ten weeks going through numerous applications and interviews before finally landing acceptable work.

After two months on his new job, Joe realized that he was still not the easiest person to get along with, but had clearly overcome the behavioral acting out which had led him to the brink of divorce and criminal charges.

Adjustment Disorder with Mixed Disturbance of Emotions and Behaviors

Adjustment disorders with mixed disturbance of emotions and behaviors involve not only distressing feelings, but actions on these feelings which are likely to have life-damaging consequences for you or others.

Lorraine was a 55-year-old pillar of the community. She had served on the school board, been involved in city government, headed various fund-raising organizations, and been a devoted wife and loyal mother. Lorraine's life had gone smoothly and according to plan until her 26-year-old son was arrested on drug trafficking charges. Shortly thereafter, Lorraine's husband, Ned, was diagnosed as having Alzheimer's disease. Lorraine's usual cool composure and task-oriented approach to dealing with stress soon began to come unraveled.

The first thing to go was Lorraine's sleep. She found herself lying in bed, staring at the ceiling, wondering what to do. She would go downstairs and reread the paper, which she had already read twice, flip on the TV, and look for anything to keep her occupied until she felt a wave of exhaustion come over her which might lead to a few hours of sleep.

Although Lorraine secured the best legal help she could for her son and sought the best medical attention available for her husband, she continued to feel powerless over the plight of two of the people she loved the most.

Lorraine's friends noticed that she had become increasingly anxious. She cared little for socializing with them or serving as the sparkplug for many of the volunteer services she belonged to.

The breaking point came when Lorraine was arrested for shoplifting a $9 pair of sweat pants from a Kmart store. The guard on duty noticed that Lorraine had several hundred dollars in her wallet, and she told him her husband had a net income of over $100,000 per year.

Lorraine had never engaged in any form of thievery before, and her behavior was so shocking that most prominent members on the various boards that Lorraine belonged to simply refused to believe the accusations.

Over the course of our initial visits, Lorraine confided to me that she had tried to be a helper and manager for not only her loved ones, but for her entire community. Lorraine's life was one of service to other people, and this behavior had seemed to work well up until the time of the problems with her husband and son. After a couple of hours of self-examination, Lorraine realized that she was always trying to help other people without ever helping herself. She told me that she took the sweat pants because she had always wanted a pair, and no one had ever given her any. She said that she could always find other uses for the money with her husband, son, grandchildren, and others in need.

Yes, Lorraine had reached a breaking point. Her neglect of herself, coupled with feelings of helplessness and hopelessness, had pushed her over the edge.

Although Lorraine was dismayed over her behavior, with a little retrospective analysis she quickly became aware that her stealing was related to the medical and legal problems of her husband and son.

Lorraine's approach to coping with these difficult stressors was to set aside a specific amount of time each week to try to help her husband and son. Lorraine would consult her husband's doctor, check on how he was feeling, and provide her husband with daily doses of support and encouragement despite his failing memory. Lorraine then decided to take good care of herself by doing some things she had always wanted to but never gotten around to, such as taking a class in stained-glass work, beginning to ride a bicycle, and purchasing a quality camera and taking photography classes.

Lorraine learned to recognize her sphere of influence and accept the things she could not control. Perhaps more importantly, Lorraine learned to balance her obligations to taking care of others with her obligation to taking care of herself.

Within four months of the theft, Lorraine had recovered from her adjustment disorder with mixed disturbance of emotions and behavior, and returned to normal.

Adjustment Disorder with Mixed Emotional Features

Adjustment disorder with mixed emotional features involves a maladaptive reaction to a stressor which includes at least two of the following: anxiety, depression, irritability, hostility, anger, frustration, or despair. Other emotional features such as disappointment, guilt, envy, jealousy, or rage may also be present. This type of adjustment disorder is not limited to just one particular type of emotion such as depression, but a fluctuation both within and between emotions of different types.

Rosanna, a 30-year-old teacher, wife, and mother of two small children, is having a great deal of difficulty adjusting to the fact that her husband, Bill, would be spending week nights in a nearby city while working to complete his master's degree in engineering. Rosanna agreed to support Bill in his project and realized that the time Bill would have for her and the children would be minimal.

The first few weeks after school began, Rosanna seemed to manage fairly well. She was starting to adjust to the fact that Bill wasn't around, and she and the children began to entertain themselves. But, after a month and a half, Rosanna began to get depressed. She found herself crying and missing Bill in the evenings, and developed such characteristic signs of depression as disturbed sleep, change in appetite (her appetite increased), increase in weight (she gained 11 pounds), and withdrawal from enjoyable activities.

The children in Rosanna's class began to notice that she was irritable and edgy much of the time. She found herself snapping at students in a way highly uncharacteristic of her usual warm and patient approach.

Rosanna noticed that when Bill was at home during Christmas and semester breaks, and while she was with Bill over the summer, all of her symptoms disappeared. Things went back to normal quickly— that is, until it was time for Bill to return to school again.

Rosanna was suffering from a cyclical pattern involving an adjustment disorder with mixed emotional features; it was reactive to the stress of her husband's out-of-town academic pursuits.

As Rosanna and I both suspected, once her husband earned his master's degree and moved back home full-time, her emotional problems disappeared quickly.

Adjustment Disorder with Physical Complaints

Sometimes people react to psychosocial or other stressors with physical complaints. The usual depression, anger, anxiety, or frustration which occur typically when most people are facing severely stressful situations are blocked out by people whom we call "somatizing individuals." These people have a way of ignoring their emotions, but these feelings don't go away. They tend to surface as physical complaints like fatigue, headache, backache, or other aches and pains that are not diagnosable as physical disorders.

Even if you are an emotionally healthy person, you may find that minor aches and pains seem to be a lot more severe when you are undergoing severe stress.

Dean, a 26-year-old landscape designer, is forced to take a leave of absence because he strained his back. During his absence, the business goes under, and he finds himself unemployed. While Dean's back strain had been improving during his two-week medical leave, news of the company's closure hit Dean hard. His back pain became more severe, and he began to have headaches every morning.

In Dean's mind, these complaints were real. He had always been an honest, hardworking man, and was a dedicated employee. Dean was not the kind of person who would malinger or make up physical complaints that weren't really there.

What was significant about Dean's telling that he no longer had a job was his sense of indifference. He used words indicating that he was upset about what had happened, but there appeared to be no real punch or feeling to what he was saying. In fact, Dean talked about the loss of his job with the same amount of emotion as he would use to describe a weather report in a distant city. Dean had blocked out his frustration, disappointment, and anxiety with the hope that these feelings would disappear. Unfortunately, his painful feelings manifested themselves as physical complaints: the backaches and headaches.

Due to his work-related back injury, Dean was eligible for vocational rehabilitation training. He received further education in landscape architecture, and once he was on course with his profession, Dean's backaches and headaches disappeared. Although the disability payments Dean received were far less than his lost income, he redirected the course of his life by pursuing more education and creating greater career opportunities.

Adjustment Disorder with Withdrawal

A diagnosis of an adjustment disorder with withdrawal should be used when the manifestation of the adjustment to a stressor is social withdrawal without significantly disturbed emotions or behaviors.

Jackie, a 46-year-old English professor at a community college, is noticeably and appropriately upset at the death of her father. Jackie had a very close relationship with her dad, and his death, while later in his life, did come as a surprise.

Jackie sheds some tears over her loss and initially accepts the support and comfort of her siblings, husband, relatives, and friends. Jackie continues to teach classes at the college, although her typical ebullience is replaced by a perfunctory task-oriented manner. Jackie initially pulled away from others as she went through the grieving process. But after this customary six-week period of acute mourning, Jackie didn't seem to be bouncing back. She refused to go out to the movies with her husband, continued to pass up her weekly bridge games and, other than going to work, almost never left the house. When Jackie's friends called and tried to get her to go out with them, she politely excused herself for one reason or another, and cut the conversation short.

On the job and at home, Jackie seemed neither depressed, angry, or anxious. Her teaching continued to be acceptable, and she continued to maintain her house.

But Jackie's husband and friends know that something is wrong. Jackie is not her normal self.

With the support and encouragement of weekly counseling sessions, Jackie was able to express most of the grief she felt. Once these feelings of sadness had been fully ventilated, Jackie told me that they disappeared. To use Jackie's own words, "Once I really got in touch with all of the sadness and tears I had about losing my dad, I felt like I basically cried myself out. When there were not nearly as many tears left, I felt a real sense of relief and was willing to get on with my life."

Jackie's reaction to the stress of losing her father had manifested itself in her withdrawing from other people. Once the underlying emotion of distress and sadness was fully let out, the adjustment disorder with social withdrawal disappeared.

Adjustment Disorder with Inhibition of Work or School Performance

By now, it is already apparent that feelings of anxiety, depression, frustration, disappointment, or despair are common reactions to severe stressors. It is therefore not unusual that reactions to a stressor could effect your job or school performance.

This is what happens in adjustment disorders with inhibition of work or school performance. Although anxiety, depression, and other emotions may be apparent, they are not severe enough to warrant the diagnosis of adjustment disorders with emotional disturbance.

Luke is a 19-year-old college freshman who recently moved from his home town to attend a university in southern California. Luke's grades throughout high school had been excellent, and he had received a partial scholarship. Shortly after arriving in southern California, Luke began to feel uneasy. He missed the familiarity of his home environment and found himself calling his mom and dad for reassurance every evening.

Although Luke made friends, he longed for the security of his home town.

Luke was able to keep the lid on his anxiety for the first couple of months, yet his grades were not what anyone expected. Despite having an IQ of 130, and making straight As and Bs in high school, Luke barely maintained a C average during his first semester.

Other areas of Luke's life seemed to be going well. He began dating various girls at school, became involved in a political action committee for students, and engaged in numerous hobbies such as rowing, cycling, and swimming with his college friends.

Luke's reaction to the developmental stressor of moving away from home and going to college had triggered his adjustment disorder with academic disturbance.

Through weekly counseling sessions with his psychologist at the university health-care center, Luke became aware of the nature and extent of the stress he was experiencing, and developed an understanding that his sub-par academic performance represented a wish to return to a more safe and secure environment. When Luke faced this reality, he realized it was time for him to grow up, and within the next two months his grades became more consistent with his intellectual potential.

Adjustment Disorders Questionnaire

Directions: Answer the following questions as honestly as possible. Do not deny or minimize your responses, but do not answer yes to questions that do not reflect how you really feel.

1. In the last three months, have you been unusually upset or worried about a stressful incident that has happened to you—for example, loss of a job, death of a loved one, separation, divorce, accident, serious illness, retirement, or moving away from home?
2. Do you or other people that know you feel that you are having more trouble handling this stressor than most people would?
3. Did your reactions to this stressor cause you problems or discomfort in your life?
4. Did your reactions to this stressor cause you problems at school, your job, or affect your ability to take care of your home?
5. Did your reactions to this stressor cause you problems with your family or cause your family to worry about you?
6. Did your reactions to this stressor interfere with your relationships or friendships?
7. In the past three months, have you received treatment (including medication, counseling, or hospitalization) because of your reactions to the stressor?
8. Have your problems with respect to this stressor lasted for less than six months?

Scoring: If you answered yes to questions 1 and 2, yes to any of the questions 3–7, and yes to question 8, you are likely to have an adjustment disorder.

   Remember the qualitative differences with respect to adjustment disorders.
   Adjustment disorders with depressed mood are characterized by feelings of hopelessness, irritability, fatigue, and feeling low.
   Adjustment disorders with anxious mood are characterized by feelings of nervousness and anxiety.

Adjustment disorders with social withdrawal are characterized by the desire to be alone more than usual.

Adjustment disorders with inhibition of occupation or school performance are characterized by disturbances in these areas.

Adjustment disorders with disturbance of conduct (behavior) usually involve reactions to stressors such as fighting, driving recklessly, or breaking the law.

Adjustment disorders with physical complaints involve such physical problems as headaches, backaches, and fatigue, which seem to be caused by stress.

SUMMARY

Adjustment disorders are so common that they may be considered the common cold of mental health.

All adjustment disorders are time limited, and resolve themselves in one of three ways: (1) the stressor disappears and the problem is resolved, (2) the stressor continues for over six months and you develop another clinical disorder, or (3) the stressor continues, you adjust, adapt, and improve your functioning.

While the time-limited nature of an adjustment disorder makes it seem reasonable for you to ride it out, or grin and bear it, stress-coping strategies such as those discussed in the chapter on stressors and those in the next chapter can easily be applied to overcome this common psychological disorder.

CHAPTER **12**

TIPS ON GETTING AND STAYING NORMAL

AFTER ANALYZING YOURSELF WITH THE PSYCHOLOGICAL TESTS IN THIS BOOK, YOU might ask, "Okay, so I'm screwed up. What can I do about it?" Certainly, if you have an actual clinical disorder, consult a professional. But statistics show that 60 of the 80 million people who will need help at some point for a psychological or a substance-abuse problem will never get it.

Fortunately, the sciences of psychology and psychiatry have developed the tools necessary to eliminate most emotional suffering. The problem is that the tools have never been organized into a coherent approach that people can utilize effectively.

Brilliant theoreticians like Sigmund Freud, Kurt Lewin, Abraham Maslow, Fritz Perls, and B. F. Skinner, and recent conceptual leaders in the field like Albert Ellis, Wayne Dyer, Joseph Wolpe, and Peter Lewinsohn have provided us with most of the psychological tools necessary to take care of ourselves.

Let's now look at twelve basic tips on how to get and stay normal in an often difficult and sometimes nearly impossible world.

Tip 1: **Your problems are not all inside your head.** It's almost impossible to stay normal when you're in an abnormal or chronically difficult situation. B. F. Skinner has been quoted as saying, "Before you change yourself, try to change your environment."

Despite what all those self-help psychology books might tell you, many of your problems may clearly be reactions to the situation in

296

which you're living. How possible is it to be normal and stable when you're living with a physically abusive alcoholic husband, a faithless wife, or a spouse who continues to write checks and drain your savings accounts to pay for his drug habit.

Can you maintain a normal and balanced life when you've been working twenty-five years for a company that is about to be merged with a larger company and you realize that your years of hard work do not ensure job security?

Is it likely that you will not develop a serious alcohol or drug problem if all of your friends and most of your family members are consistently abusing alcohol and drugs and encouraging you to join them?

Legendary gestalt psychologist Kurt Lewin taught us that your behavior is a function of your interacting with your environment. Your environment includes everything from where you live, to your spouse, to your job.

So before you go on an extensive journey to try to figure out what's wrong with your mind, it's absolutely essential to take a clear, focused look at all aspects of your environment to determine what opportunities you have, or what barriers interfere with your potential to become the unique individual you really are.

Right now, take a clear, focused look at the different areas of your life and see how your environment measures up. I have found it highly effective to have my patients rate their situations on a five-point scale with respect to limitations and opportunities. −2 represents a very difficult or constraining situation, 0 represents a neutral situation, and +2 represents a highly opportune situation for the fulfillment of your needs and values.

So put this five-point scale to use. Begin by rating your job. Look at the different areas of your job and see whether it offers you the opportunities to fulfill your needs and values, financial and otherwise. Do you have upward mobility? Are your hours of work acceptable? Are your relationships with supervisors and coworkers all they could be? Are you hanging on to a paycheck on a month-to-month basis with virtually no intrinsic meaning and little job security?

Think about the many dimensions of your job. Try to make an overall evaluation of the extent to which it offers you opportunities to fulfill your needs or prevents you from living your values. If you feel your job is basically constraining and not taking you where you want to go, rate it a −2 or −1. If, on the other hand, you feel relatively fulfilled and pleased with your job, rate it a +1 or +2.

Now do the same thing with your relationship or marriage. If you are in volatile or difficult relationship with a man or woman who is abusive or grossly negligent with respect to your needs, rate this situation as a −2 or −1. If, however, you feel that most of your needs and values are being fulfilled or satisfied by your spouse or lover, rate it a +1 or +2.

We often have trouble rating the extent to which our partners meet our needs because of our own insecurities. Many people have stayed in disastrous relationships because of the fear of being alone. I call this phenomenon "the security of the miserable." Someone caught in this trap feels it would be far better to continue the unhappy but predictable existence rather than to risk the unknown.

A third crucial area to assess is the geographical location in which you are living. How happy is a person whose main joy in life is surfing if she never leaves Phoenix, Arizona? Is it possible to receive your M.D., Ph.D., or juris doctorate degree if you never leave Podunk? Or, more generally, does the city in which you live offer a college or university which will allow you to pursue your educational goals?

Your living situation can be threatening to your very survival. How safe is it to live in a neighborhood that is riddled with crack houses and gang violence?

The final important area of assessment with respect to your situation is the social network you are involved in, who your friends are.

One of the most powerful determinants of your behavior will be the kind of people you associate with or befriend. Would you really feel as if you fit in, hanging out all afternoon with six of your friends who were stoned while you were not smoking pot? Or, on the contrary, would you feel comfortable being around friends who are straight while you are loaded on alcohol?

Once you have assessed the situational constraints and opportunities regarding your present physical, social, and occupational environment, decide whether to (1) accept the situation, (2) try to change or correct the situation to one that it is more responsive to your needs and values, or (3) leave.

The order of these options cannot be overemphasized. Sometimes people will exaggerate the problems they are having in an essentially good situation. Other people give up quickly and find themselves moving from town to town or city to city and never resolving ordinary stressors which they would face anywhere.

But, more typically, many people stay in miserable situations which have virtually no hope of improvement and feel that this is the norm and that they must learn to tolerate it. This is a myth that has created a tremendous amount of undue suffering. You really *do* deserve better.

Take a clear, focused look at your situation. If you can do anything to correct or improve your situation, do it. If not, find a better situation in which your needs and values are more likely to be met.

Tip 2: **Your emotions, both pleasant and unpleasant, are your friends.** Your feelings are there to help you. The sooner you learn to recognize, experience, and express them, the sooner you'll be on your way to living a normal, happy life.

As a human being, you are entitled to experience and express a wide range of feelings, including anger, sadness, fear, guilt, envy, jealousy, disappointment, frustration, and despair. Some of these feelings can be pretty unpleasant, and most of us try to avoid experiencing them if at all possible. We usually have no trouble experiencing emotions like joy, acceptance, ecstasy, jubilation, delight, and enthusiasm.

Keep in mind that your emotions are telling you something important about your values and needs. It is absolutely normal to be angry when somebody continues to hurt your feelings. It is absolutely normal to feel sad when your mother or father dies. Guilt is a normal reaction when you violate your own conscience, and disappointment is a normal reaction to not having your expectations met.

If you try to block out, suppress, or deny unhappy feelings, they don't go away, but build up and become stronger. Many theoreticians believe that depressed patients are people who have not learned how to fully express and ventilate their sadness. When the sadness is blocked out, the patient becomes chronically depressed. The same is also likely to be true of such feelings as guilt, anger, and fear. People who try to hide their fear are the ones who come across as the most anxious.

Tip 3: **In order to stay normal, you need to know how to stand up for yourself and be assertive.**

This tip is closely related to Tip 2, but goes beyond it. Not only do you recognize what your feelings are, but you are able to express them clearly and appropriately to other people.

Contrary to what a number of people think, being assertive does not mean being aggressive. It means being able to express your feelings, both positive and negative, and clearly get the point across to the people with whom you need to communicate.

How many times have you found yourself biting your tongue when somebody hurts your feelings and saying to yourself, "I'd better not say anything to him or I might make him mad."?

If you don't tell people where you stand, they can continue to victimize you or take advantage of you. They may not even know that they are hurting your feelings as they continue to contribute to the resentment you feel.

Then, usually, something occurs which you consider to be the last straw, and you either end the relationship or lash out with inappropriate anger.

In a nutshell, being assertive means:

1. Be immediate in communicating. Tell people your emotions when you are actually feeling them.
2. Be clear when communicating your feelings. Try to spell out for people specifically what they are doing or not doing and how it affects you.
3. Be genuine and sincere when expressing your feelings. Try not to use assertiveness as a tool to force your will on other people. If your feelings are real, then learn to express them appropriately and clearly when you feel them.
4. Use the sandwich effect when you are assertive with people and are expressing constructive or critical information to them. Tell someone something positive about themselves, which is then followed by something constructive or critical, and finally followed again by something positive at the end.

Let's look at how this works.

Bob, a very dear friend of mine, recently disappointed me by not showing up for a dinner date with me and my wife.

When I talked to Bob on the phone, I used the sandwich effect as follows:

Positive   "It's really great to hear your voice, and I'd love to get together with you as soon as we can."

Critical   "I was really disappointed that you didn't show up for
         our dinner date. What happened?"

Positive   "I hope we can get together before I have to go back
         home."

Tip 4: Before you can let go of problems from your past, you must first learn from them.

Most of us have psychological skeletons rattling around in our
unconscious closet. Lingering resentment, anger, fear, disappointment, or grief often lead to nagging insecurities and a difficulty in
developing our potential.

But have you ever asked yourself what is the purpose of these
ghosts from the past?

I believe that the purpose of any problem which seems to be
lingering in your mind is to let you know that you have not clearly
resolved this issue and have not learned your lesson.

If you go back to the function of your feelings, you will recall that
each emotion serves a particular purpose. Anger serves a purpose of
protecting you. Fear does the same. Sadness serves the purpose of
letting other people know that you have had a loss and giving them
the chance to support and comfort you. Guilt tells you that you have
done something wrong, and the misery you experience with this
emotion is a valuable experience which prompts you not to repeat
the mistake.

So go over your past and take a look at what might be cluttering
your mind. Are you feeling anger towards your dad who was abusive
or negligent? Do you feel sadness about your mom's never giving
you the attention and love you felt you deserved? Do feelings you
have from the past tend to clutter up your present relationships?
Does the anger you have towards your abusive ex-husband interfere
with your ability to trust and relate to your present husband?

There are no quick and easy answers to how to let go of the past.
But keep in mind that whatever feelings you are hanging onto are
likely to be lessons which you have not learned completely. It is also
probable that you have not found a substitute for these emotions
and, in that case, these ghosts from your past will continue to linger
until you find an appropriate alternative. Your feelings all serve purposes or needs, and before you can let go of them, you must find
other ways to meet your needs.

Let's look at one example of how this works:

Tammy, a 26-year-old secretary, came to my office with complaints of lack of intimacy, distrust, and anger towards her husband Bill. Upon interviewing Tammy at length and talking with Bill, we all agreed that the problem came primarily from Tammy's past. Subsequent history taking indicated that Tammy had been neglected by her natural father and sexually molested by her brother and her cousin between the ages of 8 and 12. She was raped by a male acquaintance at the age of 13, and when she married at the age of 18, it was to an abusive alcoholic who routinely beat her.

Tammy had a tremendous volcano of anger, hurt, resentment, and distrust of men. All of these feelings were being displaced or dumped onto Bill. Tammy and Bill both realized that he did not deserve it.

After several sessions, Tammy became aware that the distrust she was throwing onto Bill served the purpose of protecting her from further hurts. She reasoned that if she didn't trust Bill, he couldn't hurt her. Although Bill was not hurting her physically or emotionally, Tammy was stuck in an anger mode with respect to men.

After much reassurance from Bill and numerous sessions with me, Tammy finally became aware that she could exercise a realistic caution with respect to Bill and allow him to earn her trust gradually, over time. It was impossible for Tammy just to come out and say, "Bill I love you and trust you completely, and I know you would never do anything to hurt me." On the other hand, she did begin to show signs of opening up as she honestly observed Bill's behavior over the months to come. If Bill's behavior had changed and he had become abusive with her, then it would be completely normal for Tammy to either confront him and eliminate the behavior, or get out of the marriage quickly. Before she could let go of her anger, Tammy developed the alternative strategy of realistic caution to protect her while she adjusted.

Tip 5: In order to stay reasonably normal, you need to know what your basic needs are and go about meeting them.

Human beings are not really all that different from each other. We all have the same basic makeup. Psychologist Abraham Maslow felt that human needs fell into a pyramidlike structure, with the most basic needs such as hunger and thirst being at the base of the pyramid and the highest level needs—self-actualization and spiritualization—at the top of the pyramid. Maslow theorized that before your high-order needs could become known, your lower-order needs must first be met.

PERSONAL NEED PYRAMID

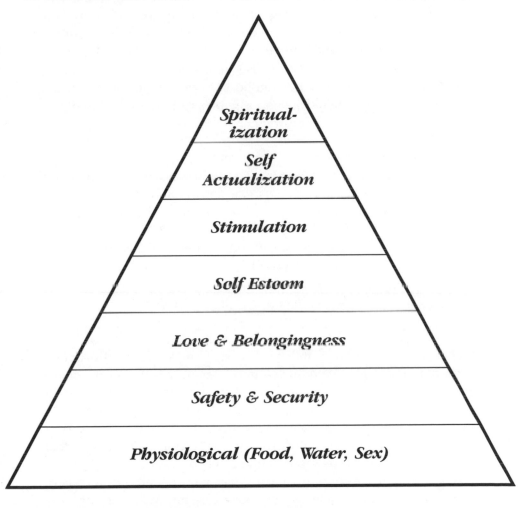

Spiritual-
ization

Self
Actualization

Stimulation

Self Esteem

Love & Belongingness

Safety & Security

Physiological (Food, Water, Sex)

spiritualization needs (your relationship with God)
self-actualization needs (developing your full potential)
stimulation (excitement and variation in your environment)
self-esteem (feeling good about yourself)
love and belongingness needs (a sense of acceptance by others)
safety/security needs (a reasonably safe and secure environment)
physiological needs (hunger, thirst, oxygen, and sex)

To look at the principle of basic need satisfaction and how it works, think to yourself how artistically creative you could be if you didn't know where your next meal was coming from. Or how you could develop a sense of self-esteem and feel good about yourself when you were constantly under the threat of physical violence.

But just knowing your basic needs is not enough. Once you realize your needs, you have to have a good plan of how to satisfy them.

The following problem-solving principles can be applied easily to help you meet your basic and higher-order needs:

1. Specify which need is not being met.
2. Assess your resources with respect to how to go about meeting the particular need, both personal and situational.
3. Brainstorm and develop as many alternative plans to meeting your need as you possibly can.
4. Evaluate your ideas and select the plan most likely to succeed.
5. Implement the plan into your life.
6. Assess whether the plan worked.
7. If it did not work, implement an alternative plan.

Most of us fall into the trap of not having some of our basic and higher-order needs met, and we just stay stuck, feeling frustrated, without trying to change things. A good example is the recent divorcée who is lonely and lost in a sea of uncertainty after ten years of marriage. While the feelings of sadness and distress may serve as a sign for eliciting comfort from others, if our divorcée does not go out and try to make new acquaintances or connections, it's unlikely that she will meet her needs for love and affection.

A less extreme example is the person who is chronically bored. Most such people are actually very boring themselves. The only way to overcome boredom is to create excitement in your life. Instead of complaining, develop a plan of what you can do to create excitement and enthusiasm. Implement the plan in your behavior, check your feelings, and go from there.

Tip 6: **In order to stay normal, you must engage in behaviors that are normal and healthy.**

The psychological discipline of behavioral medicine has taught us that there are certain things which are not only good for your physical health, but also for your mental health and self-esteem. Unfortunately, when you are feeling your most down or depressed, you are not likely to feel like doing things that will make you feel better.

Many of us operate under what I call the "motivational fallacy": the idea that you should do what you feel like doing only when you feel like doing it. If the world operated on this principle, everything would quickly come to a halt.

You see, it really doesn't matter whether you feel like it or not; you can improve your mood and raise your self-esteem significantly just by performing the right behaviors on a regular basis.

Several classes of behaviors have been found by psychologists to be very beneficial for your emotional health and self-esteem. Let's look at some of the most important ones:

(1) *Pleasant-events scheduling.* This is a technique developed by Dr. Peter Lewinsohn at the Oregon Research Institute to help patients overcome depression. Dr. Lewinsohn has patients schedule enjoyable behaviors daily. Patients are required to do things like go to movies, go out for ice cream, read a book they've always wanted to, go for a drive in the country, or do other things that have made them feel good in the past, or that they feel may make them feel good in the future. Dr. Lewinsohn noted that people who are depressed don't do the things that make them feel good, and that they can reduce depression markedly simply by engaging in these behaviors.

In short, whether you feel like it or not, put yourself on autopilot and do the things that used to make you feel good, or the things you think might make you feel good.

(2) *Large-muscle activities.* Large-muscle activities involve anything in which the major skeletal muscles of your body are involved. Walking, swimming, or cycling can all be considered large-muscle activities. Weight lifting or circuit training also qualify. These activities can also be pleasant events.

In 1990 research from scientists in Scandinavia found that simple skeletal muscle exercise, independent of aerobics, was associated with the release of natural opiatelike substances called endorphins, which are associated with feelings of euphoria.

(3) *Aerobic activities.* Many research studies have documented the effectiveness of aerobic training not only in improving your cardiovascular conditioning, but also your mood, self-esteem, and overall level of well-being. A recent Swedish research study discovered that beta-endorphins are released after 90 minutes of sustained aerobic exercise.

Use the following formula to help you determine your ideal aerobic training zone. Subtract your age from 220 to get the maximum number of heartbeats per minute that is not dangerous.

Then multiply this number by .6 to get your minimum aerobic level training heart rate. Next, multiply 220 minus your age by .8 to determine your maximum heartrate training zone. For example, if you are 40 years old, your aerobic training zone would be calculated as follows: $220 - 40 = 180$, $180 \times .6 = 108$ (minimum aerobic heart rate). Next, multiply $180 \times .8 = 144$, which would be your maximum aerobic heart rate. You therefore need to keep your heart rate between 108 and 144 beats per minute for the ideal aerobic training zone. You should do aerobic exercise a minimum of 30 minutes per session, yet my patients and I have found that sessions of 1 to $1\frac{1}{2}$ hours make you feel even better.

To summarize, when you are feeling at your lowest, you are the least likely to engage in activities and experiences which have given you pleasure in the past. You must overcome this behavioral inertia and drag yourself up and throw yourself into these activities. Once you get going, the momentum shifts, your mood changes, and it is much easier to continue.

Side tip: Many people find it much easier to begin a regular exercise routine by working out with a friend. Try it for yourself and see whether you can form a mutual-support network.

Tip 7: It is normal to be calm and relaxed, so quit fighting and learn to let go. Your mind and body were actually designed to be calm and relaxed, yet we respond to the stressors we face in life by getting stuck in an alarm mode. In order to break out of this mode, you need to practice relaxation training on a regular basis. While volumes have been written on various meditation, relaxation, and biofeedback techniques, let's look at one of the oldest and most effective methods. It has never failed to work for me or my patients. The following exercise is based on the progressive relaxation technique developed by Edmund Jacobson. It utilizes the idea of muscular fatigue: once you tense, hold, and then relax a specific muscle group, it will become more relaxed then it was to start with. It often helps to tape-record this script and listen to it 3–7 times per week.

Script

Begin by getting in a comfortable position and arrange to spend an uninterrupted 15–20 minutes giving yourself permission to relax. Make sure that you don't have to answer the phone, the door, or respond to any other demands around you.

Now close your eyes and take three deep, comfortable breaths. When you breathe in, let your stomach rise, and when you breathe out, let it fall.

In the back of your mind, say two words to yourself. With each breath in, say to yourself "safe," and with each breath out, say "secure." Let these two words go on playing in the background of your mind with each breath in and out.

Now make a tight fist with both of your hands and hold it for a count of ten. During this time, really focus on the tension and tightness in your fist and forearms. After ten seconds, take a very deep breath and, as you exhale, release, relax, and let go. Focus on the surge of relief that flows into your hands and forearms.

Tighten the muscles between your elbows and shoulders. Feel the tension and tightness in your bicep and tricep muscles and hold it for a count of ten. Take a deep breath and, as you exhale, release, relax, and let go. Focus on the sensations of relief that flow into your upper arms.

With your arms hanging loose and limp, lift both of your shoulders up towards your ears as high as you can and hold it for a count of ten. Focus on the tension and tightness in your upper back and shoulders. Take a deep breath and, as you exhale, release, relax, and let go. Focus on the loose comfort that flows into your upper back and shoulders.

Remember to say to yourself with each breath in "safe," and with each breath out, "secure." Now keep your eyes closed but lift your eyebrows up as high as you can and at the same time pull them together, creating tension and tightness in your forehead. Hold it for a count of ten. Focus on the tight band across your forehead. Take a deep breath and, as you exhale, release, relax, and let go. Feel the soothing relief flow into your forehead.

Pull your eyebrows down and together, creating tension and

tightness in your brow, and hold it very tightly for a count of ten. As you do, feel the excessive tension right above and between your eyebrows. At the count of ten, take a deep breath and, as you exhale release, relax and let go. Smooth out your brow smoother and smoother with each breath out.

Now squint your eyes tightly and wrinkle up your nose. Tighter and tighter and hold it for a count of ten. Then take a deep breath and, as you exhale, release, relax, and let go. Feel the surge of relief flow through and around your eyes.

Next pull the corners of your mouth back as far as you can, like a giant exaggerated smile, and hold it. Feel the tension and tightness in your cheeks and let it be there. And, at the count of ten, take a deep breath and release and relax and let go. Feel the soothing relief flow through and around your cheeks.

Remember to say to yourself with each breath in "safe" and with each breath out "secure."

Now bite your teeth firmly together, creating tension and tightness in your jaws and hold it, feel it, and focus on it for a count of ten. Then take a deep breath and, as you exhale release, relax, and let go. Feel the relief that flows through and around your jaws. As you relax your jaws, you may notice that your mouth sags open slightly. If it does, that's a good sign your jaw muscles are relaxing.

Next push the tip of your tongue against the roof of your mouth so you can feel tension and tightness in the muscles under your chin and in front of your throat. Push firmly and hold it for a count of ten. Take a deep breath and then release, relax, and let go. Feel the relief stream down the sides of your face, under your chin, and into your throat.

Now push your head back against the surface behind you, creating tension and tightness in the back of your neck. Never do anything to cause pain, only some muscle tension and hold it for a count of ten. Take a deep breath and, as you exhale, release, relax, and let go. Feel the soft, comfortable relief flow into the back of your neck.

Now pull your head down and forward, touching your chin on or near your chest and hold it. Feel it and focus on it for a count of ten. Take a deep breath, and relax and let go. Feel the release of tension in the back of your neck.

Now take a deep breath, fill your lungs, and hold your breath for a count of ten. As you do, notice the tension and tightness throughout your chest and torso. And at the count of ten, release, relax, and let go. Let the general sense of relaxation flow through every muscle, fiber, and cell in your body. Go on breathing easily and naturally, at your own pace and in your own way. Let the rest of your body be as relaxed as possible, but take one more deep breath and hold your breath for a count of ten. Feel the tension and tightness return. Then release, relax, and let go as you exhale. Again feel the relaxation flow through your body. Notice that every muscle in your body tends to become more relaxed when you exhale. Go on breathing naturally and easily, at your own pace and in your own way.

Next, tighten up your stomach muscles as you push your lower back against the surface behind you. This simultaneously tones and tightens your stomach, while stretching your lower back. Feel the tension and stretch in your lower abdomen and back, and hold it for a count of ten. Take a deep breath and, at the count of ten, release, relax, and let go. Feel the relief flow through your abdomen and into your lower back as it gets loose and limber.

Allow your upper body to continue to relax deeper and deeper with every breath out, without even having to think about it.

Tighten up your hips and buttocks and feel the tension and tightness through these muscles. Hold it tightly for a count of ten. Take a deep breath and, as you exhale, release, relax, and let go. Focus on the surge of relief that flows through your hips and buttocks.

Now tighten up your thigh muscles. Hold it for a count of ten and notice how you feel the tension in the top and bottom of your thighs and the inside and outside of them and hold it. Feel it and focus on the tightness. Take a deep breath and, as you exhale, release, relax, and let go. Again, feel the surge of relief that flow through your thighs.

Finally, point your toes straight ahead, creating tension and tightness in your calves and arches and hold it for a count of ten. Feel the tension and tightness in your calves and arches and hold it.

At the count of ten, take a deep breath and, as you exhale,

release, relax, and let go. Feel the delightful relief flow through and around your calves and arches.

You don't have to tighten any more muscles now, and it's okay just to relax. Remember with each breath in, think to yourself "safe," and with each breath out, "secure." Now count backward to yourself slowly, from ten to one. Notice the little pause at the end of each breath out, and notice how this pause serves as a stepping stone to even deeper levels of relaxation.

So with each breath out, count backward from ten to one, and allow yourself to go deeper and deeper with each number. Ten . . . nine . . . eight . . . seven . . . six . . . five . . . four . . . three . . . two . . . one. . . . Very good.

Now that your body is relaxed, tell yourself that your mind is perfectly calm, crystal clear, and totally aware. Your body is loose, relaxed, and comfortable. Your spirit is easy, light, open, and free. And, most importantly, realize that when you are in this optimal state of relaxed, clear, calm, well-being, you will be able to easily handle any stressors or demands which may arise.

To return, take three deep refreshing breaths, open your eyes, stretch, and go about your day feeling relaxed and refreshed.

Tip 8: **In order to feel normal, you must discover your personal sphere of influence.** Learn to control the things you need to control, accept the things you cannot control, and develop understanding or wisdom to realize your boundaries. You've probably noticed a strong similarity between Tip 8 and Reinhold Niebuhr's serenity prayer. There is great wisdom in it:

> "God grant me serenity to accept the things I cannot change,
> Courage to change the things I should change,
> And wisdom to know the one from the other."

How many times do you find yourself spending useless hours worrying over things that you have virtually no influence over.

On the other hand, there are obviously some very difficult problems you are going to face in life which will require sustained and diligent efforts to cope with or overcome.

One of the best ways I've found to help myself and my patients

YOUR PERSONAL SPHERE OF INFLUENCE
Learning What You Can & Cannot Control

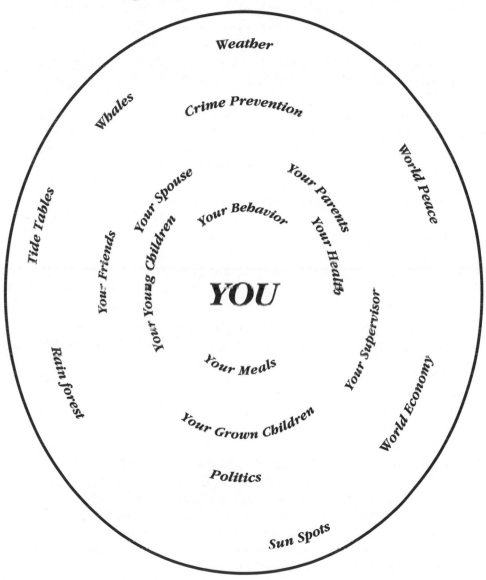

with these long-term and difficult problems is a technique called *time-structured problem solving*. Let me explain how this works.

After you have determined what the problem is, you set aside a specific amount of time to work on it at regular intervals. This may involve 30 minutes a day working on your tax problems, an hour a week talking with your accountant, a staff meeting with your co-workers for two hours a week, or one hour of undivided attention each day with your disturbed daughter or son.

After you have spent what you feel is a reasonable and fair amount of time trying to take care of the particular concern, you need to feel good about your efforts. There is a difference between completion and finishing. If you feel complete, you realize that the problem may still be unresolved, yet you are comfortable with the amount of effort you have exerted. If you feel incomplete with respect to your efforts, your problem will tend to drain your energy and keep popping into your mind at inopportune times. Once the problem is finished or resolved, it will disappear, and the next problem can be engaged.

In short, spend your energies focusing on the things which you can influence and control. There are many problems, issues, obligations, and projects to which you can devote energy and receive rewarding outcomes. Don't needlessly waste your energy, time, and life pouring out worry and concern over something which is oblivious to your efforts. Instead, use time-structured problem solving for chronic or difficult problems.

Tip 9: **When your body gets and stays completely relaxed, you cannot be upset no matter what you think about.** Combining the power of relaxation training with discovering your sphere of influence, you can desensitize things which are upsetting to you.

Physician Joseph Wolpe discovered that when he was able to induce a profound state of relaxation in phobic patients and gradually have the patients think about or rehearse distressing thoughts while maintaining the deep level of physical relaxation, the phobia would disappear. Your emotions are based on your physiological responses, and if you maintain a profound level of physiological relaxation, distressing emotional responses are unable to appear.

But you already know that your emotions serve a function or purpose. So before relaxing and desensitizing distressing thoughts, first determine if your emotional reactions to these thoughts or situations are compelling you to take some action to correct them. Once you are certain that there is nothing you can do about the problem, the next thing to do is make a list of events or thoughts, starting with the least distressing and working your way up to the most distressing. For instance, if you are afraid of closed-in places, the first item on your list may be being in a large room with one or two people. The next item may be standing in a smaller room by yourself. Toward the distressing end of the hierarchy, you may imagine yourself packed in an elevator full of people, and your most distressing thought may be being tied and bound in a dark closet.

Then, induce a profound state of relaxation using the relaxation script provided in Tip 7. Begin to let yourself relax into the distressing thoughts or situations as you work your way up the hierarchy, starting with the least distressing thought.

It is crucial to notice any anxiety whatsoever, and immediately remove the upsetting thought from your mind and focus on getting yourself relaxed again before you continue.

I have often found it very helpful with my patients to suggest to them that the more upsetting the thought or situation gets, the more relaxed their body becomes.

Tip 10: **Your emotions can be invested, just like your money can.** In order to stay normal and healthy, you have to make wise emotional choices that will generate personal and spiritual rewards for you.

What hooks do you hang your life on? The question of value is different from the question of need. We all know that we need food, water, security, and self-esteem. But what about your values: how much emotional energy do you put into any object, activity, or person in your life?

Pretend for a moment that you are an emotional octopus with eight arms. Each of the arms represents one-eighth of the amount of total emotional energy you have to invest.

How many arms do you put around your spouse? Lover? Your job? Your friends? Your children? Your recreations and hobbies?

People who are what we call codependent tend to put most—if not all—of their arms around one person. This is potentially dangerous because any variation in the highly valued person's behavior or availability often wreaks havoc on the person who is codependent.

But there are other forms of unwise emotional investment as well. Look at the workaholic, who has seven or eight arms wrapped around his job.

Many of the top corporate executives, doctors, lawyers, and professional athletes have most—if not all—of their arms wrapped around their careers. This is often beneficial in the sense that the people who are at the top of the ladder receive large, measurable returns.

But have you ever asked yourself what is the cost they pay for this success?

I once knew a professional football player who poured his heart and soul into his football career, only to have a career-ending knee injury. The young man was devastated and severely depressed for over two years.

Perhaps a more healthy way of investing your emotions is to diversify.

An emotionally diversified octopus may have two arms around his spouse, two arms around the children, two arms around the job, one arm around recreations and hobbies, and one arm divided among various friends.

Although this principle seems safe, I have run into people who have been highly emotionally diversified and all of the people, objects, or activities they are committed to are providing negative returns.

So first ask yourself: "What is really important to me?" Once you know this, create a personal time pie. I have my patients draw a 24-hour circle that represents one day. Seven to eight hours are blocked out for sleeping, seven to eight hours for working, and the remaining seven to eight hours are the critical area of where you decide how to express your values. If you can express your values in your job, you have solved half the problem.

If your time pie doesn't measure up to your stated values, it's time to restructure your life and start living what you believe in. It's not enough just to know what is valuable, you've got to show it in your everyday behavior.

Tip 11: In order to be normal, you must know how to say the right things to yourself.

We all have a little voice inside of our head that talks to us. Psychologists call this "self-talk." Your little voice may tell you things in the morning like: "I've got to get up and go to work," "I've got to take a shower," "I'd better get a cup of coffee before I go back to sleep," "I'm exhausted," and so on.

Spend a few minutes several times a day just listening to the kinds of things you say to yourself. If you find yourself saying things like: "I

can't do this," "I'll never succeed," or "I'll probably blow it again,"
you are obviously setting yourself up for failure.

The power of your beliefs, expectations, and self-talk is crucial in
determining not only your behavior, but your emotions and self-
esteem.

I found it very useful to have my patients develop a motto for the
day.

Some very effective slogans are:

> "I'm eager to spend valuable time with my loved ones."
>
> "I'm going to see how much energy and enthusiasm I
> can generate at work today."
>
> "My mind is perfectly calm, crystal clear, and totally
> aware."
>
> "I had just the perfect amount of sleep last night and feel
> refreshed, revitalized, and ready for this new day."
>
> "I am resilient, resourceful, and can easily handle the
> stressors and problems which life throws at me."
>
> "This, too, will pass."
>
> "At my own pace and in my own way, I will resolve my
> problems."
>
> "Every day and in every way I am getting better and
> better."

Although you can use different mottoes for each day, it is often
effective to have a general motto by which you live your life. One of
my favorites is by Oscar Wilde: "To live is the rarest thing in the
world; most people exist—that is all."

To me, living involves a range of emotions and experiences which
are all part of the joy of being a human being. Certainly life doesn't
come with any guarantees, and there are always going to be ups and
downs. But if you can learn to accept this and enjoy the often-won-
drous ride of life, you will have an optimistic outlook on your existence.

Closely related to the idea of a motto is the self-fulfilling prophecy.
This means that you tend to create for yourself what you expect. The
self-fulfilling prophecy serves as a kind of motto, but in many cases
the motto is negative. "I can never do it," "This is too difficult," "I'm
worthless or no good," are all examples of negative self-fulfilling
prophecies. People who think these thoughts tend to behave in ways

which set themselves up for failure. Break this habit. Think of your problems as projects which you, a resourceful and strong individual, can resolve.

Use the power of your beliefs, expectations, and positive self-talk to enhance your life. Don't be a Pollyanna or act naïve, but keep a goal-directed, realistic attitude. Look at your problems as projects which you're trying to accomplish.

Another way of creating a positive frame of mind is by using a cognitive-therapy technique called *reframing,* in which a distressing event is reconceptualized in a positive or at least a neutral mind set.
Example 1:
Negative: "I won't be able to survive if my husband leaves me."
Positive: "I'll try my best to save my marriage. But if I can't, I know deep inside that I'm a resourceful survivor."
Example 2:
Negative: "I worry every day that if the company is taken over, I'll be terminated. I'm too old to get a new job."
Positive: "I'm concerned about the pending merger and I will take steps to find another position. With my experience, I'll be a real catch for some company."

When you are facing life's toughest challenges, be on your own side. You can't afford the luxury of wallowing in self-pity or self-doubt. Of course, life can hit us with some terrible blows. But examine your thoughts to make sure that they are not dragging you even deeper down into despair.

Abide by the first law of holes:

> When you are in a hole,
> stop digging.

Tip 12: **Perhaps the most powerful advice of all in maintaining normalcy in an often-crazy world is to initiate, develop, and maintain warm, trusting, loving relationships.**

Psychologists and marriage counselors have discovered that there are at least eight keys to healthy relationships:

(1) Clear, immediate, specific, genuine communication. Let your beloved know how you feel when you feel it. Express your appreciation to your husband when he pays attention to you, but also let him know when you feel neglected.

(2) Know the politics of your relationship: who is the boss of what.

Share responsibilities with your loved one in a fair and equitable way. One partner may handle the bills, while the other takes care of the yard.

(3) Learn how to let go of past resentments, while still protecting yourself. Don't trust your husband blindly if he has hurt you. Pull back a little, be cautious, but give him a chance to regain your trust over time.

(4) Establish and follow reasonable and fair rules for your relationship. Develop a set of expectations for each other that you both can live with.

(5) Demonstrate and accept mutual respect. Acknowledge that you and your partner are different and may have different needs. Your wife may need to go shopping just as badly as you need to play golf.

(6) Give the people you love all of the time and attention they need of which you are capable. Usually 30 minutes a day of undivided attention to your beloved works wonders, but people vary in the amount of attention they need.

(7) Give the people you love the attention they deserve when they do the things you support and, after communicating, try to ignore negative or dysfunctional behavior. If you disapprove of your husband's smoking, try leaving the room when he lights up.

(8) Use contiguous conditioning—what I call the "magic bullet"—for fixing relationships. This means that you can learn to like and eventually love someone you are continuously having an enjoyable time with. For example, if you are angry or resentful toward your husband, but you both love to garden, arrange to work together in the garden. During this time you will associate your love of gardening with your husband, and this good feeling can help break down past resentments.

CONCLUSION

No matter what diagnosis you think you may have, you and I both know that you are normal. You have done the best you could, given your own history, circumstances, situation, strengths, and weaknesses. You have at least gotten by. You are a survivor. Congratulations! But isn't life more than just surviving?

The science of psychology and the medical specialty of psychiatry have developed many of the tools necessary to eliminate most emotional suffering. Competent, caring professionals in these fields stand ready and willing to help you. But to get help you've got to acknowledge that there's a problem and want to overcome it.

And for those of us who are free of major psychiatric disorders, remember, just because you're psychologically normal, doesn't necessarily mean that you're happy.

The tips discussed in the final chapter should be taken seriously. They represent some of the most powerful insights from the greatest minds in the history of the science. In the weakest sense they are a kind of psychological tool kit. And, in a truer sense, a kind of psychological road atlas, which not only directs you safely to where you want to go, but makes the journey an exciting and meaningful one.

BIBLIOGRAPHY

Alzheimer's Association. *Standing by You: When the Diagnosis is Alzheimer's.* Alzheimer's Disease and Related Disorders Association, Inc., Chicago, 1990.

American Psychiatric Association. *Diagnostic and Statistical Manual of Mental Disorders, Third Edition—Revised.* The American Psychiatric Association, Washington D.C., 1987.

The American Psychological Association Division 42. Highlights from a symposium on new perspectives on anxiety. Pragmaton, Chicago, 1990.

Ekkehrd, Othmer, et al. Psychiatric Diagnostic Interview Revised. Western Psychological Services, New York, 1981.

Kinney, Gean and Leaton, Gwen. *Loosening the Grip: A Handbook of Alcohol Information—Third Edition.* Times Mirror/Mosby College Publishing, St. Louis, 1987.

Korchin, Sheldon J. *Modern Clinical Psychology: Principles of Intervention in the Clinic and Community.* Basic Books, Inc., New York, 1976.

Levenkron, Steven. *Treating and Overcoming Anorexia Nervosa.* Warner Books, New York, 1982.

Liska, Ken. *Drugs and the Human Body: With Implications for Society—Third Edition.* Macmillan, New York, 1990.

Mace, Nancy L. and Rabins, Peter V. *The Thirty-Six Hour Day: A Family Guide to Caring for Persons with Alzheimer's Disease, Related Dementing Illnesses, and Memory Loss in Later Life.* Warner Books, New York, 1981.

McGuire, Christine and Norton, Carla. *Perfect Victim*. Dell Books, New York, 1988.

Nathan, Ronald G. and Charlesworth, Edward A. *Stress Management: A Conceptual and Procedural Guide*. Biobehavioral Press, Houston, Texas, 1980.

National Institute of Mental Health. *Depression Awareness, Recognition, and Treatment (D/ART)*. National Institute of Mental Health, Rockville, Maryland, 1990.

National Institute of Mental Health. *Schizophrenia: Questions and Answers*. U. S. Department of Health and Human Services, National Institute of Mental Health, Rockville, Maryland, 1986.

National Institute of Mental Health. *Useful Information on Anorexia Nervosa and Bulimia*. U. S. Department of Health and Human Services, National Institute of Mental Health, Rockville, Maryland, 1987.

National Institute of Mental Health. *Useful Information on Phobias and Panic*. U.S. Department of Health and Human Services, National Institute of Mental Health, Rockville, Maryland, 1988.

National Institute of Mental Health. *Useful Information on Suicide*. U.S. Department of Health and Human Services, National Institute of Mental Health, Rockville, Maryland, 1986.

Reisberg, Barry. *A Guide to Alzheimer's Disease for Families, Spouses, and Friends*. The Free Press, A Division of Macmillan, Inc., New York, 1981.

Rodin, Judith. "Body Mania," *Psychology Today*. January/February, 1992. Pages 56–61.

Rosen, Marjorie and Eftmiades, Maria, et al. "A Terrible Hunger," *People Magazine*. February 17, 1992. Pages 92–98.

Schlaadt, Richard G. and Shannon, Peter T. *Drugs—Third Edition*. Englewood Cliffs, New Jersey: Prentice Hall, 1974.

Selye, Hans. *Stress Without Distress: How to Use Stress as a Positive Force to Achieve a Rewarding Lifestyle*. Bergenfield, New Jersey: New American Library, (Times Mirror), 1974.

U.S. Department of Health and Human Services Public Health Service Alcohol, Drug Abuse, and Mental Health Administration. *You are Not Alone: Facts About Mental Health and Mental Illness*. National Institute of Mental Health, Rockville, Maryland, 1991.